# Raising
# Global Children

**Ways Parents Can Help Our Children
Grow Up Ready to Succeed in a
Multicultural Global Economy**

By

**Stacie Nevadomski Berdan**

and

**Marshall S. Berdan**

ACTFL
AMERICAN COUNCIL ON THE
TEACHING OF FOREIGN LANGUAGES

Books published by American Council on the Teaching Foreign Languages (ACTFL) may be purchased for educational, business, or sales promotional use. For information, please email headquarters@actfl.org or call (703) 894-2900.

FIRST EDITION

Printed on acid-free paper.

Berdan, Stacie Nevadomski
Raising global children: ways parents can help our children grow up ready to succeed in a multicultural global economy / Stacie Nevadomski Berdan and Marshall S. Berdan
Includes bibliographical references.
ISBN 978-0-9705798-4-3

Library of Congress Control Number: 2013951437

The views expressed in these chapters are solely those of the authors. They do not necessarily represent the official position of the American Council on the Teaching of Foreign Languages.

Book Editors:
Martha G. Abbott, Executive Director, ACTFL
Howard R. Berman, Director of Membership & Administration, ACTFL
Chelsea A. Bowes, Web/Communications Specialist, ACTFL

Copy Editor: Sandy Cutshall, Senior Editor, Print Management, Inc.
Jacket Design: HDN Studio, Inc.
Text Design: HDN Studio, Inc.

*Raising Global Children* is dedicated to
the parents who believe in it,
the teachers who encourage it,
and the children who embrace it.

# Raising Global Children

# Foreword

My own first international experience came in my junior year in college when I participated in a study abroad program in Madrid and lived with a Spanish family. Every single experience I had that year, from learning to bargain at the market to having to defend the U.S. involvement in Vietnam, helped shape me as an adult. It was truly a turning point in my personal development that has served me in innumerable ways in my career as an educator and, in particular, in developing insights into cultural perspectives, some that mirror my own, and others that are quite different.

I can't really pinpoint what caused me to seek out the study abroad opportunity that changed my life, but I have been recommending that all young Americans do something similar ever since. The world that our young people are facing today is fundamentally different from the one in which my fellow baby boomers grew up. Look no further than social and other online media to witness this difference. As the adults who raise them and as the educators who teach them, we have an obligation to help prepare our youth for the world in which they will be working and living. This world requires that they develop competence in other languages, understand other cultures, and develop an openness to interacting with the world around them.

*Raising Global Children* provides the rationale and the concrete steps that parents and educators should take to open up the world to young people. The Berdans have done an excellent job of outlining how, in both small ways and major ones, adults can influence and shape the development of a global mindset among children. With their extensive experience in traveling, living, and working abroad, the Berdans have firsthand experience guiding their own children in expanding their horizons, not only through thoughtful travel experiences, but also by providing opportunities for them within their local community to foster this "outward thinking" toward the rest of the world. They also provide practical suggestions to all parents on how to support the development of this "global mindset" and cultivate it as a family.

ACTFL is pleased to be publishing this book because we believe that *Raising Global Children* clearly illustrates how parents and educators can open up the world to the young people in their lives—a world that is increasingly at their fingertips—by developing the necessary skills and attitude to fully embrace it!

**Martha G. Abbott**
*Executive Director*
American Council on the Teaching of Foreign Languages (ACTFL)

# They Are the World

Why are a businesswoman and her travel writer husband writing a book on parenting? Let me tell you a story.

I had just finished speaking at a university in Nashville, Tennessee. The professors told me that my message was spot-on, exactly what today's students needed to hear from a global business leader. The career counselors talked about making passports mandatory for students beginning in their sophomore year. A small group of globally minded students shared their hopes and dreams for pursuing international careers. I left the campus in a buzz of good feeling that my message was getting across.

Then I got chatting with the van driver who had come to take me back to my hotel, a middle-aged gentleman who was born and grew up in the area and was now married with two middle-school age children. Making small talk, he asked why I was in town. I responded that I was speaking about global careers and the need for more global awareness among young Americans. His reaction was quick and visceral: "We don't NEED to know about the rest of the world! If we put our noses to the grindstone, work hard, and create jobs here in America, we'll be back to normal in no time—the way things used to be!" He claimed not to "want to put a fence around America," but, he said, "we have everything we need, and the world needs us much more than we need them."

I politely disagreed, offering a few words about how large mature economies like ours naturally grow more slowly than do rapidly developing markets. But I didn't want to argue. He fell silent, as did I. This encounter left me wondering: How can I get someone like him to help his kids?

My high was gone, and I mulled over how I could expect to help more young people understand the importance of developing a global mindset if their parents were blind to the realities of globalization and had either passed on this ignorance to their children, or at the very least, hindered their ability to understand the world. Could parents who are not globally minded raise children who are?

I was reminded of some of the other major disconnects I've witnessed of late. Businesses are clamoring for globally minded employees. Yet government agencies, universities, and not-for-profit organizations are churning out reports about how low rates of foreign language fluency and limited global exposure among American college graduates hamper business growth and national security. I compared this to when I lived and worked in Hong Kong in the late 1990s and reflected on how much better prepared Hong Kong professionals (whose native language is Cantonese) were to work globally—because they had to be. Their preparation didn't begin at the university level, but in elementary school with immersion in English and Mandarin and a truly global curriculum. It is still that way—if not even more so—according to recent conversations I have had with former colleagues there. But it's not just geographically small places like Hong Kong and Singapore that are dependent upon trade. It's the same for many countries around the world where 18- and 19-year-olds routinely enter the global workforce upon graduation—a very important distinction.

We know that at senior levels, American professors, business executives, and government leaders tend to "get it," and many are calling for greater global education. But at the grassroots level, too many Americans still seem to think like that van driver, that somehow, things will go back to the way they "used to be." My college talks tend to be well attended, but many there—and most of those who follow up actively after hearing me speak—are international students, not Americans. I am saddened by this and yet I recognize the exceptional qualities they possess. Most graduated from secondary school speaking two or even three languages and are already equipped with what academics and business leaders have come to call a *global mindset*: the ability to operate comfortably across borders, cultures, and languages. These students have the best of both our country and their own: a multicultural upbringing with postsecondary education here in the United States and the opportunity to find rewarding and high-paying jobs throughout the world.

Of course there are also American-born students with a wonderful grasp of international affairs and a positive attitude about working globally themselves. Many such students graduate proficient in another language or even two, despite the difficulty of doing so posed by American educational curricula. But too many American students, even at the college and graduate school level, seem curiously indifferent to the wide and changing world beyond U.S. borders.

At the elementary and secondary level, this disconnect is even larger. In my conversations with teachers and administrators in school districts across the country, a few common sentiments have emerged. Teachers who are interested in broadening the curriculum to include more foreign language learning, cultural education, and greater global awareness are often limited by a combination of budget cuts and parochial priorities. Parents, some fellow teachers, and local politicians simply do not recognize the need to begin global education until high school at the earliest, with many preferring to postpone it until college.

Yet most education experts say that it is not practical and probably not even possible to teach college students all they need to be career-ready upon graduation. For example, many colleges would like to make second language proficiency mandatory to receiving an undergraduate degree no matter what the major. But how can they advocate such a requirement when many students are not even able to study a second language for the first time until college? It is neither reasonable nor fair to expect all students to become proficient in a second language at the college level without a significant amount of time spent studying combined with some immersion. And so campuses focus on the knowledge needed for graduates to secure their first job. But that first job is often only that—an introduction to the workplace. What is increasingly needed to go beyond that first job to a successful and rewarding career is a global mindset, and recent academic research has revealed an inconvenient truth: College is far too late to start teaching this global mindset.

Given my most recent professional work as an international careers expert who speaks and writes about the need for global awareness in college graduates, I felt compelled to join this conversation and share what I know about the expanding global jobs market, the importance of cross-cultural awareness, and the need to better prepare our children—including my own two daughters—to compete with well-qualified job seekers from around the world. I felt so passionately about it, in fact, that I recruited my husband, Mike, a travel writer and former high school English teacher, to assist me in producing a go-to resource that will help other parents, individually and collectively, bring the world into their child's life. Mike brings a wealth of practical knowledge, global experience, and a lifelong commitment to learning languages (including English).

And as you will no doubt be pleased to hear, it doesn't have to take a lot of time, and it doesn't have to cost a lot of money. Raising global children is **not** just for wealthy families; it is for **every** family. But how to accomplish it is hardly self-evident. That's why I decided to write a comprehensive, how-to guide—one grounded in solid research and analysis, but written in an accessible style without jargon—that helps both parents and teachers understand **why** raising global children is important, **what** raising global children means, and **how** to develop a global mindset. The result is this book, and I hope you enjoy it and learn from it. Perhaps you will even find yourself challenged by parts of it.

This book is different, though, in that it doesn't conclude at the end of the last chapter. I will continue to work with the growing movement of parents, bloggers and tweeters, language teachers, social studies professionals, librarians, and school superintendents—anyone and everyone who wants to share the world with kids—to create a positive and organized force to make a positive difference. Together we must demand a better global education for our young people and our families. And by demanding better, we will succeed in doing better.

When people ask me what else I hope to accomplish by writing this book, I say that I would also like to effect change in the national curricula for K–16 by infusing it with cultural education. By this I mean that teachers will teach **all** subjects through a global lens, not just social studies and language. We have the opportunity to do this as the Common Core State Standards—which the vast majority of states have adopted—are now in place in school districts across the country. It's important to note that this approach is not an "add on," but an "add to" as school districts select materials with global awareness as part of their overall curriculum. Administrators, superintendents, and advisory boards can support the process by facilitating links across all subjects to foster global awareness.

I hope this book will inspire a groundswell of concerned parents, teachers, administrators, politicians, professionals, and business leaders to work together to advocate for greater global awareness. We're going to need every person, platform, and blogger doing his or her part to make an impact on the national scale. But it's a worthy goal: The future of our children begins with us. But it will take time. Each community, district, and state will do it differently and at its own pace. Some have even suggested that it may take a full generation to change our students. I'm not sure about that, but I do know one thing: If we work together to demand changes in our schools, and we take responsibility to help our own children to become more globally aware, then we can make a difference.

In the following pages, you will read stories from many other parents, educators, and global experts in the hopes they will inspire you to help raise the next generation of global children. This book is written for all of our children. And this is why a businesswoman and mom teamed up with her husband to write this book.

Stacie Nevadomski Berdan

# CHAPTER 1

# A World of Change

*The United States is a dominant player in the world, and, as a result, we have a responsibility to think bigger than ourselves. We must all teach our children to live in a big world, even if we live in a small town.*

**Anna C. Catalano**, board director and mother

Globalization is everywhere and it's here to stay. For the first time in human history, the world is coming together as a single entity. Although country borders still exist, people within them are experiencing a shift to an increasingly borderless economy that includes politics, culture, and international relations. Most nations have realized that they need others to prosper as the world continues to shrink and people of different nations, cultures, and religions come into deeper and more frequent contact, not only with their geographical neighbors and traditional partners, but potentially with everyone else around the world. Globalization reflects the expansion of one's worldview as we come to realize that wherever we come from, we are now one people with an increasingly common destiny.

But just because we are becoming more interconnected does not mean that we know how to deal with the benefits and obstacles associated with it. The world as we know it is changing, and we must adapt to succeed. For some, especially those with economic or intellectual incentives, adaptation will be relatively easy. For others, it will be a protracted struggle. But there is no reason why we as a nation should compel the next generation to repeat the same adaptation process. Instead, we must see to it that our children develop the flexible qualities of character and mind necessary to handling the challenges that globalization poses. To become global citizens, they must learn how to communicate and interact with people around the world.

## Globalization Then and Now

The roots of today's globalization are hardly new. They stretch back hundreds of years to the first long-distance traders. Native Americans had water-based trade routes in pre-Columbian times from what is now Alaska all the way down to Patagonia. The Vikings began crossing the North Atlantic as early as 1100

A.D., and the Chinese sent armadas exploring sea routes to Africa in the 1300s. However, it wasn't until the 1400s that the nation states of Western Europe got involved, with the Spanish, Portuguese, and Dutch setting up trading posts along the coasts of Asia, Africa, and South America. Eventually, the Europeans realized that it was more efficient and profitable for them to procure the natural resources they desired themselves, thus opening the door to exploration and colonization. Meanwhile, European ideas, such as civil administration, science, and Christianity began to penetrate other parts of the world. People of different cultures came into prolonged contact with one another and the world began to "shrink," however slightly. Advances in technology, particularly in the modes and efficiency of travel, accelerated the process, gradually but perceptibly. By the middle of the 20th century, people and goods could move from just about anywhere to anywhere else with relative ease and efficiency. World War II disrupted the progress of economic globalization while at the same time proving the globalization of another, equally pervasive human enterprise—warfare.

But progress and technology resumed their symbiotic march forward and, by the turn of the 21st century, have brought us to the point where American consumers don't think twice about having their hardware manufactured in China, their clothes made in Latin America and Asia, and their food come from just about any place on the globe. And if that means that American factories have closed up and their jobs have moved overseas, well, so be it. According to conventional economic wisdom, we would more than compensate for those lost jobs and increased imports by exporting to the newly industrializing and increasingly affluent other countries of the world what we do best—technology, high-end finished products, and financial services.

Perhaps even more conspicuous in our lives today is the other main manifestation of globalization: communications. Over the last 100 years, we have gone from Morse code and underwater cable lines to televisions, PCs, and smartphones. Now, thanks to the Internet, anyone who is connected can have instantaneous, direct one-to-one communication with anyone else also connected anywhere in the world. Be it for business, personal enrichment, or just entertainment, we are now all part of what can legitimately be called a "worldwide web." Knowledge, in particular, has become democratized. If you have a question about any topic in most any language, you simply log onto the Internet and have an answer—although not necessarily a correct answer—within minutes, perhaps even seconds, of hitting the search button.

*Communications has changed the world and the Internet ties us all together. But just because the world has grown smaller does not mean the long-standing rivalries between nations disappear. You can't erase history, but you can study it to figure out how to work across cultures that are, oftentimes, steeped in history filled with animosity.*

**Don V. Cogman,** business leader and father

*Social media has changed our world and could do a great deal to broaden Americans' views of the world. It can be used to surmount the traditional media barrier that limits and even trivializes important news about other countries to a sound bite or two. However, it can also be isolating and reinforce negative perceptions because many users choose to receive information that fits their worldview.*

**Steve Finikiotis,** business leader, emerging markets

Globalization is not without its challenges. Although it has brought the world beyond our borders into our offices, kitchens, and family rooms, it has also contributed to the loss of control over the "information overload" environment within which children are raised. Radio, television, and other one-way media have been replaced by the two-way Internet which also allows for an exponential growth in access to information, and not just information produced by some organized or commercial entity, but by anyone anywhere with access to posting and sharing. We're interacting with people all over the world, including those of other races, cultures, and nationalities. This can threaten our sense of self. Few of us are completely comfortable with all aspects of globalization. It's easy to be overwhelmed by a plethora of rapidly changing global news, trends, and crises. Being overwhelmed typically begets fear, fear that we are all being swept up into one increasingly homogeneous, one-size-fits-all world. That fear tends to force us backward into a more isolated existence—a world that is less global. And although it's happening to people all around the world, Americans are particularly sensitive to it because we have, for such a long time, been the country that seems to have needed no one else's help. But globalization pulls all of us into a swirling melting pot. Rather than be afraid or stick our heads in the sand, we must accept the new reality and adapt to the new conditions.

*The United States has dominated the world politically and economically for decades and, as such, we haven't had to learn to speak other languages or learn much about cultures beyond our borders. But this is not sustainable. Other nations educate their students about their own country and the rest of the world. They learn a language or two, as well as English. These students have a much greater advantage when it comes to operating in a multicultural workplace.*

**Julian Ha,** executive recruiter and father

Ignoring the parts of it that we don't like won't make globalization go away, even if we really wanted it to, which we probably don't. We may sympathize with protests against global multinationals, but at the same time we appreciate being able to buy inexpensive clothes manufactured in Bangladesh, drink coffee or tea grown on plantations in Ethiopia or Indonesia, and watch the latest YouTube dancing craze.

But there is more to be derived from globalization than just consumer goods and entertainment. It is only when we accept that globalization is an ineluctable part of 21st-century life, however, that we can begin to prepare for it. And that means helping our children develop global awareness so that they can proactively participate in the new global society. Failing to teach them to embrace it for all it is worth will only condemn them to being left further and further behind since—rest assured—millions of others throughout the rest of the world will.

*Globalization affects everyone. We can't put our head in the sand and hope it goes away. We must learn to deal with it, and help our communities and schools understand that it's about learning how to* **thrive** *rather than how to* **survive.**

**Steve Miranda,** international educator, business executive, and father

## Globalization Gives Rise to the New Global Worker

Nowhere is this "keep up or be left behind" dichotomy more potentially detrimental than in the job market. A half century ago, American businesses were the undisputed kings of the hill in international business, a position that they had been able to claim largely as a consequence of America's having won World War II, with only a minor amount of the actual fighting taking place on our soil. Today, however, there can be no denying that American businesses face ever fiercer competition on an increasing number of fronts. First, there were the former economic powers that were rebuilt after the war, specifically Britain, France, Germany, Russia, and Japan. In turn, these were joined by emerging economic powers such as China, India, Singapore, and Brazil. Even former "basketcase" countries, such as Ghana and Ethiopia in Africa, and Pakistan and Bangladesh in Asia, are now undisputed economic players. The overall result is that for the first time since our nation's founding, contemporary American parents face the very real possibility that their children may actually have a lower overall standard of living than they do.

Moreover, these trends are accelerating. Goldman Sachs predicts that by 2030, when today's toddlers are slated to finish college, the four BRIC nations [Brazil, Russia, India, and China] will own more global gross domestic product (GDP) than the G7 [the United States, United Kingdom, France, Germany, Italy, Canada, and Japan]. The National Intelligence Council's *Global Trends Report* shows that China will surpass the United States as the world's largest economy by that same year.[1] PricewaterhouseCoopers predicts that by 2050, the E7 [China, India, Brazil, Russia, Indonesia, Mexico, and Turkey] will be more than 50% larger than the G7 countries when measured by GDP at market exchange rates.[2]

*There is only so much more the United States can grow, even in the best of times, when there are dozens of economies growing between 10–15% a year. We must adapt as a nation, and we must help our students adapt as they become global workers.*

**José D. González,** professor and father

*Africa is going to be so important in the 21st century. It has some of the fastest growing countries in the world—Ghana, Ethiopia, Rwanda, and Tanzania just to name a few. China and India understand this and are heavily involved in building relationships and investing money in infrastructure and local businesses in these countries. In contrast, the United States is missing the boat economically because we think of Africa as a place of poor people. We need to appreciate the opportunity, diversity, and world views that exist across the continent and get involved.*

**Dr. Liesl Riddle,** professor and mother

This does not mean, however, that it is a matter of our country versus theirs. By now, almost all large American companies have bought into globalization—some proactively, some reactively—with the result that from engineering to marketing, manufacturing to agriculture, government to education, they are now working and acting globally. Consequentially, they all increasingly need globally oriented workers, both here in the United States and at their overseas facilities. In the words of a major bipartisan report, "Globalization is driving the demand for a U.S. workforce that possesses knowledge of other countries and cultures and is competent in languages other than English . . . Most of the growth potential for U.S. businesses lies in overseas markets [while] our own markets are facing greater competition from foreign-owned firms, many of which manufacture products on U.S. soil."[3] The U.S. Department of Education's top official for international education recently joined the U.S. Departments of State and Defense in noting that it "wants to ensure that more American students have the skills to compete in a global workplace, and not just build up 'deep, deep expertise' among a small group of graduates in foreign languages or cultures." Similar needs for globally minded graduates apply to government and national security agencies as well as universities and not-for-profits.

Tomorrow's college graduates are just as likely to compete for jobs in and with people from as far away as Beijing, Buenos Aires, and Bangalore, as they are from Boston or Boise. But the ability to work across cultures is no longer a nice-to-have skill set for elite executives; every year it becomes more essential to finding any job at all. A machine operator at a plant in Wichita that exports aircraft parts to Brazil needs to know how to interact effectively when Brazilian customers visit. A nurse's aide at a Houston hospital who serves a large Hispanic community has to deal with family members in ways that encourage, rather than discourage, patient compliance with doctor's orders. A farmer in Western Pennsylvania can open up potentially rich new revenue streams by understanding exactly what qualities in wild-crafted American ginseng appeal most to the Korean market. The examples go on and on.

Unfortunately, not enough young Americans have the skills and aptitudes that global organizations feel they need. One HR executive quoted in a Randstad study called American students "strong technically" but "cross-culturally short-changed" and "linguistically deprived." Another said "if I wanted to recruit people who are both technically skilled and culturally aware, I wouldn't even waste time looking on American college campuses."[4]

Despite the fact that hundreds of thousands of educated, intelligent Americans are looking for work, many good jobs in America are still going to non-Americans. This is also true for multinational companies around the world looking for global workers. A recent Forbes Insight survey, for example, found that more than a third of the executives surveyed plan to hire even more foreign nationals in the coming years for executive positions in the United States. A McKinsey

Global Institute (MGI) study found that worldwide, 40% of job growth in advanced market economies, including the United States, is likely to go to foreign nationals in the coming decades. And while some Americans are finding jobs abroad, particularly in China and India, those without global skills and experience will find they have fewer and fewer opportunities. One survey of more than 10,000 HR and recruiting personnel worldwide found that most require international study experience among candidates, especially at the executive level.

*In today's information-based economy, the jobs go to workers who have specialist knowledge irrespective of their location. To stay competitive, young Americans should develop a global mindset—and some specialist knowledge—so that they can be prepared to add value anywhere those skills are needed.*

**Abraham Minto,** certified public accountant

*Looking at the explosive growth of the global marketplace, it's becoming increasingly clear that corporations need workers with a combination of technical and disciplinary skills as well as linguistic and cultural competencies to be effective in markets around the world.*

**Dr. Frank D. Sanchez,** college administrator

Clearly, those who are best prepared for the new realities of the job market are the ones most likely to first be hired, and then to succeed. For students who are contemplating a career in international business, research, or diplomacy, a global mindset is truly imperative. But all future job seekers, regardless of their field, will benefit from having the soft skills—especially communication, analytical abilities, cross-cultural competence, and flexibility—that are part of a true global mindset. As a driver of career success, a global mindset is moving from a "nice-to-have" to a "must-have" trait. Many would say that it is there already. But it is not only in the competitive business setting that international skills are needed. Our ever-more complex world demands that we raise children with the knowledge, stability, and personal and social skills needed to operate successfully in all fields. Learning how to interact appropriately with people from other countries and cultures will be essential for them as well, whether they end up going into government, academia, or the not-for-profit sector. And nowhere will it be more important than it is for those who set their sights on addressing the urgent global topics and issues— from climate change and renewable energy to terrorism and interfaith dialogue—that are essential to advancing peace and prosperity worldwide. More than any other kind of work, finding solutions to such global problems requires the ability to forge solutions through internation-al dialogue and collaboration.

Global awareness also makes us better citizens and participants in our own democratic process. Understanding international developments on a mac-ro level helps in understanding U.S. foreign policy and the positions taken by elected officials. What may seem to be unfathomable events in Russia or the Middle East become clearer when we grasp the underpinnings of their cultures. Lawmakers in Washington, D.C., make decisions that affect not only Americans, but the rest of the world. Each individual's understanding of these issues—especially when reflected in the way he or she votes—can matter a great deal.

> We live in a global world. Products come from all over the world. People at universities come from all over the world. We can't exist on our own. The more you can understand and appreciate how things operate and how decisions are made, the more you realize that our actions have consequences on people outside the United States. If we don't think about those things, then we're not living up to the American ideal of morality or of equal opportunity for all. We have a responsibility to think about our role within our interconnected world.
>
> **Therese Miranda-Blackney,** graduate student

> Having a global mindset not only helps us understand the world beyond our borders, it helps us understand others within our borders. It helps us get along with others, something that we really need right now in our divided environment.
>
> **Dr. Jeffrey W. Overby,** professor and father

## Globalization on Our Doorstep

In addition to sending our children out into a brave, new, increasingly glob-al world, globalization also means that that world is arriving on our doorstep. Wherever we live, we should expect to be sharing our schools, communities, neighborhoods, clubs, and houses of worship with people from increasingly diverse backgrounds, the ones that globalization brought here. Cross-cultural competency matters as much in the communities in which we live as in the offices in which we work. Naturally, some places have experienced this influx of new cultures more or earlier than others. Leading the way are those communities that are the home to the types of companies and industries that attract highly skilled immigrants. While these tend to be in the Northeast and along the West Coast, a growing number of corporations located in the heartland have joined their ranks in establishing localized bastions of multiculturalism. And, of course, there is also the natural increase of established immigrant populations as the children and grandchildren of 20th-century immigrants move out of traditional immigrant neighborhoods and claim their share of the American dream.

As both a traditional and contemporary global melting pot, the United States is actually better positioned than most countries to raise global children. Considering the diversity inherent in our history, you might think that doing so should be a natural extension of our culture. But unfortunately, it's not. The fear of foreigners, or xenophobia, is widespread and particularly prevalent among those who haven't met many people from other countries and who have never traveled abroad themselves. It can become positively virulent, however, among those who think—rightly or wrongly—that their jobs are threatened. For them, raising global children may be an uncomfortable idea, one that translates into resistance when it comes to revamping school systems to properly prepare even their own children for the global economy that awaits them.

## Many Americans Brands Are No Longer American-Owned

Another interesting twist to the globalization-hits-home story is the number of prominent American brands and old-line American companies being bought by foreign interests. Smithfield Foods of Virginia, the world's largest pork producer and processor, was recently acquired by Shuanghui International Holdings for $7.1 billion in what is generally believed to be the largest ever acquisition of a U.S company by a foreign buyer. The AMC movie theater chain, which began as a family-owned business in Kansas City, Missouri, was bought by the Chinese company Dalian Wanda Group in 2012. Entenmann's baked goods are now owned by Mexican firm Grupo Bimbo, the largest bakery company operating in the United States. Burger King is owned by 3G, a Brazilian private equity company, which also has the controlling stake in Anheuser-Busch InBev; Budweiser's CEO is Brazilian born. South African Breweries bought Miller Brewing Company years before in 2002. Some piece of Americana is being acquired every year and although manufacturing sites generally remain in the United States, the intersection of local business and global managers create change. These changes affect workers, local communities, and consumers. People from many countries around the world are accustomed to U.S. expansion in the form of McDonald's and Coca-Cola, and that just might be what's around the corner for Americans: more international brands in our local stores.

## Global Education Is Proven to Be Better General Education

Neither global education nor learning a second language is a component of the standard American school curriculum. But that doesn't mean it is wise policy, based on years of empirical data. Even without including foreign language learning, research on global education shows that it also benefits general education by supporting critical thinking, especially in terms of encouraging a consideration of multiple perspectives, a skill identified in much research as supporting success across a range of academic disciplines and careers. Moreover, the reflective practices and consideration of varying perspectives that well-designed global education programs foster have been demonstrated to support analytical skills in all areas of education.

Effective global education programs can also encourage brain development by helping children come to grips with questions of personal, community, and national identities. Some researchers have found that the complex perspective issues that naturally arise in global education can assist with "open-ended, creative problem-solving," and with the ability to "reflect on contexts," useful skills not just for global life and work, but here in the United States too.[5]

With respect to foreign language education, the benefits are especially clear. Decades of research have amply demonstrated that learning foreign languages:

- Supports academic progress in other subjects;
- Narrows achievement gaps between different demographic student populations;
- Aids both basic skills and higher order, abstract, and creative thinking;
- Enriches and enhances cognitive development (especially if done early);
- Enhances a sense of achievement;
- Improves scores on standardized tests;

- Promotes cultural awareness and competency;

- Improves chances of college acceptance and achievement;

- Enhances career opportunities; and

- Benefits understanding and security in one's community and society.

*Young Americans will depend on and most likely work in a world far beyond our borders. Early exposure to different languages and cultures prepares young people for the constant transformation that will be required in their future careers. Acquiring the kind of intercultural communication skills that today's employers value will offer them an economic, as well as intellectual advantage. Having the opportunity to learn about other countries at a young age—and even better, to prepare them to study abroad as part of their college education—opens students' eyes to a new way of thinking about the world, instilling a more informed approach to problem-solving in cross-cultural contexts. Whether their ultimate career interests lie in public service, business, science and technology, academia, arts and culture, or any combination of the above, the global perspective gained through international education will serve today's students well throughout their lives.*

**Dr. Allan E. Goodman,** leader in international education, former dean and professor, and father

## Raising Global Children

In order to give our children the best opportunity to thrive in the new global world, we need to give them a global education. Working together, teachers and parents can raise global children, expanding their personal horizons while opening up a world of personal and professional opportunities.

When it comes to specific advice on how to raise globally minded children, we recognize that not only do we all live in different geographic locations, we are all at different stages in our lives financially, emotionally, and globally. Some of you may already be engaged in raising globally aware children and are looking for additional ideas to supplement your actions. You may have younger children, teenagers, or a mixture of ages. Or you may not even have children yet, but are interested in learning how best to prepare for their arrival. Others may under-stand the need for—and excitement of—opening the world for your children, but have little international experience and are unsure where to turn for resources. Some of you may even be afraid that your own lack of global awareness will be a barrier to helping your child become the globally aware individuals that you know they need to become. We all have different means and desires and so each person's approach to raising global children will be a little different.

We imagine that for every parent who already has the means to encourage global thinking, there are probably 100 who appreciate the value, but have little global awareness themselves. And you may not live in a town or even a part of the country that has much access to multicultural learning opportunities. No one has all the information to answer the variety of questions about lifestyles and paths, so it's best to tap into a network of globally minded people for insight, ideas, and inspiration. Whatever you're looking for on the spectrum of raising global children, this book is filled with proven parenting strategies, practical tips, and real-life examples culled from the experiences of hundreds of globally minded individuals and families.

## The Cost of a Global Education

Some people think that raising global children is only for the well off. This is **not** true. Raising global children does not have to cost much money, nor does it require hundreds of hours of free time. The single most important part of raising global children is to instill in them the right attitude. Traits such as curiosity, empathy, compassion, and flexibility cannot be bought, they must be taught. To be sure, travel, ethnic restaurants, and cross-cultural museum exhibits can enhance a child's global mindedness. But so, too, can the treasure trove of books, music, movies, magazine, and maps available at the local public library. Our point is not to advise you to pile on the costly extracurriculars, but to enjoy exploring the world with your child in the many different ways highlighted throughout this book. Incorporate an idea or two into your schedule as you see fit, and think long-term about the actions you can take to help your child become more globally aware. And while some things suggested here do indeed cost a lot of money, there are plenty that don't cost much, and others that don't cost anything at all. Just by reading this book you have expressed an interest in the topic, which is far and away the most essential first ingredient in raising a global child.

*It doesn't take a lot of money or high-level academics to learn about other countries and cultures. But it does require putting aside any fear. We're all just people after all.*

**Claire González,** teacher educator, former teacher, and mother

But even parents can't do it alone: we need teachers to do as much as they can to bring the world into the classroom. To that end, we'll also be sharing with you ways that you can get involved and advocate for more global education in your local school. In order to do so, however, you'll need to understand what is meant by the term global education and follow the debate that continues to swirl among academics and politicians on a national level.

Based on academic studies and original research, we define global mindedness in Chapter 2 in order to set the course for all the practical advice that follows. Instilling a global perspective combines parenting and teaching skills to strengthen appreciation for, rather than fear of, all that is different and new. A child raised with a global mindset is a child for whom the world presents a plethora of adventure and opportunity. Building this type of global awareness requires both a solid grounding in the child's home culture and a strong base of core life skills, such as careful observation, deep listening, and curiosity. And not surprisingly, the earlier a child starts attaining these qualities the better. Chapter 3 discusses the practical methodologies of raising children with the mental agility, emotional stability, and personal and social skills needed to operate successfully in today's multicultural global marketplace.

Adding language to the mix creates even richer dimensions, not only in the cultural doors that it opens, but in the benefits it bestows upon general education and career opportunities. Although the vast majority of Americans aren't proficient in another language, it does not have to remain that way. Parents can take action, be it in their child's school or at home, to establish a strong foundation for languages. Chapter 4 contains plenty of research, as well as ideas and tips, on how best to help your children achieve proficiency in a second language. You might even be inspired to start learning one yourself!

But it doesn't have to be all work, and it doesn't have to cost much as shared in Chapter 5. A child's cross-cultural curiosity can be inspired by eating a variety of cuisines in restaurants or cooked at home; by doing puzzles and playing board games involving geography, animals, and people from around the world; and through friendships with kids from other cultures. Libraries are a valuable resource for families looking for books and music about faraway people and places.

For those able to explore for themselves firsthand, international travel will put real flesh to the bones of second-hand knowledge, solidifying cognitive understandings while also dispelling stereotypes and misperceptions. But traveling with children can be a daunting experience and takes a great deal of planning and preparation. Chapter 6 opens up the world of travel as a very real possibility, including how it can be done for less than you might imagine.

By the time they are in their teens, children are generally able to go on mission trips, exchange programs, and other supervised cross-cultural adventures without you. Teenagers are at a very special place as they spread their global wings on their way to becoming adults. That's why we've devoted Chapter 7 specifically to them, sharing the ways they can become more globally aware through teen-based travel, community service, high school course selection, and college preparation.

This book has been written for those who may despair of improving broader global education for American children in an atmosphere of budget cuts, xenophobic grandstanding, and reactionary wagon-circling. Beyond working at an individual level as parents, families, and educators, we need to band together to advocate for better global education nationwide. There is something in this book for every parent and teacher, and we must work individually and collectively to make a difference, one child at a time, one family at a time, one school at a time.

## Real Stories from Real People

We surveyed approximately 1,000 people across a wide variety of geographic locations, ages, income levels, and educational backgrounds who consider themselves to be at least one of the following: successful internationalists (defined by living a global lifestyle or having a successful international career), parents or teachers who are trying to raise globally minded children, or students and young professionals who, having grown up in an increasingly global world, have developed a global mindset. We designed the survey in consultation with a seasoned research expert. Invitations were sent to people we know personally and professionally, as well as to the members of respected nonprofit organizations, such as the American Council on the Teaching of Foreign Languages (ACTFL), the National Network for Early Language Learners (NNELL), the World Affairs Council (WAC), and the Institute of International Education (IIE).

The information collected provides an insightful complement to the dozens of survey and research reports conducted by think tanks and academics that you'll find referenced in the text and detailed as notes at the end of the book. Some results were expected, some were surprising, but they were all exciting in the way they confirmed the commitment that more and more families are making to prepare their children to face a global future.

In addition to the raw data accumulated in the quantitative surveys, we chose 50 individuals to interview in depth. The stories of these individuals and their families appear as quotes and anecdotes throughout the book. Interviewees include:

- A mother of three who decided to homeschool her three children and created a global curriculum that includes hosting couch surfers and exchange students;

- A respected senior U.S. diplomat who grew up as a third-culture kid and is deeply committed to world understanding;

- A 20-year-old who describes a life-changing experience when attending a youth leadership conference in North Philadelphia;

- A mother who fought against budget cuts in her school district's language program and won;

- An immigrant from India who moved to the United States with her new husband, launched a successful career, and is committed to instilling in her children the gift of curiosity;

- A woman who grew up in a blue-collar working family and founded a not-for-profit organization on the belief that if a child who lives in poverty has academic fluency in a second or third language, more doors would be opened for him or her academically and professionally;

- A 15-year-old who witnessed how poverty and joy coexist while on a community service trip to Thailand and Cambodia;

- An international business executive who believes that raising global citizens is a necessity today and offers the examples of his own adult children as proof; and

- A family that hosts an exchange student every year to bring the world into their home since they can't afford to travel internationally.

Probably the most interesting and useful discoveries we made, however, are the three common strands that run through almost everyone's stories about why and how they think they developed their own global awareness. **First**, every person noted that curiosity about people, places, and knowledge in general made a huge difference. Some talked about an inherent curiosity, while others mentioned ways their parents and teachers encouraged it in them as children. **Second**, almost everyone noted a solid grounding in their own "home" culture, one that enabled them to feel comfortable exploring outside their environment. For some this meant fervent patriotism, while for others it boiled down to what can be called good parenting skills. **Third**, most people had a specific moment in time or experience they look back upon as "the" moment that shifted their thinking and, therefore, the path they would take in life as a globally minded adult. These threads are not grand nor are the experiences described necessarily earth-shattering. But the combination of the three factors seems to have made these people willing and able to think differently. These common themes and the colorful stories that accompany them will inform and shape the advice throughout the book by offering specific, practical tips that you can consider in raising your own children. Together, we'll cover a lot of ground as we create a roadmap of sorts with options for you to pick and choose from.

In these pages you will also meet a diverse group of parents and teachers who have made raising global children a priority and who share both their successes and their failures because they want others to be informed and spread the word. You'll hear from parents who found ways to access global exposure in their own communities—be they large cities or small towns—and others who have found a way to explore the world with their children through travel. You'll read about the power of a teacher to open the eyes of a child who is inspired to learn about other cultures and alternative ways of looking at a problem. You'll learn how the diversity of food, music, art, and film found in most metropolitan areas can transport you and your children to faraway places. You'll read about how opening your home to an exchange student may be the one thing that inspires your children to want to learn another language—or enables them to embrace other people and differences. You'll hear from parents who believe that community service is one of the best ways to encourage empathy and respect for diversity. Some of these young people also share their stories in a section dedicated to teens, which offers practical advice on how they can pursue global adventures in safe yet fun ways.

# CHAPTER 2

# What Raising Global Children Means

*The world is global and although having a global mindset may help kids get a job, it's not just about business. It's also about opening their eyes and their minds to the big, wide, wonderful world.*

**Michelle Morgan Knott,** mother

Any discussion of raising global children has one overarching challenge: There is no widespread agreement on just what is meant by the various terms commonly employed. Academics in particular have come up with subtle, but important on some level, differences in the way they define terms like "global mindset," "global mindedness," "global awareness," "global education," "international education," "global citizenship," "world studies," and "education for international understanding"—the result of which is a nomenclatural minefield that some researchers call "the big terminology debate." Such distinctions, however, are not particularly germane to this book which is not being written for academics, but rather for parents and teachers interested in raising children able and ready to thrive in a global society, a society that has begun to permeate our neighborhoods and is now an inherent and irrevocable part of our children's lives.

Therefore, we will confine our usage to the terms "global mindset" and "global mindedness" according to a simple definition broadly accepted by most academics, organizations, and companies, which is: "an ability to live in and work successfully across multiple cultures—including, but not necessarily, in other countries." This is a functional definition based on what people can accomplish personally and professionally, and as such, is widely used in hiring and promotion decisions. But that doesn't mean that having a global mindset is only for international corporate employees or diplomats. It is just as important for a technician running a machine in a plant in Minnesota that supplies parts to a company in Shanghai. And, of course, as noted throughout this book, it's not just about jobs.

True global mindedness is not just a career skill, it's a much more encompassing set of life skills. It implies a multitude of abilities that has as much to do with innovation and problem-solving as with an ability to appreciate different cultures. Global mindedness matters in the communities where we live just as much as in our workplace since global mobility means that we are increasingly sharing our neighborhoods, schools, religious institutions, and clubs with people from ever-more diverse backgrounds. But according to the National Research Council, Americans' "pervasive lack of knowledge about foreign cultures and foreign languages threatens the security of the United States as well as its ability to compete in the global marketplace and produce an informed citizenry."[1] For most of us, appreciating instead of fighting diversity will aid happiness as well as career success in the years ahead. In addition to being able to compete on a global scale collectively as a nation, global awareness also enables us to enjoy the benefits and pleasures of a bigger, broader world.

> *The United States has a lot going for it because we draw people from around the world. We need to keep doing so and find a way to tap the cultural and language resources recent and past immigrants can offer to engage and educate more Americans about the rest of the world.*
>
> **Julian Ha,** executive recruiter and father

> *As a business executive and former expat, I see huge differences between children and young adults with a global perspective and those without it—differences in conceptual capacity, world view, broad thinking, and openness to diverse experiences and people. Having a global mindset is a major competitive advantage for young adults entering the workforce.*
>
> **Diane Gulyas,** international business executive

> *Today's global workers need a granular view of other countries in order to be successful. They need to have the context of other markets: the history, politics, culture, value chains, and regulations, for example. This not only takes a while to learn, but it takes a sincere interest.*
>
> **Steve Finikiotis,** business leader, emerging markets

Creating the mindset that will enable our children to succeed personally and professionally in a globalized world requires that we help them develop a resilient and confident sense of themselves and their own background; knowledge of, curiosity about, and respect for other perspectives; and the flexibility to work across cultural boundaries while maintaining their own goals. We believe that using common language will help us all as parents and educators to focus on meaningful content in global education, and may also help sidestep some of the thorny politics that have dogged this topic.

## What We Do NOT Mean by Global Mindedness

In advocating global mindedness, we'd like to clarify what we do NOT mean:

- Memorization of disconnected facts about dozens of different cultures, as if global-mindedness were a prize to be won at a geography or history bee (what educator William Gaudelli calls "trivial pursuit pedagogy");

- Dilettante tastes of "exotic" foods, films, or ideas that encourage seeing other cultures as separate, strange, or intellectually curious;

- Fluffy "love of the world" that tries to erase differences or eliminate analysis in favor of what some anti-globalists call "ga-ga cultural relativism;"

- Self-righteous hand-wringing about America's needing to right every ill in the world; and

- Global knowledge gained for the sake of one-upsmanship, with facts collected only to prove American superiority.

Such practices, if not downright counterproductive, will do little to prepare our children to function in the multicultural world they will face as adults.

## Getting Past Controversy in Raising Global Children

We've often wondered why global education—which we equate to the importance of teaching technology to children—is so controversial. It should be what our kids call a "no-brainer." For better or for worse, the world has grown more interconnected, and we must both accept and learn how to deal with it. For starters, teaching children about the world beyond their borders has never been simple. Most national education systems place a high value on developing national pride and identity, thus imbuing global education with an ethnocentricity that highlights, often unjustifiably, their own country. The United States is no different and has historically had a love–hate relationship when it comes to learning about the rest of the world. There has been recent pushback against global-mindedness from defunding the Foreign Language Assistance Program (FLAP) to "America first" diatribes by grandstanding politicians playing up to self-righteous groups of supporters who are nothing more than the modern equivalents of the 19th-century "Know-Nothings." Contemporary anti-global attitudes come from a long, if not distinguished, line of similar sentiments. Educator Kenneth Tye's *History of the Global Education Movement in the United States* recounts challenges to balanced U.S.-based teaching about the world going back more than 100 years, including:

- Late 19th and early 20th century curricula which sought to assimilate waves of immigrants into "the American way of life" via schooling in U.S. history, civics, and values;[2]

- Post-World War I curricula that contrasted President Wilson's peace initiatives with the global rise of totalitarian regimes, and advocated isolation and protectionism;[3]

- Patriotic curricula during World War II, which included many positive images of our then ally, the Soviet Union, and historically unjustified characterizations of our foes, particularly the Japanese;

- Cold War McCarthyist curricula equating internationalism with "godless Communism" and demanding punitive loyalty oaths from educators;

- A flowering of global and foreign language education, starting in the 1960s as educators disillusioned with the Vietnam War sought alternatives, from the influential *International Education for the 21st Century* to Jerry Brown's Global Learning, Inc.; but whose efforts raised hackles among supporters of traditional, U.S.-centric curricula;

- A major Reagan-era backlash which accused globalists of reflexive pacifism, anti-Americanism, redistributionist goals, and antipathy toward capitalism, and which resulted in "America the Great" curricula mandates for many school districts and educators;[4] and

- Further defunding of programs related to social studies and non-academic "electives" (including global education and foreign languages) following the passage of No Child Left Behind, with its mandated hyper-focus on literacy and math.

By 2003, the Federal Government was spending 25% **less** on foreign language education per capita for schoolchildren (adjusted for inflation) than it spent in 1967. Since then, we have seen a further retreat from supporting any type of globally focused education within the Obama administration. When neo-isolationists attacked candidate Barack Obama for supporting foreign languages in 2007, he fought back, decrying "the problems we get into when somebody attacks you for saying the truth . . . We should want children with more knowledge." President Obama—who, it bears remembering, had attended kindergarten in Indonesia and whose father came from Kenya—came into office championing the need to open the eyes of American schoolchildren to the larger world via stronger foreign language education. "For all the young people here, I want you guys to be studying hard because it is critical for all American students to have language skills," he said. "And I want everybody here to be working hard to make sure that you don't just speak one language, you speak a bunch of languages. That's a priority."[5]

Since taking office, Obama has been distracted by other more pressing concerns and his administration hasn't been much different than his predecessors. At the time of publication of this book, his major education speeches had all focused on technology and accountability, and rarely mentioned global or foreign language education. And FLAP funding was cut on Obama's watch, albeit under a divided Congress. Clearly President Obama has faced tough economic, diplomatic, and political challenges during his presidency, but his apparent abandonment of foreign language learning is still disappointing.

Other top administration officials have been more outspoken, but no real progress has resulted. Former Secretary of Defense Leon Panetta called the "sad history" of foreign language education in the United States "scandalous," and said that improving global education is "essential to our ability . . . to protect our security."[6] Panetta has been promoting the importance of language learning in the United States since the 1970s. U.S. Army Foreign Area Officer Rich Outzen cited "problems with the teaching of foreign language and culture" as "an incapacity we've had in the Force," to which former U.S. Secretary of State Hillary Clinton replied "Amen to that," and suggested that we "look for ways that we can better coordinate our language and culture education programs."

More promisingly, the U.S. Department of Education seems to be changing its course, albeit slowly. It recently announced plans to invest in programs that will improve the global competency of all American students, adapt educational best practices from other countries, and be more active in "educational diplomacy," or diplomatic engagement through education-related endeavors, such as the global exchange of students and scholars. It's an important step since the Center for American Progress and the Center for the Next Generation released a report in August 2012 (*The Race That Really Matters: Comparing U.S., Chinese and Indian Investments in the Next Generation Workforce*) which shows how much more these two countries are investing in education and how, as a result, American graduates are going to be even less prepared to compete.[7]

*Some in education believe the United States has an invincible ignorance complex, in effect believing no matter how far we're falling behind, we're still better than everyone else in the world. I'm concerned this notion will shatter as we fail to raise our own standards in education and advance larger percentages of our nation's diverse populations. In some cases, the solutions (i.e., models, systems, cultures) may be found elsewhere in the world*

**Dr. Frank D. Sanchez,** college administrator

While government dithers, the private sector continues to demand more global skills. A study by the National Security Education Program via its Language Flagship—a national initiative to change the way Americans learn languages through a groundbreaking approach to language education for students from kindergarten through college—involving surveys and focus groups among more than 100 senior U.S. executives, concluded that increasing language and cultural skills is "critical" to American business, including developing and keeping new deals, overseas marketing, and winning the global war for talent. As one survey participant said, "the lack of language skills among U.S. businessmen is an enormous barrier to increasing U.S. participation in overseas markets."[8]

America's business leaders are crying out for more globally-educated talent to grow our economy while our military and national security leaders are calling such talent crucial to our security and national defense. Yet nationwide, funding for global and foreign language education has been cut. Why?

Certainly the Great Recession and its lingering after-effects are big reasons. But foreign language and global education has also become an easy political target in these highly polarized times with partisans on both sides seeking to score easy points among their most active and vocal bases. Those on the Right decry global education as anti-American propaganda meant to undermine God-given American "superiority," while those on the Left often focus on the divvying up of the world by soulless corporate Godzillas. Despite their diametrically opposite perspectives, both paint globalization in the blackest of hues, and thus inadvertently work together to block any productive response to it.

Moreover, there have also been some unproductive debates among proponents of global education themselves, including, according to Kenneth Tye and William Gaudelli:

- Whether global education should have a moral dimension, encouraging students toward what educator D.B. Heater calls "appreciation that people have rights and duties toward one another . . . sympathy for the unfortunate," and "readiness to act responsibly to help resolve the world's problems."[9]

- Whether American global educators are responsible primarily for strengthening student pride and self-identity as Americans, or primarily for what ethicist Martha Nussbaum calls "cosmopolitan awareness" (i.e., a sense that students "are, above all, citizens of a world of human beings").

- Whether global studies should be combined with American studies in comparative fashion to emphasize interconnections in history, economics, and other fields, or kept separate to emphasize America's uniqueness.

- Whether cross-cultural education should focus on transnational cultures or on multi-cultural groups within the United States.[10]

- Whether global studies needs to be taught differently to different cultural and socio-economic groups.

- What we should call global education, and whether relabeling the field is useful.

Although these topics do warrant further discussion (if you're interested, you should explore the Notes at the end of the book to learn more), we prefer to let such debates remain within the confines of academic circles. As parents with limited time, our attention would be best spent on practical efforts at the local level and not in engaging in philosophical, national-level debates.

*A nationalistic tone pervades the wider culture today, which can make teaching very frustrating. It often comes across as anti-intellectualism, limiting a student's interest in learning about other cultures—the very thing they must learn to be able to work in the global marketplace.*

**Dr. Jeffrey W. Overby**, professor and father

*Despite the obvious need for developing global awareness in our students, as a country we tend to be short-sighted and focused on ourselves. We teach to tests instead of providing a great, well-rounded education. The tendency toward American exceptionalism spills over into our classrooms limiting intellectual curiosity about other people and places outside the United States, while the mainstream media reinforces this point by offering up information low on content and high on drama and entertainment instead of providing in-depth information about happenings around the world that are very important.*

Brent Riddle, transportation planner and father

*We are very concerned that at a time when business leaders are calling for employees who can communicate and understand the cultures of our business partners around the world, the statistics point out that our students are woefully underprepared to meet these demands.*

Martha G. Abbott, language educator and administrator

## The Content of a Global Mindset

So what does it take to raise children capable of living and working effectively in a global economy? Since 2004, Dr. Mansour Javidan of the Thunderbird School of Global Management in Glendale, Arizona, has been conducting a good deal of research on the concept of a global mindset. In *Conceptualizing and Measuring Global Mindset®: Development of the Global Mindset Inventory*, Javidan's rigorous scientific study of the drivers of expatriate success has shown that a global mindset crosses professions and countries.[11] He and his Thunderbird Global Mindset Institute team posit the following components of a global mindset:

- **Intellectual capital:** Defined as knowledge of global industry and competitors and measured by global business savvy, cognitive complexity, and cosmopolitan outlook. Practical reduction: Do you have both the knowledge of global industries and the ability to understand complex global issues to get the job done?

- **Social capital:** Involves building relationships of trust and is measured by intercultural empathy, interpersonal impact, and diplomacy. Practical reduction: Do you have the ability to work well with colleagues who are different from you in order to inspire productivity?

- **Psychological capital:** Reflects and is measured by one's passion for diversity, quest for adventure, and self-assurance. Practical reduction: Deep down, are you curious enough about the world to explore and respect other cultures, and to interact and collaborate with them?

It's important to note that while these three types of capital interact and influence each other, a person may be stronger in one or another. Dr. Javidan's research corroborates similar findings from research Stacie Berdan conducted in 2006 with more than 200 internationalists, i.e., professionals who had successfully worked overseas, to inform her first book, *Get Ahead by Going Abroad*.[12] Respondents there identified five life skills critical to success in cross-cultural situations:

- **Adaptability/Flexibility:** Internationalists must appreciate cultural differences and tolerate ambiguity. Foreign environments require the ability to work around obstacles and find alternative ways to accomplish tasks. Global work and living require solving problems in different ways and adapting to the various ways that other people analyze and resolve issues.

- **Excellent communication skills:** How people speak, listen, and intuit can make or break a cross-cultural experience. Internationalists must learn to understand and be understood, especially when differences in language, culture, politics, and religion increase the odds of miscommunication. Nonverbal cues, such as culture, body language, reading between the lines, and interpreting the environment, are critical.

- **Ability to build teams and relationships:** Internationalists look beyond stereotypes and get to know people as individuals. They also appreciate the rewards of bringing together different types of individuals. This requires not only the organizational, time, and people-management skills that are important at home, but also the ability to reach across cultures and draw together people from different backgrounds.

- **Patience and persistence:** Successful internationalists maintain grace under pressure, going with the flow when things don't work as they expect. "Local time" and "local custom" mean different things in every country. Savvy global workers know that waiting and watching often outperforms rushing in and demanding immediate answers or changes.

- **Intellectual curiosity:** Internationalists are interested in—and open to— dealing with whatever comes their way, and they enjoy new environments. This curiosity drives them to learn about the world, especially history, geography, literature, and economics. The knowledge they acquire leads to an even better understanding of how to work across cultures.

In an effort to complement these two pools of research, both of which focused exclusively on business professionals, we recently conducted quantitative and qualitative research with approximately 1,000 individuals who identified themselves as having a global mindset. Out of a list of 13 traits, respondents were asked to identify which they thought were the top five ingredients of a global mindset. More than half of the respondents selected these five:

- Open-mindedness (89%),

- Ability/Willingness to listen carefully to others (67%),

- Interest in other cultures (67%),

- Flexibility (59%), and

- Curiosity (58%).

You may have noticed the pattern that exists across all three bodies of research.

*Having a global mindset will affect every part of your life and only in a positive way. It's absolutely worth whatever time you dedicate to do it. It's never too late—and never too early.*

**Jeanette Miranda,** undergraduate student

*Embracing a global mindset only enhances who children are; it doesn't invalidate what parents are teaching in terms of beliefs and values.*

**Liz Allred,** higher education adviser

## Instilling a Global Mindset

Javidan's team found that not all components of the Thunderbird Global Mindset Inventory can be learned equally at all ages. Its research shows that properly designed academic collegiate courses can strengthen intellectual and social capital. Psychological capital, however, seems to be largely fixed by adulthood. Thunderbird faculty, with all their commitment and training, had little effect on the degree to which students wanted to learn about the world, were excited and open-minded about other cultures, or felt self-confident in such exploration.

Our survey echoed this result. The five qualities that our respondents ranked as most important in a global mindset really should be developed in childhood since they are much harder to acquire later. Moreover, they are best taught in the early years at home and in school settings. Accordingly, 95% of our respondents agreed that global education should begin in kindergarten, if not earlier.

In follow-up interviews with approximately 50 respondents, we asked each if they could identify the moment in time when they first became excited about the world and, in retrospect, were propelled on their way to developing a global mindset. Their responses fell into five categories:

(1) Small event that blossomed into something big:

- *I loved looking at pictures of buildings and great architecture in books from the library. I wanted to see them and that meant exploring places outside Texas.*
- *I was enthralled with the pictures of faraway places and people who looked very different from me in the pages of* National Geographic. *I wanted to see and meet them for myself.*
- *My parents hosted an exchange student for two weeks, which was my first real foreign interaction. I was determined to study abroad one day, too, and so began taking Spanish in school.*
- *I had a pen pal in India. I wanted to meet her and see what her life was really like.*

(2) One big event:

- *My grandparents took me to Europe when I was 12. I was hooked and decided to study French, which led to a French minor in college and a semester abroad.*
- *I decided to study abroad. After graduation I moved to London, studied further, got a job, moved to Hong Kong, and then returned to the United States 10 years after that initial study abroad.*
- *Traveling to another country is one of the most powerful, positive experiences anyone can have. It can stimulate interest, inform a young mind, and develop innate curiosity. It certainly did so for me during my first trip to Greece when I was 12 years old. I wandered around Athens fascinated by the cobblers and souvlaki vendors. It made me realize that culture is rich and interesting.*
- *When I was in elementary school, my mother went back to school for a journalism degree. As such she was required to watch, analyze, and critique the news. She taught me how to do it with her, and we spent hours watching the news together. I remember being very confused in 1979 when the news presentations about Iran seemed to turn on a dime: a country historically presented as a stable ally and friend of the United States suddenly was portrayed as a country filled with people who hated Americans and everything America stood for. It inspired in me a desire to study the language and culture and teach others about it to do my part to improve cross-national understanding.*

(3) Steady stream of global interaction:

- *I attended public schools in California that had tremendous diversity. I made friends with people who looked different than I did and came from different places, but I realized that we were all the same.*
- *My parents sent me to Concordia Language Villages for the first time when I was 7 years old. I loved exploring language and culture and returned every year for 9 years.*
- *My parents loved to travel: My dad did so for work; my mom was an armchair traveler. I saw that they approached global interaction differently, but the result was the same.*
- *My parents were always very open to interacting with new cultures, taking us to a variety of cultural events and restaurants. It inspired an openness to and a natural curiosity for difference.*

(4) For as long as I can remember:

- *My mom had the greatest influence on me, always talking about the world beyond our town, state, and country. I started taking Spanish in first grade, and I have loved the language and culture ever since.*
- *For as long as I can remember, my parents shared their love of the world through maps, games, puzzles, and travel, and I loved learning about so many interesting places beyond the United States.*
- *My parents were from Italy. I wanted to know more about where they came from so I could better understand them and the rich cultural heritage they passed on to me.*
- *I grew up in an immigrant household understanding that the world was not only about the United States. It was always natural for me to think about more than one country. I spoke Chinese before I spoke English.*

(5) Inspirational teachers:

- *I took French in high school where my teacher noticed my interest and inspired me to keep learning, which I did through college and graduate school. I also studied abroad in France. I now teach all over the world, most recently in Spain, Poland, South Africa, and the United Arab Emirates. However, it all started with my French teacher.*
- *I had an awesome sixth-grade social studies teacher. He opened up the world of geography, teaching me to read maps, both technically and as a way to understand culture.*
- *I learned about Australia in first grade, and I loved what I learned. My teacher encouraged me to do a further project, which I happily did. As*

*I grew up, I was determined to go and eventually studied abroad there in college.*

- *My high school Spanish teacher encouraged me to keep taking Spanish after I fulfilled my 2-year requirement so that I could apply for the school exchange program as a senior. I followed her advice even though I wasn't that interested in Spanish. But she knew the trip would inspire me to not only continue studying Spanish in college, but to study abroad and seek out a career in which I used my language skills.*

The first thing worth noting here is that these experiences run the gamut from only reading about other cultures to actually living them at an early age, from a family that inspired global awareness to one that did not. There is, therefore, no one single doorway through which children pass on their way to becoming global citizens. A global awakening can occur in many ways, which means it's important to provide your children with as many opportunities to experience the world as possible. You never know which event might be the one that inspires them. But for young people to be susceptible to that inspiration, you must stimulate and encourage their curiosity. Every person interviewed mentioned curiosity as one of the traits that contributed to their global mindset. They were curious about other people, places, and things, and each found a way to fulfill that curiosity through various forms of global engagement.

The second important point is that the vast majority who remembered one single experience as being the impetus for their global awakening said that it occurred somewhere between the ages of 9 and 14. Many later solidified that initial experience with a trip overseas in high school, an exchange or study abroad program in college, or a job overseas early in their career, but the seed itself was sown at an earlier age.

These anecdotal stories, combined with the business and academic findings previously cited, confirm the common-sense knowledge that we as parents and educators already know: We must instill in our children the interest to learn about the world early on. Global perspective can be strengthened at any age, but the best time to start developing a global mindset is in childhood, ideally right from infancy. Research on early childhood global citizenship education being done in nursery and early primary schools in Scotland and France suggests that young children thrive on exposure to the concept of citizenship, both within their own culture and across cultures. The researchers concluded that early childhood education should include, among other things, exposure to how their own lives are linked to those of other people throughout the world via the interconnectedness and interdependence of modern living.[13] Evidence suggests that the traditional approach of not introducing global education until secondary school is far too late, and that the most effective schools begin teaching global education to the young child.[14]

While experts agree that children's personalities are at least partially innate, parents know that family choices and opportunities at school are crucial in determining whether or not any given child achieves his or her true potential. This is at least as true in global competence as in any other area. Children are powerful sponges, soaking up whatever experiences parents and teachers lay before them. The more experiences your children have when young, imparted in the safety of the home or school, the more open they will be later on in life.

> Global mindset is a major competitive advantage as young adults mature and enter the workforce. Not everyone can live overseas, but we can all use parenting techniques and support educational practices that encourage and nurture curiosity about the world and its interconnectedness.
>
> **Diane Gulyas,** international business executive

> A global mindset isn't optional any more. It's not nice to have, it's necessary in order to have a significant, positive impact on the world we all live in.
>
> **Therese Miranda-Blackney,** graduate student

A common concern of parents wishing to instill a global mindset in their children is the necessity of travel abroad. For many, this is impossible because of professional or other responsibilities and/or the lack of financial resources. For them, the reassuring news is you don't have to physically leave the United States in order to bring your children up with a global mindset. Schools and families with the resources for international travel, however, are probably at an advantage: 96% of survey respondents—and 97% of educators—agreed that travel outside the United States helps children develop a global mindset. But it is also clear that international travel is not necessary for a global education: 85% agreed that travel within the United States can also be helpful in developing a global mindset, while 94% of educators believe it can help. And there are other things that you can do instead as noted throughout this book.

Global mindedness is truly about mindset, a different level of awareness of yourself and your culture in relation to the rest of the world. We asked respondents what specific actions that they have taken in their own lives. The results both inform the structure and content of much of this book by providing a clear path that you, as parents, can follow, most commonly by selecting and implementing the components that are most relevant and/or doable for you. Naturally, the more comprehensive you can be the better. And as already mentioned, the earlier you begin, the better your prospects of success.

## Survey Results from Global Thinkers

Approximately 1,000 people took the online survey, ranging in age from 17 to 65 and hailing from almost every state in the Union. They included teachers, superintendents, and administrators, as well as parents with everything from newborns to college graduates, successful internationalists without children, and young professionals who have grown up globally. The percentage of respondents who agreed with the different variables are given below, with educators on the left and global thinkers from other walks of life on the right. There was no restriction on the number of activities that could be chosen.

| Educators | Importance to Developing a Global Mindset in Children | Other Global Thinkers |
|---|---|---|
| 98% | Encourage children to study a second language | 98% |
| 97% | Travel outside the United States | 96% |
| 97% | Encourage children to ask questions | 96% |
| 97% | Expose children to other cultures through music, visual arts, dance, film, books/literature, museum exhibits | 96% |
| 96% | Celebrate difference and appreciate diversity | 95% |
| 98% | Encourage learning geography through games, puzzles, current events, and history | 93% |
| 97% | Discuss current events | 93% |
| 95% | Learn or practice a second language with children | 93% |
| 92% | Try ethnic foods at restaurants and cook them at home | 88% |
| 95% | Ask questions about what they're learning in school | 87% |
| 94% | Travel to different places within the United States | 85% |
| 93% | Have credible sources bookmarked for quick reference, as well as a dictionary and an atlas/globe/world map in a common room in the home and use them | 81% |
| 86% | Host foreign exchange teachers/students from other countries | 68% |

When we asked respondents to choose the three most important factors from the same list, they responded in the following order:

1. Expose children to other cultures through music, visual arts, dance, film, books/literature, museum exhibits;

2. Encourage children to study a second language; and

3. Travel outside the United States.

We also asked both groups what actions parents could take to support global education in schools, pre-K through 12. The answers below reflect what respondents believe will help.

| Educators | Actions Parents Can Take to Support Global Education in Schools | Other Global Thinkers |
|---|---|---|
| 94% | Advocate for second language learning in school/district as early as kindergarten | 90% |
| 93% | Support global education initiatives and extracurricular activities with global content | 87% |
| 91% | Advocate for enhanced social studies/geography learning in your school/district | 78% |
| 92% | Support international exchange and sister-city programs | 74% |
| 89% | Volunteer in schools to help with geography clubs, international night, and the like, as well as share global talents and/or travel adventures | 71% |
| 75% | Participate in fundraising activities for global studies | 60% |
| 79% | Call and write to your political representatives, including members of Congress | 48% |

It's clear from the responses that educators think that parents can make a difference if they support global education in schools. This is probably no revelation to most parents since schools want to partner with you to ensure they have your support. Most educators appreciate that they can do a much better job of educating our children if they collaborate and communicate with parents. The top three initiatives identified by global thinkers are the same three identified by educators, with "advocate for second language learning in school/district as early as kindergarten" topping both lists at 90% and 94%, respectively. Remember that 98% of both noted that encouraging children to learn a second language was the number one means of developing a global mindset.

When we asked educators what percentage of parents at their school had a global mindset, the response was disheartening but not surprising. More than

40% responded "a little" or "none at all." We followed up with a question about global education support given to teachers by their administration. More than 50% said "a little" or "none at all."

What does it all mean? Most importantly, parents and educators must work in conjunction to foster the development of a global mindset in their children and charges. Parents need to begin as early as possible and be as comprehensive as possible. They also need to work with teachers, schools, and districts to encourage more global education and especially language classes in the formal education process, and the sooner the better. Eventually, we'll reach the point where we stop calling it global education because it will be standard education.

## Real Stories from Real People

### Steve Miranda, *international educator, business executive, and father*

My father emigrated from India to the United States in 1961 in order to pursue his educational dream. Unable to join him right away, my mother waited a year before bringing my two brothers (ages 1 and 2) and me (age 3) to South Bend, Indiana, where my father was pursuing his Master's Degree in Civil Engineering at the University of Notre Dame. Later, while completing his PhD at Ohio State, our family would grow to include one final sibling, a sister. My father's dream was both simple and profound: To move his family to a land where both he and his children would be presented with more opportunities and fewer obstacles than in the country where he had grown up. At that time, the country that offered the best promise was the United States. By any measure, his dream has been fully realized with all four of his children holding graduate-level degrees and positions of high responsibility across corporations, nongovernmental organizations (NGOs), and academic institutions.

My wife and I have strived to continue in this spirit of exploration and adventure by always encouraging our three daughters to "work hard, learn a lot, and have fun." In fact, it's the rare day that goes by when I don't find myself repeating this exact phrase as I drop them off at school or bid them farewell as they head off on their latest work, travel, or educational adventure. I repeat this phrase because I believe deep in my heart that it contains the keys to having a meaningful and happy life for anyone dealing with our increasingly complex world. Namely, the satisfaction that comes from full effort, the knowledge that we must always grow in what we know, and the belief that true joy comes from the journey.

One of our parenting cornerstones has always been to help our daughters understand that in almost any situation, what is important is NOT to figure out "who is right" or "who is wrong," but rather to focus on "why is there disagreement?" As such, we've encouraged them to find people who hold the opposite view than they do and seek to understand why they hold that view. As they've interacted with people from around the world, they've emerged with two key takeaways. The first is that there are very good reasons why people believe what they do, and making an effort to educate oneself on the relevant cultural, religious, historical, and social context is critical. The second is that once you understand where they're coming from, you find your own beliefs have a lot more "holes" in them than you initially thought! As the world continues to become even more diverse and the opportunities for interaction with people who are "not like me" continue to grow, we believe this approach will serve them very, very well.

### Jacqueline Stack, *teacher and mother*

Students in technical high schools are often stereotyped as being "non-academic" or "headed only to the trades." The stereotype-mongers sometimes suggest academic enrichment opportunities like global education are "wasted" on technical students. But anyone who thinks that hasn't seen how eagerly my students have embraced the global experiences I have been able to offer them. These experiences are already starting to open up new opportunities for my technical school graduates with global awareness.

After 20 years teaching in the public schools and six years in the technical school system, I jumped on the global education bandwagon in 2010. While participating in a U.S. Department of State International Research and Exchanges (IREX) Teaching Excellence and Achievement Exchange to the Ukraine, I realized just how similar young people there were and felt a call to share the delights of that discovery with my students.

As I enthused about Ukrainian food, music, and youth culture, my students caught my excitement and asked to be put in touch with young Ukrainians. This led to snail mail exchanges between Manchester, Connecticut, and Zhmerynka, Ukraine, in which student after student, sharing the usual, universal adolescent hopes, dreams, and problems, had the sudden and wonderful realization that despite cultural differences: "They are just like us." Together with those students, I wrote a follow-on grant to IREX that supported a day in New York City visiting the United Nations, meeting with a Ukrainian diplomat, and enjoying the Ukrainian Museum of Art and dinner at a Ukrainian restaurant. Each participant's global mindset was enriched forever.

With support from our school's administrators, I followed up that experience by working with fellow teachers to develop a freshman Global Studies curriculum, one that introduces students to our ever-shrinking world and the importance of having the tools to effectively engage with global peers. To that end, we have woven a thread of global themes throughout our academic and technical courses in an attempt to endow each of our students with the gift of a global mindset, made real via direct interaction with secondary students on the other side of the world.

In the years since, we have expanded our Ukrainian student-to-student communication program, enriched by the real-time communication now possible via email and Skype. We have also added opportunities for additional global experiences for students through two additional grants from IREX. First, in 2012, our social studies and information technology students participated in a semester-long project, "Our Inter-Connected World," with students in Kyrgyzstan. Those students learned to identify cultural universals depicted through art, a project that culminated in a visit to the Yale University Art Gallery. Guest speakers and authors spoke to them about the importance of a global mindset in their chosen careers. Culinary students researched recipes, developed a mini-cookbook, and created a Kyrgyzstani luncheon.

This year brought a new set of technical school students eager to experience global interaction, and we have been able to add a peer-to-peer program with students in Ghana. This program incorporated email, Skype, and snail mail exchanges, museum visits, culinary exploration, and other programs that had been proven successful before. We also added a project in which our high school students researched, developed, and presented lessons in African children's literature for second graders at our local elementary school—a way of "paying forward" the chances they had been given for an expanded awareness of the world. Our students also explored literature aimed at African teenagers and their hopes, dreams, and problems, once again expanding their awareness of both similarities and differences across borders.

These programs have been transformative for most participants. This is evident by their interest in university programs that have a focus on studying abroad. They discuss employment in a global marketplace where business travel to China is commonplace. They commit to volunteerism in Haiti during April vacation where their technical skills are utilized in the rebuilding of the island's infrastructure. In addition, their military service to our nation often starts in the summer before their senior year. The "new volunteers" share how an understanding of the peoples of the Middle East is a prerequisite if peace is to be realized. The students coming up behind them in the technical school ask how they can be part of a program where they can experience the same global mindset-building experiences. And for all our graduates, awareness that people around the world share their hopes and dreams has helped make the world a less scary and more welcoming place, with greater and more hopeful possibilities for their careers and their lives. What more could an educator hope for?

# CHAPTER 3

# Building a Launch Pad:
# How to Prepare Children to Become Global

*As they grow up, my three daughters will have a hundred times
more opportunity to interact with the world than I did. Globalization,
technology, and the ubiquity of communications have brought the
world into our neighborhood, and with the world in their backyard,
our children must understand how to both live and thrive in it. Raising
children to be global citizens isn't a choice; it's a necessity.*

**Steve Miranda,** international educator, business executive, and father

Trees need roots before they can grow branches, and birds need to be able to perch before they can attempt to fly. Likewise, children need a solid grounding in their home culture and a strong base of core life skills before they can begin to develop a global mindset. In the previous chapter, the life skills identified as being most helpful in developing a global mindset were identified. The majority of these skills are also the basics of a solid developmental foundation. We'll review these skills and their relevance to raising global children later in the chapter. But first, let's touch briefly on the parenting and educational cornerstones that form the foundation for all healthy childhood development.

There are literally hundreds of parenting books out there, and it's easy to criticize middle class parents as "an insecure, easily gulled consumer group" (as a recent *New Yorker* article did). Many of you have read of now-debunked parenting "wisdom," from the alleged need to physically discipline children daily to the supposed importance of praising their every move. But behind the hype of afternoon talk-show debate among popular parenting "experts," there is agreement on many, if not most, fundamentals among real clinical experts. And in a book related to child rearing, it's important to share with you some of the basics, even at the risk of re-telling you what you already know. All children need and deserve:

- A sense of security, belonging, and love;
- Physical safety and well-being, including rules promoting healthy eating, plenty of sleep and exercise, and other good self-care habits;

- Ample exposure to books, music, cooking, art, and other sensory delights and challenges so as to stimulate creative mental, spiritual, and physical growth;

- Solid and loving discipline to help develop good work and life habits; and

- Guiding and modeling in developing good manners and empathy, so they can get along with others and find a positive place for themselves in the world.

And of course, good parenting—as well as good teaching—requires dedication and commitment to finding what works for each individual child.

> *Raising a "global child" is about raising a kid who respects others, no matter where they are from.*
>
> **Curtis S. Chin,** international business executive and former U.S. ambassador

## Grounding in Home Country and Culture

Beyond these basics, one of the best ways parents can help their children prepare for a global life is to give them a solid grounding in their home culture. The sense of "home" develops early in ways that are remarkably similar in all the places the world's children call home. This is because, in the words of Dr. Lei Zou of Yale University's Gesell Institute of Child Development, "the fundamental development of child cognitive and psychosocial functioning is universal." As the Gesell website puts it, "all children typically grow through patterned and predictable stages." Via research and observation, "normative patterns" have been "established for each developmental age." Of course "each child progresses . . . at his or her own rate . . . a fluid process that cannot be rushed." But the basic structure of infant and child development—from wiggling to sitting to scooting or crawling to walking to running, from gurgling to babbling to talking, from "Me! Mine!" to parallel play to cooperative play to best friends—is well understood.

Understanding this process is important because it offers a rational explanation of how and when to teach children about the larger world. It's important to note that part of this basic cognitive and psychosocial development is a well-studied process of growing awareness that proceeds outward gradually, like layers on an onion, from the child, to immediate family, then to extended family, community, nation, and eventually to the entire world. First, infants become aware

of themselves and their ability to manipulate the world, then of people immediately around them, then that those people may come and go, while others
less well-known may intrude (the awareness that initiates stranger anxiety at 8
or 10 months). Then, as toddlers, children gradually become more fully aware
of themselves as separate from others, and of their home and community as
different from other homes and communities. This awareness, however, tends
to be highly localized (e.g., we have a white house, Johnny has a blue house;
I like the playground with the duck slide more than the one with the fish slide).

In the preschool years, children absorb massive amounts of information. As a
result, this is an ideal time to share the sensory joys of foods, art, music, and
other delights from many lands. But in these same years, children have trouble
sorting fact from fantasy, or cause from effect, and they often create magical
explanations. Stories of life in India or Mexico can blur with stories about Cin-
derella, or the Little Red Hen or anything else long ago or far away. In these
years, the sense of home also comes together, forming the deep-seated emotional bonds that years later develop into patriotism and/or the love of home
best exemplified by Dorothy as she clicks the ruby slippers in the penultimate
scene in *The Wizard of Oz*.

Only gradually, starting at age 5 or 6, do children begin to understand their
world in a more nuanced and logical way. Only then can they really learn that
gorillas are real but goblins are not, that Japan is a real place but Candyland is
not. That is why, around the world, "real" school (as opposed to play-school,
preschool, or kindergarten) tends to start at age 6 or 7. These early school years
are also ideal times for games, books, movies, and other materials introducing
the wider world.

During their elementary and middle school years, children become very concerned with acceptance and belonging. They develop the ability to set and
achieve their own goals and develop a sense of self-worth based on confidence and competence. Finding their own standing within a known community
is crucially important, but so is giving them a chance to reach out and challenge
themselves. They'll learn to come to grips with new cultures, languages, and
communities, and succeed in finding new places for themselves. This growth
can be enormously helpful in developing the self-esteem and confidence that
are necessary for cross-cultural aptitude.

In their teenage years, children begin to diverge from the family, hopefully
equipped with the skills, aptitudes, and know-how necessary to live a self-
sufficient and purposeful life. These are the prime years for participating in

language exchange programs and international travel. Another way to help point teens toward successful adulthood (and to enhance their college applications) is to encourage community involvement. Opportunities abound for community activism on behalf of immigrant communities, refugee groups, international students, global environmental issues, and other causes that expose teens safely to diverse cultures and forces, all of which can be powerful tools for building a global mindset.

Of course, while the broad outlines of the child developmental process are universal, the particulars most assuredly are not. There are as many ways to raise a healthy child as there are happy families, especially in the culturally diverse United States. The question of "what is home" to an American and her family can be more complicated for expatriate, multicultural and/or multiracial families, families with one or more immigrant parents, and families with religious or other deep ties to countries other than their passport country. Yet thoughtful families can invent creative answers to the question of what home is that reflect the wonderful diversity of each family's situation.

> It is crucial to help young children understand their place in the world, and also to find their right size. They should know that their parents and family treasure them. They should also know that they are not the most important people in the universe, that the world is large and complex and that other people have their own stories, rights, and goals. Sometimes this lesson is lost when we have children to give our own lives meaning; it's not good for a child to have so much power. The best thing for a child is to be part of a family, a community, a tradition, a sense of purpose that includes them, but is larger than they are. That is a good home.
>
> **Roya Hakakian,** journalist, author, and mother

Whatever approach you decide to take, it's important to make conscious decisions and take action to give your children a sense of home, community, and belonging, however you chose to define them. Considerations include:

- Who is your child's immediate family, and how is your child encouraged to find a unique and meaningful role in that family?

- Who is your child's extended family? How are ties and a sense of connection with it created and maintained over time, especially with older generations (including those who have passed on)?

- Who is your child's immediate community of friends, neighbors, and special local places? How can your child best enjoy and learn from all the cultural and personal riches of your community?

- Of what region is your child's community a part, and what foods, languages, arts, music, or other cultural or natural aspects of that region can enrich your child's life?

- What other nations, communities, or traditions are part of your child's heritage, and how can your child be encouraged to learn about, appreciate, and take pride in them?

Together, the unique ways your family answers these questions will create a rich, multilayered, and deeply meaningful sense of "home." That sense appears to be especially important in the crucial early developmental stages when stability is critical to your child's developing sense of self, family, and community.

The importance of groundedness and sense of place also applies in school, where experts agree that being secure with one's self and confident among others is crucial to facing issues and formulating a world perspective. Indeed, as families and communities shift, and a sense of home for some students becomes weakened, some educators argue that "the psychological sense that one belongs in a classroom and school community is . . . a necessary antecedent to the successful learning experience."[1] Clearly a sense of belonging and a strong self-identity provide solid grounding for success in many areas of life, including living and working across cultures. Without it, children risk feeling unmoored.

*India is a big country with a great deal of diversity, especially in festivals and foods. Now that we're here in the United States, we celebrate U.S. holidays, but we also get together with people from other parts of India to celebrate all kinds of Indian festivals and there are very many since India has such diversity across its different states. This allows our children to have a broad appreciation and understanding of their heritage as well as their new home allowing them to be more globally aware.*

**Indira Pulliadath,** pharmacoeconomist and mother

# Moving Abroad: Raising Children Outside the United States

Although neither feasible nor practical for the vast majority of Americans, raising children overseas will certainly expose them to the world and help them become global citizens, both in short order. Most families move abroad because one parent accepts a job and agrees to relocate for a few years, sometimes with multiple assignments in different countries. Depending on that job, you will probably receive some sort of expat package and assistance as you settle in for the typical initial 2–3 years. However, some parents—often teachers—also decide to take a sabbatical from their jobs and move themselves for a year or so to live in another country. The two experiences will be different, but the benefits for children will be similar.

Immersion in a different culture is intellectually stimulating and forces children to examine their culture and their place in the world. Your children's adaptation, tolerance, and acceptance of different things will broaden their horizons. They will learn firsthand what "different" means—and that it doesn't mean "wrong" or "bad." If you go to a non-English speaking country, your kids will get a head start on a second language. If they attend local school there, they'll experience a different school system with diverse teachers and students. But to ensure that they are benefiting from this global experience, it's important to note that it will not come naturally, even though many who have done it say that it's easier for children than adults. It's important, therefore, to model behavior that teaches children to appreciate different cultures and languages—and all of the nuances therein. And although it may sound exciting and even glamorous, it can also be difficult for a family to adjust to a new culture, especially one that is significantly different from their own.

Generally speaking, the younger the child, the less disruptive the move will be. In any case, it's important that you consider all the pros and cons before moving your children overseas. Do your research and confer extensively with others who have done so.

## Third Culture Kids

The term "third culture kids," or TCKs, was coined in the 1950s by anthropologist Ruth Hill Useem in her writings about children of expat families in India. The term was then popularized by sociologist David Pollock to refer to anyone who "having spent a significant part of the developmental years in a culture other than the parents' culture, develops a sense of relationship to all the cultures while not having full ownership in any."[2] TCKs especially include anyone whose family makes frequent moves across national and cultural boundaries, such as the children of army officers, missionaries, "global nomad" expats, and others whose jobs require regular changes of venue.

Frequent early cross-cultural experience has its advantages and disadvantages. Third culture kids usually have a great appreciation of a variety of cultures. They take pride in telling stories about their host culture, and they learn to value its more outward aspects such as food, music, dress, and attitude. These experiences teach them valuable lessons about life as they learn to appreciate how others live and are able to accept people for who they are regardless of their status or race. However, most third culture kids tend to feel they don't completely fit in anywhere. Still, growing up among different cultural worlds allows them to see the world, learn and use many languages, and experience diversity firsthand for themselves.[3] Their friendships invariably cross the usual racial, national, or social barriers. In some ways, President Obama may well be our most famous "third culture kid," having spent part of his early life in Indonesia where his mother was involved in development work while she was married to young "Barry" Obama's then-stepfather.

To learn more about third culture kids, check out TCK World.

> Life as the "army brat" son of a career U.S. Army officer and registered nurse moving from post to post in the United States and throughout Asia, including Taipei, Bangkok, and Seoul, made me a bit of a "third culture kid." And, whether it was their intent or not, my parents were raising global children, exposing me and my siblings to new foods, new thinking, and new worlds very different from their own childhoods growing up in rural Washington state and Baltimore, Maryland. Growing up for me was a life of packing up and moving, making new friends, and attending new schools every 2–3 years.

> **Curtis S. Chin,** international business executive and former U.S. ambassador

> For the past 20 years, we have lived in and out of the United States: Bolivia, Thailand, Hong Kong, India, Germany, and Israel. Our children have grown up around the world, speak at least two languages other than English, and are comfortable traveling alone in most big cities, and in and out of international airports. Although we have missed out on many family milestones, close gatherings of friends, and the acquisition of a dream home or automobile, I wouldn't change it for the world! I

*hope my children are better communicators and more compassionate*
*people who see the world through different lenses.*

**Sharon Elliott Sullivan**, international educator and mother

*I'm American and my husband is Austrian. Our boys (one adopted,*
*one biological) were born in China, and we live in Shanghai, which*
*has been a great home for all of us. We've taken the legal steps to*
*give our boys the gift of dual U.S.–Austrian citizenship; we'd do triple*
*citizenship if we could. They speak English with me, German with their*
*dad, and Chinese with their nanny, so they are native speakers in three*
*languages, and as adults will be able to live easily in the U.S. or EU and*
*probably in China, as well. 'Home' is our multi-cultural family and our*
*wonderfully diverse little alley in Jiangsu District which is very Chinese,*
*and also full of families from around the world. We also visit relatives*
*in the United States and Austria often enough that our boys feel real*
*connections to their other "native countries."*

**Clancey Houston**, global health care consultant, business leader, and mother

## Cultivating Patience—and Delayed Gratification

Another good general parenting and educational practice that helps prepare children for life and to work across cultures is teaching patience. Unfortunately, teaching patience has been a challenging task for both parents and teachers throughout history. Jewish scholars from Talmudic times tell us God tried Job partly to show how difficult, but important, it is to teach patience to those in our care. The instant gratification of today's 24/7, on-demand culture makes it even harder.

Yet teaching patience is crucial. In his influential book, *Emotional Intelligence*, Daniel Goleman speaks of delayed gratification as a "master skill" that underlies many other abilities. Goleman details the famous 1972 "marshmallow experiment" by Stanford psychologist Walter Mischel, in which 4-year-olds were offered one marshmallow right away, or two if they waited alone without eating the first one till the experimenter returned.[4] Only about one-third of the children were able—or willing—to wait. In follow-up research 10 and 12 years later, the children who had waited for the second marshmallow were doing better in social interactions and academics than their instant gratification (single-marshmallow) peers, including averaging 210 points higher on their SATs. Still later surveys found the two-marshmallow kids had more stable careers and lower divorce rates. By almost any measure, the two-marshmallow kids had more successful lives, and the "marshmallow divide" predicted that better than any other factor tracked, including age, race, family income, number of siblings, and age of parents at birth.

As noted in Chapter 2, patience and the ability to wait and watch before rushing to conclusions or decisions have clear links to global success, and are among the top skills identified by many researchers as being crucial to a global mindset.

So how can you teach patience? While there are no magic formulas, here are some tips that might be helpful:

- Avoid hurrying children as much as your life allows, and try to arrange schedules so as to reduce chaos when rushing is inevitable, especially with small children. Children who experience adults being patient with them are more likely to be patient with others, and life in general.

- Model patient behavior by, for instance, waiting politely in lines at the bank or grocery store, or by playing word games instead of cursing in traffic jams.

- Don't rush to respond to a child's every cry for help, from a baby's whimper to a preschooler's call to have a shoelace tied. Real needs must naturally be addressed, but not always at a moment's notice. A little frustration can do wonders for teaching children both patience and self-sufficiency.

- Take time satisfying wishes and whims. For example, requested toys and games can go onto a "long, long list" of asked-for goodies and only when a coveted item has stayed on this list long enough to clearly not be an impulse wish (usually several months) can it be considered for purchase.

- Limit exposure to videos, TV, computer games, and other media that feature passive consumption of rapid-fire images, instant gratification, and bombardment with corporate advertising.

- Encourage reading, board games, time in nature, and other activities that help slow things down for children in our too-hurried, hyperactive world.

- Model appropriate behavior in your own lives, including working at responsible jobs, saving up for desired purchases and resisting impulse buys, studying or otherwise preparing for future goals, and healthy exercise and food habits.

- With older children, talk explicitly about the importance of planning ahead and preparing for the future, and help children find their way to do so financially (via allowances and small jobs), educationally, and socially.

- With tweens and teens, explicitly reward good planning, and allow the natural, albeit non-harmful, consequences of impulsive behavior to play out so as to discourage it.

## Encouraging Curiosity, Questioning, and Analysis

Of all the traits assessed in our surveys, curiosity and the ability to question things stand out as the most common—and probably most important—attributes needed for developing a global mindset. This makes intuitive sense: a child has to be curious and interested in the broader world before being motivated to learn more about it. As noted in Chapter 2, our quantitative survey respondents ranked curiosity and interest in other cultures as two of the top three attributes necessary in developing a global mindset. But in our one-on-one interviews, every single person mentioned curiosity, essentially seeing it as one and the same with interest in other cultures. Moreover, almost all interviewees remarked that being open-minded and empathetic was assumed—you couldn't be expected to succeed cross-culturally if you weren't. Curiosity has inspired many people to pursue avenues they otherwise would not have had they been left to regular school offerings or family outings.

Similar comments came from many of those who participated in our research. For instance:

~ *Children need self-confidence, open-mindedness, and independence, but patience is paramount.*

~ *Open mindedness, curiosity, adaptability, and empathy are the requisite tools for a global life.*

~ *What helped me succeed globally was a willingness to try new things and extreme curiosity.*

~ *I succeeded because my parents taught me to be curious, open-minded, and explore life to its fullest.*

Again, there is much that you can do as parents and teachers in the early years to encourage and stimulate your child's curiosity. Examples include:

- **Encourage questions.** Ask them yourself. Answer theirs. Invite your children to ask more. Make kids feel that asking questions is not a waste of time, but rather a valuable way to learn. A curious child can be demanding in terms of time, but this time demand can be deflected away from busy parents to grandparents, older siblings, other family members, neighbors, friends, teachers, colleagues and (with older children) books, maps, and the Internet. But asking questions per se should never be discouraged. The toddler who wants to know "why, why, why?" is more likely to become the teen who explores issues deeply and the adult who succeeds in figuring out how to make things work.

- **Encourage curiosity.** If your children explore things about which they are curious, they learn about those things through repetitive exposure and independent exploration. This in turn creates a sense of knowledge and mastery of a new subject, which then encourages further curiosity.

- **Encourage independent thinking.** There are always multiple ways to achieve goals and make things work. Encourage your kids to seek their own solutions to problems by refraining from stepping in yourself with the answer. Independent thinking should not, of course, become an excuse for rudeness or self-centeredness. But many parents shut down true independence in a heavy-handed focus on decorum, resulting in what Albert Einstein called a strangling of "the holy curiosity of inquiry."

- **Model curious behavior yourself.** One of the most powerful answers a parent can give to a child's question is "Gee, I don't know. That is such a good question! Why don't we look up the answer together?"

- **Play games and do activities with your child that encourage curiosity and exploration,** such as scavenger hunts, and collecting things that fall in complex categories like insects, leaves, and stamps.

*Curiosity is the driver for global thinkers. We are stimulated by the world and by our environments. Rather than shrinking from difference, diversity, or foreign circumstances, we thrive in it.*

**Steve Finikiotis,** business leader, emerging markets

*While technical skills are important, I believe that instilling a sense
of wonder and curiosity about why people, countries, and cultures
"do what they do" is the single best attribute we can pass on to our
children. Technologies go out of style. Curiosity never does.*

**Steve Miranda,** international educator, business executive, and father

*The other young Americans who were living in Taiwan with me who
were incurious about the lives of the Chinese people all around us got
far less out of the experience than the ones who tried hard to interact
and understand.*

**Scott D. Seligman,** historian and author

*It's interesting to me that there are so many diverse cultures all over the
world, and everywhere you go there are always customs and traditions
unique to that area that can't be found anywhere else.*

**Paige,** eighth-grade student

## Encouraging Careful Listening and Observation

Other important basic life skills to teach children are good listening and careful observation. Both will prove useful in many areas of adult life, and especially in living and working cross-culturally. As referenced in Chapter 2, the ability to learn and integrate new information is critical to the flexibility and responsiveness that the research for *Get Ahead by Going Abroad* identified as one of the top five skills necessary to success in working overseas. Moreover, 91% of respondents in our most recent survey strongly agree that encouraging adaptability in children will aid in later global success. Good listening skills are equally central, not only for learning and integrating new information, but also for being able to understand and relate to the varying needs and wants of friends, neighbors, colleagues, and customers across cultures. Possessing these skills also indicates that we want to understand others, which matters a great deal when working with people who are different from us.

The ability to listen well and observe thoughtfully starts young. Here are some tips that can help you strengthen these skills in your children:

- Model good listening skills by taking time every day to listen carefully and thoughtfully to your children and reflecting appropriate answers back to them so they know they have been heard.

- Model good observational skills by noticing what is going on in your children's lives, as well as in the larger world.

- Play games that encourage close observation such as "I Spy," matching games, "what has changed" picture puzzles, and scavenger hunts.

- Engage in word games, riddles, and puns that encourage listening closely for hidden clues and subtle distinctions.

- Read books that require memory and analytical skills, such as age-appropriate mystery stories; and read and discuss alternate versions of favorite stories.

- Spend close observational time in nature, both at the macro-level (e.g., hikes and nature walks; nature scavenger hunts) and at the micro-level (e.g., in your own backyard, garden, and neighborhood). Activities like bird-watching, animal tracking, and leaf-printing are excellent for fostering close observational skills.

- Encourage children in all the creative arts, including finger paints, self-portraits, clay sculptures, journaling, photography, graphic design, and neighborhood dioramas from the recycling bin. An artist's eye (or writer's eye) is one well-trained in observation.

*I was brought up in a small suburb of Jackson, Mississippi. I didn't have much multicultural exposure from an international perspective, but I was exposed to racial differences. Just living in a diverse community enabled me to develop an open mind and encouraged me to see "different" as something to be appreciated and enjoyed.*

**Dr. Jeffrey W. Overby,** professor and father

*We all seem to lead busy lives filled with immediate "to do" lists. As a result, we often don't have enough time to pause, reflect, and think. As parents, we need to make time for conversation with our kids about events happening in other parts of the world to people we don't even know. Whether or not we want to believe it, we're affected by things that happen everywhere on the globe. The earlier the age at which kids are able to realize that significance, the greater the likelihood they act accordingly as adults.*

**Anna C. Catalano,** board director and mother

## Encouraging Independence and Avoiding Being Overly Protective

The last of the general parenting and educational basics critical to raising global children is to encourage independence and calculated risk-taking by balancing reasonable concern for safety with a child's natural impulses to try new things. Kids who learn to take chances from the earliest age, including making mistakes, falling, and picking themselves up again, have the best chance to grow into curious, resilient adults able to face the challenges of a diverse world. Rather than trying to cushion every possible blow and prevent every cut or scrape (emotional or physical), you would be better off teaching your children that the world at times has sharp edges, and that they need to—and you trust them to—take appropriate precautions. This, in turn, will prepare them for true adventures while also being able to stay safe along the way.

Many of us need to take a step back from the hyper-vigilant "safety culture" that has become so prevalent in our society. Naturally, none of us wants our children to get hurt, but a growing body of research suggests that a more balanced approach to these circumstances may in fact help children be safer over time, as well as become more self-confident. Some studies link parental over-protection to the difficulty that some Millennial young adults show in assuming full adult responsibilities.

The problem is not limited to the United States. British child development experts despair over how little rough-and-tumble outdoor play schoolchildren now get in the United Kingdom, and others describe similar issues in Australia.[5] Over-protection of children, guided potentially more by tort lawyers and parental fears than by anything advised by child development experts, appears to be a growing problem across the developed world. Yet this trend seems far less troubling in the developing world—which begs the question whether a strong sense of adventure, nurtured in childhood, is actually a contributing factor to the more rapid development of the so-called "Third World" countries.

What are the long-term effects of a culture of excessive safety-consciousness, liability, and assigning blame to someone else for anything that goes wrong?

In light of the clear differences, one also wonders about the long-term effects of such a culture upon Western national psyches. Such questions have long been part of the UK's "nanny state" debates. Maybe they should be part of the debate about economic shifts between the United States and China and the rest of the developing world. Too many American kids seem to be growing up emotionally handicapped by rules that say, "Don't run here, don't try that, don't climb anything you might fall from because it's not safe." Changes in the design of American playgrounds speak volumes about just how risk-averse we have become as a society.

*When we expose our children to a world filled with many different types of people, places, and things, we teach them about dealing with situations and solving problems without being in familiar territory. This is an important life skill for anyone to have no matter where they live or what kind of job they do.*

**Brent Riddle,** transportation planner and father

Similar sentiments were voiced by many of those interviewed. And a full 89% of our survey respondents agreed that parents should avoid over-protecting children if they want to encourage later success. Again, no one is advocating throwing safety out the window. But it's worth asking ourselves as parents whether we might be overdoing safety consciousness when we listen to the lawyers more than what our own hearts and minds tell us our children need.

## Real Stories from Real People

### Rebecca Weiner, *entrepreneur, author, and mother*

My daughter Sarah often seems braver in China than at home. She climbs higher, runs faster, tries tougher exploits, and cries less when she falls in favorite Chinese haunts like Shanghai's Zhongshan Park than at home in New Haven's Edgewood Park. Certainly the contrast can't be explained by overall comfort in China. Sarah doesn't love being left with Chinese ayis (nannies) while I work, and squirms at the attention the Chinese lavish on young foreigners. Yet she lists Zhongshan among her favorite places anyway. When she goes there without me, I hear tales of bumper-car rides that turned ayi green but which, Sarah boasts, "didn't bother me."

No doubt the difference stems partly from simple excitement, running around halfway across the world while regular playmates back home are sleeping. But I long suspected deeper factors, and a pair of incidents brought these factors into focus. Once at Edgewood I saw a wild-eyed little boy race up an artificial climbing wall, over a catwalk, across an artificial boulder designed to encourage safe rock-climbing, and straight off into thin air. The boy flailed for a split second like Wiley E. Coyote running off a cliff, then plunged to the "wood-fiber safety surface" below.

That event and its aftermath lit light bulbs. As it happens, a few months earlier, I had seen a very similar scene in Zhongshan Park with another small boy, a real boulder, and concrete. The two incidents offered almost clinically perfect contrasts in parental reactions. Both falls resulted in large scrapes and bruised egos. The Zhongshan boy's concrete landing actually drew blood; the Edgewood boy's wood fiber landing didn't. But the real impacts came from parental behavior. Both moms rushed in for the mandatory quick-check that eyes still blinked, limbs remained attached, and digits still wiggled as directed, then gave quick maternal hugs. But there the similarities ended.

The Shanghai mom berated her son for failed judgment. "Ni zenme mei kan?" she asked ("why weren't you looking?") Then she picked him up, dusted him off with a strong admonition to look before future leaps, bandaged the scrapes with a clean hanky, and sent him back to play.

The Connecticut mom wailed about her "poor baby," prompting wails from her child in response. Sympathetic bystanders clucked about climbing rocks without railings, and wondered about liability. Others kicked the safety surface, asking if it were deep enough. I heard no one suggest that the boy himself should have been more careful.

Many related contrasts rose to mind, such as the creaky yet beloved old Zhongshan amusement rides, whose sometimes rusty metal edges would long since have been banned from most American parks; the lovely handmade mosaics in the Zhongshan sidewalks that can be bumpy and uneven; the parents who bring kids to Zhongshan on bikes and motorcycles, sans kid seats, trained from babyhood to "hang on;" and all the brave Chinese kids running and leaping and climbing on those wonderful creaky, rusty playgrounds, making Sarah braver in imitation. In the meantime, signs around Edgewood remind visitors that sidewalks can be slippery when wet, and that speed bumps are bumpy.

The Zhongshan boy, in a couple of minutes, was back up leaping boulders, watching his trajectory more carefully. The American boy did not, while I watched, try to climb again. I had a strange sensation, considering the two incidents, of watching their futures unfold, the Zhongshan boy's full of bold leaps based on careful calculations, the Edgewood boy's more restrained. It was easy to see who would be tomorrow's CEO, or world leader. And I know which I'd rather have Sarah imitate.

### Indira Pulliadath, *pharmacoeconomist and mother*

When my son was in preschool he did not mind when I packed Indian dishes in his lunch box. But as he grew older, that became a definite "no-no" with him refusing to bring them saying, "I feel odd because people stare at my food and make fun of it." My husband and I absolutely did not want him to feel alienated at school, so we complied with his wishes and sent him to school with typical American food.

Over the years as our kids have been growing up, we really have had to do a delicate balance between exposing them to our culture while at the same time taking care to not overdo it lest they feel isolated among their friends. Having moved to the United States 14 years ago, my husband and I really value a lot of the things that are American. But at the same time, we think that it is very important to expose our kids to our own rich and varied heritage. In fact, because of our diverse background and perspectives, we would like them to understand not only Indian culture and values, but also be familiar with other cultures too. We believe that having a multi-cultural or global perspective early on in life helps to develop tolerance as well as appreciation for the differences that we see in today's diverse society. Hence we habitually talk about other nationalities, encourage learning new languages, and even play games that help to increase their knowledge about different countries. We also like to try out different cuisines using our international food experiences as a means to explore and learn more about different countries.

But more important than all the above-mentioned things, I encourage my kids to talk to other kids who are from a different country and to ask them questions about their country and their culture. I tell them it's ok to be naturally curious as long as they are not offensive or rude. And I think it is equally imperative that all adults also realize and practice the gospel that "it's OK to be inquisitive." I think that many times, adults try to pretend that there are no differences (even when they see them) just because they are fearful of coming across as having a discriminatory attitude. I say this based on my experiences at my workplace and the neighborhood where we live. For instance, I used to find it rather odd that when I got back to work after my vacations to India that none of my otherwise "quite friendly" colleagues would ask me many detailed questions about my trip. I am convinced that they genuinely thought they were doing me a favor by not asking! But the truth is that I would have loved to share stories about my home country, its people, and its vibrant culture.

I believe that the key to multicultural education is to encourage openness and recognize differences. Teach this to your kids as well. Encourage them to "ask questions and not to be shy." I also tell my kids that "if someone asks you anything about India, don't be afraid to talk about it." I feel that, if the kids at my son's grade school had been taught that it was OK to be curious and ask about things that look different, there could have been a better outcome to my son's cafeteria experience. If he had been asked about his food, I am sure he would have loved to explain and the mystery food would have been easily de-mystified! And more importantly, the kid who asked could have learned more about a new country and made a new friend as well!

I have been preaching these tenets in our home over and over, again and again and guess what? I think it may be working . . . just last month my son asked me to cook an Indian chicken dish, along with the homemade pizza that I usually make, when two of his close buddies came for a sleepover!

### Curtis S. Chin, *international business executive and former U.S. ambassador*

Definitions vary somewhat, but basically "third culture kids" are children (and the adults they become) who have spent a good part of their childhood living outside of their home country (or countries') culture. Typically, that can be as a "military brat" accompanying parents abroad, the child of an overseas missionary, a diplomat's kid, or the son or daughter of a business executive moving the family from one corporate assignment to the next. As the son of a career U.S. Army officer and a registered nurse, I grew up moving from post to post—both in the United States and Asia—every two or three years.

That experience helped nurture in me a sense of flexibility and an ability to meet new people easily and feel comfortable in different environments. It might also have added to my own sense of wanderlust and excitement over the next adventure in my own career and intellectual growth and development.

Raising global children, however, does not require having to move overseas or even having to travel overseas. Instead, it is about attitude and nurturing— ideally from early on—every child's natural eagerness to learn and to explore. Raising global children is also about keeping alive a child's innate sense of wonder. But there are many things that parents can do in this regard, without even leaving their hometown. Most importantly, they can set an example through their own curiosity and interests even if they do not think of themselves as global.

One great and easy way to get started in thinking globally and getting your kids involved is to put together a family tree. Begin by writing down stories of Mom's or Dad's growing up, or a tale or two from Grandpa or Grandma. With just about every American being able to trace back a connection to some other country, writing up a family history or piecing together a family tree can lead to great family conversations and new discoveries about different places.

My family just had our first ever Chin Family Reunion in Seattle, and it was a great way for all of us to reconnect with one another and our shared history. It all began with my cousin Maylee in Los Angeles helping one of her sons with a school assignment to draw a family tree. Eventually, some 110 family members convened in Seattle for a weekend of family activities. Attendees came from Bangkok, Hong Kong, Sacramento, CA, Washington, D.C., and many points in between.

Over the previous four months, we had created shared online photo albums and thanks to the Internet (as well as relatives who never throw anything out) had tracked down census reports, old passports, and other bits of data as we traced a family tree going back to my great-great-grandfather Gong Cok Han Chin, born in April 1851 in Taishan (Toisan), Guangdong, China, and great-great-grandmother Yan Hong, born in November 1861 in Sunning, Guangdong, China. In some ways, the journey of discovery was as rewarding as the reunion itself. Learning about how distant relatives traveled back and forth by ship between Asia and the U.S. West Coast in the early 1900s also underscored how global the United States is now and was even then. Tracking down our family history and all that that entailed, including spending time with and getting to know cousins, who I do not often see, made the reunion much more than a specific date or event in Seattle.

My own family reunion journey included a trip with my dad to the small central Washington town of Ellensburg, where he grew up in the 1930s. The population then was less than 5,000 people. Today it is about 18,000. My dad's childhood home had been torn down, but accompanied by my cousin Linda and aunt Sylvia, we went on a search for the New York Café, where he had once worked. The café too was long gone, but the building it had been in was still there, and we marveled at the building's still intact Art Deco metal door handles, which had been fashioned in the shape of the letters N and Y. We then journeyed on to Yakima, Washington, where we were able to visit the house my dad had lived in as a teenager. Others' family trees may well take them back to Europe, Africa, or South America. But no matter where it leads, putting together a family tree can certainly be a great adventure for any kid, and a very concrete lesson in just how global we Americans really are.

# CHAPTER 4

# Teaching Language: "Switching On" the Global Mindset

---

*The lack of language education for American students before high school inhibits their ability to master a language and to appreciate other cultures through language learning. We wouldn't consider sending students to college with only 2 years of math or history. Language should be treated the same—as a core subject beginning in elementary school.*

**Dr. Jeffrey W. Overby,** professor and father

"Why should American children—or anyone who speaks English—learn a foreign language? After all, everyone speaks English now, don't they? And for travel we can always stick a translation app on our smartphones . . . ."

Arguments like this seem bizarre to many of us in the second decade of the 21st century. But some influential people say ridiculous things. Former Harvard President Lawrence Summers, for one, recently suggested reducing foreign language study in a *New York Times* op-ed piece on educational reform. Summers, who seems to relish juicy debates, claims that English is "the global language," and better machine translation makes foreign languages "less essential." Summers's comments sparked a lively "Room for Debate" column in the *Times* that received thousands of comments both on- and off-line and demonstrated that plenty of Americans recognize the importance of foreign languages. Yet the position taken by Summers echoes the argument that many school administrators and school boards make when cutting foreign language budgets, despite research that indicates they not only improve test scores in math and language arts, but are a critical 21st century job skill. As mentioned in Chapter 2, government support for language education has been drying up, including recent defunding of the Department of Education's Foreign Language Assistance Program (FLAP).

In addition to believing that learning a second language isn't necessary, naysayers also insist that it's too difficult and too costly. To "prove" their point, many provide an example from their own educational history, generally along the lines of "I took Spanish for 4 years, and all I can say is 'Hola!'" Yes, it can be difficult to learn another language. But studies show that if you begin teaching children at an early age, their "time on task" is longer, and they stand a much greater chance of becoming proficient. Elementary school children in particular have a far greater cognitive ability to learn a language than high school students, though the very best window of language learning, not surprisingly, is the period from birth to 5 years. Moreover, it doesn't cost any more to run a language curriculum than it does a math one. But there is no denying that many school districts have been forced to make budgetary cuts these past few years, and the difficult decision of what to cut is often based on input from parents. It is paramount, therefore, that as parents, we get involved with our school system and lobby to—at the very least—maintain whatever language program is currently in place.

As of today, the United States is the only industrialized nation where the vast majority of high schools and colleges still give out diplomas without a second language requirement. Moreover, many countries now require foreign language study in elementary school, including some where English is also the national language. Schoolchildren in England, for example, now start a second language at age 7, while those in Scotland begin at age 4.[1] India has recently added Mandarin as a requirement for all students beginning in the sixth grade, and some African nations are doing the same, albeit at different ages. Meanwhile back in the United States, even those colleges with second language graduation requirements often accept just a year or two of study, a minimal level of competence that won't get their graduates very far in the global marketplace.

There's an old joke—sad but too true: "If you call someone who speaks three languages trilingual and someone who speaks two languages bilingual, what do you call someone who speaks just one language? An American."

*We must focus on improving language learning in the United States. Our language capabilities are poor compared to many other countries around the world. We should have many more immersion programs beginning in kindergarten to enable more students to graduate from high school truly proficient.*

Steve Miranda, international educator, business executive, and father

## What Does Proficiency in a Language Mean?

The term "proficiency" is used a great deal through this book, but what exactly does it mean? According to the recently revised *ACTFL Performance Descriptors for Language Learners*, designed to reflect how language learners perform whether learning in classrooms, online, through independent project-based learning, or in blended environment:

"**Proficiency** is the ability to use language in real world situations in a spontaneous interaction and non-rehearsed context and in a manner acceptable and appropriate to native speakers of the language. Proficiency demonstrates what a language user is able to do regardless of where, when or how the language was acquired. The demonstration is independent of how the language was learned; the context may or may not be familiar; the evaluation of proficiency is not limited to the content of a particular curriculum that has been taught and learned.

An assessment of proficiency determines if the language user provides sufficient evidence of all of the assessment criteria of a particular level according to the ACTFL Proficiency Guidelines. The individual must do everything expected at a level in a sustained fashion, that is, all of the time, in order to be rated at that level."

For more information go to ACTFL's site.

---

*I first fell in love with Russia on a mission trip with my church at the age of 12, and since then, I have had a strong desire to master the language. I applied and was accepted into the CLS [Critical Language Scholarship] summer program when I was a junior in college. I had a phenomenal, adventurous summer where I grew not only linguistically, but also personally and relationally as well. Linguistically, the program was the most stretching that I have ever experienced; with 20 hours of in-class instruction per week, a pledge to refrain from speaking English on campus, and weekly sessions with a language partner, we were definitely immersed in the language. Speaking in a foreign language at almost all times was one of the most challenging things I've ever done, but my work was richly rewarded: at the end of the summer, I crossed a threshold on the ACTFL speaking scale, moving from an "Intermediate High" proficiency to "Advanced Low."*

**Hope Johnson,** international teaching assistant

# Why We Need Foreign Language Education

Weak as it is, the argument against teaching foreign languages persists. Fortunately, the argument for teaching them is strong and growing stronger, and you've probably met people who lend their voices to the chorus, citing one or more of the most prominent rationales: pragmatic (strengthening national security), practical (career enhancement), academic (understanding the nuances of literature or music), and personal (pleasure and personal growth). A sampling of the many reports, studies, and Congressional testimonies that demonstrate that America's business and government leaders believe in the importance of foreign language education for our citizens follows. All of them are persuasive in their own right; collectively, they are compelling.

## Economic and National Security Benefits

Our nation's military, national security, diplomatic, and business leaders recognize the importance of speaking languages in addition to English:

- According to the Department of Defense's own recruitment website, the "DoD has an urgent and growing need for Americans with foreign language skills," especially in "high-demand" languages such as Arabic, Chinese, Dari, Hindi, Japanese, Korean, Kurdish, Pashto, Persian-Farsi, Tagalog, Russian, Somali, Turkish, and Urdu/Punjabi. Congressional subcommittees on Defense, Intelligence, and National Security regularly hear reports on how our security and intelligence efforts are stymied by a lack of qualified language professionals.

- Reports by the bipartisan Language Flagship, a public–private initiative funded in part by the DoD's National Security Education Program (NSEP), quote business leaders stating that "the lack of language skills among U.S. business[people] is an enormous barrier to increasing U.S. participation in overseas markets," and "a globally competitive company requires an investment in cultural awareness and language skills." One Language Flagship participant's comments echoed what business people already knew: People and companies with greater cross-cultural abilities can develop new markets more easily, negotiate stronger contracts, connect better with customers, and attract higher-tier employees in markets around the world.

- In a report on National Defense Education, the Association of American Universities ranks foreign language education as highly as STEM [science,

technology, engineering, and mathematics] learning for both national security and economic strength.[2]

- A recent article from NAFSA, a leading association of international education professionals, points out that even the attempt to strengthen language
skills in the United States shows the rest of the world that we care about
what they have to say. Conversely, continued weakness in language education reinforces perceptions that the United States has a profound listening
problem.[3]

## Individual Career Benefits

Given the level of need for proficient foreign language speakers in businesses
and government, it is hardly surprising that language learning offers a tremendous career boost:

- The number of employers looking for graduates with bilingual skills has significantly increased in the past 5 years. Job postings for those bilingual
in English and Russian, Chinese, Spanish, Portuguese, and Hindi abound.
Many articles in human resources and career-related journals echo these
trends.

- Peer-reviewed studies on the personal economic benefits of language
skills are relatively sparse, in part due to the methodological complexities
of tracing language ability as a factor across industries over time. But the
studies that have been done are suggestive. One researcher found at least
some benefits to foreign language ability in hiring, salary, and promotional
opportunities even among relatively lower-paid employees such as bank
tellers, hospital orderlies, and hotel clerks. A meta-study in Canada found
significant correlation between participation in immersion language programs during school years and both employment opportunities and higher
incomes decades later. Other research links language skills to success in
overseas postings, thus strengthening the individual's job and salary prospects both at home and abroad.

- In our own survey, foreign language education consistently ranked among
the top three factors respondents listed as crucial to future success in a
global career. A resounding 98% of respondents agreed that encouraging
children to learn a second language would contribute to a global mindset,
and 93% agreed that it was helpful if the parent learned a new language
along with the child.

And—believe it or not—it hardly matters which language you decide to learn. Languages like Arabic, Chinese, Portuguese, and Russian are "hot" today, but it's impossible to tell what other languages will be in demand decades from now.

*You can never predict with exact precision what is and is not going to be economically useful as a foreign language. When I was in college, studying Albanian would have been considered a waste of time. But today an American who speaks Albanian fluently can easily get a job in Albania, Kosovo, or Macedonia. Who knew that was going to happen?*

**Mitchell Polman,** public diplomacy specialist

*When I got back from Taiwan in the mid-1970s, Mandarin was not really a marketable skill. Who could have predicted the sudden opening of China, and its dramatic rise? But by the early 1980s, employers were clamoring for people who could speak Chinese!*

**Scott D. Seligman,** historian and author

Of course there are no guarantees in life. To be effective in moving a career forward, language skills need to be strong, but organizations are usually looking for a combination of skills, including the ability to function in overseas markets but still think like an American. After all, it's as important to be able to communicate with the home office as it is with the people in the target market.

*I've watched too many people who are native-level fluent speakers of a language get edged-out by actual native speakers who are immigrants or just trying to extend their U.S. visa. On the flip side, I have seen people do very well in spite of the fact that they don't speak the language of the region of their expertise fluently, including ambassadors.*

**Mitchell Polman,** public diplomacy specialist

*I grew up bilingual speaking English and Greek. I also speak French, passable Spanish and Italian, and have studied Russian and Arabic. And although English is the 'lingua franca' of the business world, I have found language skills offer a huge advantage when working in other countries. Trying to speak another language with customers, even taxi drivers and vendors, fosters trust and creates a bond that enhances the experience manifold.*

**Steve Finikiotis,** business leader, emerging markets

Force-feeding is not the way to learn any language, and area knowledge is as important as language skills, but more on both those points below. Still, for the above and many more reasons, speaking a second language—any language— is likely to help our children in whatever field they choose enough so as to be well worth the investment in time and effort.

## Benefits to General Education

Decades of peer-reviewed research has strongly suggested that foreign language study offers tremendous benefits for general education, even if the exact connections cannot be pinned down. For instance, studies show that:

- Second language learners tend to outperform English-only learners in English, perhaps because learning a foreign language requires higher-order thinking about word order, meaning, pronunciation, grammar, and the other building blocks of language learning.

- Second language learners consistently out-test English-only learners in other core subjects, such as history, social studies, science, and math.

- Second language learning has demonstrated benefits for basic academic (and career/life) skills such as listening, reading, writing, speaking, comprehension, analysis, grouping/categorization, and the ability to memorize.

- These benefits appear to apply to children of all ages, races, ethnic, and economic backgrounds, with some of the strongest benefits coming for children from disadvantaged families; in other words, foreign language study also has a demonstrated ability to help close academic achievement gaps.[4]

*Learning other languages has heightened my awareness of my own language, helping me to better understand it grammatically as well as culturally. All languages are culturally bound and you learn this by learning the meanings of words and how some translate and others don't.*

**Brent Riddle,** transportation planner and father

## Personal Benefits

At the personal level, the benefits of language learning may be clearest of all:

- Many recent medical studies show that by challenging the executive functions of the brain, studying another language—and particularly becoming fully bilingual— improves higher-order thinking across many topics beyond language, and can thus help in raising healthy, self-confident children.

- Modern neuroscience has definitively shown that bilingualism can help with everything from babies learning how to understand their world to preventing Alzheimer's.[5]

- Beyond the many scientifically provable benefits, everyone who speaks more than one language knows the subtle, but powerful, intangible benefits in self-confidence, pleasure in expanded opportunities for friendships and relationships, and joy in multilayered bilingual jokes, music, and puns.

- Language ability also helps the individual understand and participate in cultures that are inherently multicultural. From "Chino-Latino" to Bollywood, from African diaspora culture to "Nordo-Turk," the world's fusion cultures today are legion and growing in wonderful richness. Speaking more than one of the languages involved makes these multilayered cultures that much more accessible and enjoyable. And there's nothing quite like the joys of finding camaraderie around the world based on shared languages.

*Some of my most enjoyable memories include chatting in "Span-Chin-glish" with Cuban-Chinese refugees in Caracas, communicating about green ideas in a stew of basic Spanish and pidgin Portuguese with environmental activists in Rio, and attending Saturday services in a mixture of Hebrew, English and Yiddish at rebuilt synagogues in Warsaw and Berlin.*

**Rebecca Weiner,** entrepreneur, author, and mother

*I've found that when I'm in France and speak French, locals treat me as their own. Their demeanor changes and they speak to me as someone who understands them and knows where they're coming from.*
*Language is what truly allows one to get inside a culture. As Americans, we expect it of others when they come here, but not of ourselves when we travel abroad.*

**Liz Allred,** higher education adviser

*Learning languages made my kids hungry to explore the world and really learn about what is happening in other places.*

**Laura Cubanski,** mother

As Charlemagne is believed to have said, "To have a second language is to have a second soul."

---

## Glastonbury, Connecticut

Glastonbury is a historic Connecticut River Valley town that dates back to the mid-1600s. Today it is a suburb of Hartford, and enjoys the benefits of having one foot still in the agricultural sector and the other in the industrial/service sector. It is also considered a national leader in language learning in its public school system. Spanish begins in first grade; a second language can be added in seventh, and a third in high school. As a result, some seniors at Glastonbury High graduate with varying degrees of language proficiency in three foreign languages, including Chinese and Russian.

Glastonbury's history of viewing foreign language as a necessary currency for future success began in 1957 with the former Soviet Union's successful launch of Sputnik, the world's first orbiting satellite. This prompted a nationwide concern that the United States was falling dangerously behind in the space race. Something needed to be done, and one of those things was to generate more Americans capable of speaking Russian.

Glastonbury had the good fortune to have a forward-thinking superintendent, Larry Pauquin, who in late 1957 started conversations with Mary Thompson, a foreign language teacher in Fairfield, Connecticut, who ran the state's first foreign language program for an elementary school. With the assistance of Yale University professors, Thompson wrote a grant requesting $1 million in funding to bring teachers together to create a set of language materials that would begin in third grade and extend all the way through high school.

In 1958, Glastonbury was selected by the Department of Defense to be one of only three pilot programs for teaching Russian, which was added as an optional second language in the seventh grade. Seventy students signed up that first year, many of whom ended up pursuing careers in the military. Those in business were ready for the opening up of Russia's markets in the late 1980s/early 1990s.

It was a revolutionary approach to language learning and Glastonbury collaborated with Yale University to build the first high school language library in French and Spanish. Interestingly, these language materials were bought by Harcourt Brace Jovanovich, which packaged and sold them around the world in the 1960s and '70s under the ALM label.

Despite academic budget cuts that began in the 1970s, Glastonbury's language curriculum has persevered virtually intact. Ninety-five percent of the graduating seniors have received the full 12 years of foreign language instruction, and are well on their way to reaching a high level of proficiency in college or university. This far exceeds the national average of just 40%, and gives Glastonbury High School a significantly stronger language program than even most prestigious private schools.

Glastonbury has implemented bold and innovative new methods of teaching foreign language, including cultural knowledge and under-standing (gestures, vernacular). It practices the philosophy that lan-guage cannot be taught in isolation, but needs to be married to actual language acquisition in a systematic way. Having native speakers with different world views as teachers allows children to acquire their lan-guage skills accompanied by enhanced levels of cultural, political, and historical context.

## How to Encourage Learning Languages

By now, there should be no disputing the value of learning a second language, not only for the sake of raising global children, but for a variety of other lifelong benefits. But actually learning one is something that is much easier said than done. And that applies to the language learner as well as his or her parents. Some of the things that you, as parents and educators, can do to help raise your children with the language skills they should have are presented here for each stage of development.

## Infancy and Early Childhood

We all first develop our language skills in infancy and toddlerhood. This is also the ideal time to introduce children to a second language. Research done on twins and neuroscience confirms that all babies are born "pan-lingual" (i.e., able to learn any language in which they are immersed, first by gurgling and babbling in the sounds that are the foundation of all human languages). As they grow, this complex of noises is "pruned" to the sounds used in the languages the child hears most often. The synapses in the brain that create pathways of meaning for those specific sounds are strengthened and others atrophy. Some researchers believe that languages learned in the crucial window of early childhood are learned in a deep-rooted way that no later language-learning can match—and that that window begins to close as early as 8 or 10 months.[6] Children who become bilingual or trilingual from birth learn naturally, absorbing the grammar, rules, and cadences of the language without any academic exercises, all of which are linked indelibly to the stories, folkways, and culture of that language.

For these reasons, children of multilingual families are at a significant advantage when it comes to learning multiple languages. When mom speaks one language with a child, dad another, and a grandparent or caregiver a third, that child grows up with an incredible gift. The old myth that bilingualism holds back learning a primary language simply isn't true. Instead, bilinguals appear to learn each of their two languages at a rate equal to or only slightly below that at which monolinguals learn their one. Any lapses which develop disappear by the time the child enters elementary school.[7]

*As the daughter of an immigrant mother from Italy, I grew up speaking Italian and English. When I had children, I wanted the same for them. As the topic of language development came up with my pediatrician, he informed me that children speaking two languages may have delayed speech development in English. Research proves this to be a myth and if I hadn't challenged this doctor and done what I had, my daughters would not be on their way to bilingualism now.*

    **Jennifer Maniscalco,** marketing professional and mother

*We never had to hold lessons in any of our kids' languages because I always used English with them, their dad always spoke German, and the nanny always spoke Chinese. So they simply grew up speaking all three. We also made sure to have books, toys, games, music, and videos around in all three languages for them to choose from. Now that they're in a bilingual school, they get high marks in both English and Chinese classes without special effort, so they can focus attention on*

*other areas that might be a greater challenge for them. We try to make
sure they get solid academic content in German as well.*

**Clancey Houston,** global health care consultant, business leader, and mother

*I'm a first-generation American, born to parents from Shanghai. I went
to the dreaded Chinese school on weekends and hated it. I didn't want
my kids to have that experience. Instead we identified a play-based
immersion program which allowed them to learn Chinese without
realizing it. I wanted them to enjoy language and embrace it as part
of everyday learning. They also attend The Deutsche School as their
elementary school where all instruction is in German.*

**Julian Ha,** executive recruiter and father

Consistent, regular early foreign language exposure is important for true bilingualism. The easiest way to raise a bilingual child is to have at least one
significant adult in the child's life be a native speaker who communicates with
the child only in that language, despite being fluent in English as well. If a loved
adult offers a choice, children tend to focus on whatever language they are
learning fastest; the other language will then be learned much more slowly, and
possibly not at all. Children then learn, for example, to always speak German
with Daddy and English with Mommy, or Chinese with the nanny and Russian
with Grandpa, etc.

*Many Iranian immigrants to the United States feel a duty to teach their
children Farsi, but teach it with such brow-beating that their children
grow up hating Persian culture. Some parents even praise their children
in English and scold them in Farsi. What message does that send? I
wanted my boys to love Farsi, so I taught jokes and silly rhymes, and
wrote them Farsi love letters and read to them from the great Persian
love poems.*

**Roya Hakakian,** journalist, author, and mother

Of course, ultimate language ability falls on a spectrum, and true bilingualism
is fairly rare among native-born Americans not born to immigrant parents. Even
so, true bilingualism as an ideal must be balanced with other goals.

*I wanted my daughter Sarah to be bilingual in Chinese, as I am. But
English is my native language, and I also wanted to sing her the*

*lullabies, read her the stories, and share the endearments of my own childhood. In the end I had to parent in ways that felt natural, which for me meant speaking with and reading to my daughter mostly in English, while also exposing her to lots of Chinese songs, stories, and games. As a result, she has not grown up bilingual. But she knows a lot of Chinese, pronounces it correctly—a challenge for monolingual English speakers—and writes the characters she knows more like a Chinese child than like an American learning Chinese. Now that she's learning Chinese formally in school, it's coming easily. She enjoys being a "star pupil" with very little effort in her third-grade Chinese class, and lately speaks Chinese more readily with me at home. I expect she will develop real fluency over time.*

Rebecca **Weiner**, entrepreneur, author, and mother

*I do not speak another language, but my wife is Russian and has spoken to our children in Russian since their birth. She has given them a beautiful gift of natural fluency, which is enhanced every time my in-laws come over to visit.*

Adam L. **Michaels**, international business executive and father

However it is done, consistency is key to helping a child learn a second language. Some studies suggest learners need at least 50 uses of a given word in each of its forms (e.g., listening to, saying it, and hearing it read for younger children; reading and writing it for older ones) to master that word. It takes a lot of time talking together to get to the word "broccoli" 50 times in Hindi!

But again, any language learning seems better than no language learning. No time you spend with your child is wasted, and time spent broadening language and culture can be valuable at many levels, even for languages and cultures that you barely understand yourself.

## Is Technology Effective for Early Learners?

Despite marketing claims by Disney and others, research consistently shows that language learning via technology is ineffective for young children, and that infants watching foreign language DVDs from "Baby Einstein," "Brainy Baby," and the like learn little or nothing from them. If mom or dad needs to put on a video as an electronic babysitter for a bit to finish up a work project or make sure supper doesn't burn, "Brainy

Baby" is probably better than some other things. But parents should not delude themselves into thinking Junior will actually learn French or Russian from it.

---

If you are interested in teaching your young child another language, here are some tips to help you get started:

- Have a loved adult or young-adult caregiver speak with the child in a language other than English, as often and consistently as feasible.

- As when speaking with small children in any language, use "motherese," (i.e., speak a little more slowly and a little more animatedly than you would with adults).

- Pronounce words clearly, and repeat, repeat, repeat!

- Use statements about the here and now ("Here is lunch." "What a pretty flower!" "The cat is black.").

- Use sight to complement sound ("Look at the red bird." "See the kitty running fast!"). Neuroscience tells us that sight centers in the brain develop quickly; by age 5, a child's visual brain is as developed as an adult's. Language centers lose some flexibility over time, but gain memorization and analytical ability over many years; the language centers in the brain don't approach maturity until the teenage years, and continue developing until the late 20s. So with small children, focus on what they can see, and build vocabulary around that.

- Don't neglect the other senses, either. Small children love to engage with what they can touch and taste, so engage them at that level ("Let's touch the kitty—how soft!" "How yummy the cookies smell!).

- Use contrasts and opposites ("This water is cold." "Be careful, Mommy's tea is hot.")

- Reserve questions for vocabulary you are sure the child knows ("Do you want more milk?").

- Have and read age-appropriate picture books in the target language. These can include translations of books already familiar from English, as well as stories written originally in the target language. This helps introduce the culture, and also shows the child that there is special fun to be had only in that language.

- Have and play age-appropriate games in the target language. Seek out simple and colorful puzzles and board games that provide the perspective of another culture, decorated with words from the target language.

- If you can find a playgroup of children who are native speakers in that language, include your child as often as you can.

- Hang art and posters from the target culture and in the target language on the walls. Talk about them with your children, explaining why you like them.

- Listen, dance, and sing together to songs sung in the target language. Songs are a magically easy way for children to memorize vocabulary, and the rhythms and movement of dance seem to help cement learning.

- Play games in the target language—perhaps designate certain toys as being Chinese toys or certain stuffed animals as speaking only German.

Above all, have fun! If your children see language learning as a chore, they won't like it. Make the language you want them to learn a magic key that opens a door to new worlds, not a prison sentence. Share things that are funny, silly, and even outrageous in the language.

*You know what really made my boys love Farsi? They loved learning that Farsi has a rich variety of wonderfully onomatopoetic words for all the varying types of farts.*

**Roya Hakakian,** journalist, author, and mother

## National Network for Early Language Learners

The National Network for Early Language Learning (NNELL) provides monthly information online for its members that address teacher and parent questions about early language learning. The site is an excellent resource filled with tips and information about how to help children learn another language.

## School-Age Learning

Once your children reach school age, the choice of which language to learn will be dominated—if not entirely co-opted—by what is being taught at their school. (See the advocacy section in Chapter 8 for tips on influencing what opportunities are made available.) But as parents, you might still be able to constructively influence what language your child chooses from among the school offerings and/or via after-school programs.

*I love studying languages. It's exciting! I love exploring other cultures that I wouldn't normally learn about.*

**Paige**, eighth-grade student

## Language Choice

The bottom line is that any second language will help switch on that "second soul" for your child, enabling him or her to better bridge divides with other cultures, and stand out as an individual. That said, not all language learning programs are created, treated, or respected equally. If you have the option to choose a language to study, children and their families should consider their personal interests, the prospective ease of learning, and to some extent, its future employment potential.

- **Personal interest.** If a child has an interest in a particular language, and that language is one of the ones offered in his or her school, by all means, encourage them to pursue that interest. However, it's a good idea to explain to them that the process of learning a language is similar to learning any subject; it takes a great deal of time, dedication, and study. If he or she doesn't know much about the language and it seems to have been selected for frivolous or ephemeral reasons (e.g., the cousin they admire studied Arabic; their favorite meal is sauerbraten and spatzle), it's important that parents intervene in the selection process. If parents know a language, have a personal history, or, at the very least, have a positive attitude about a language, children pick up on it. Conversely, if parents are negative about a language or culture or nervous about their children learning skills they don't have or think they are wasting their time, the kids will pick up on this as well. Personal interest does matter and can enhance the speed and effectiveness with which children learn, especially if supplemented through cultural elements such as food, music, and art.

- **Ease of learning.** All else being equal, it can help to choose a language to study that comes relatively easily. Some languages are grammar-heavy; others require memorization of word-order rules. Still others are musical, and require intonation. If a choice is available, go online and try to listen to basic phrases to get a sense of the language. You and your child might spend time flipping through age-appropriate first-year language guides, picture books, and dictionaries in different languages at a bookstore, and see which make sense. Also, consider opportunities to practice—are there native speakers or learners' groups in your area?

- **Professional potential.** In the end, one major reason for you to ensure that your children learn another language is to expand their economic opportunities. Most any language will do that, but some more than others. Spanish, in addition to sometimes being the only foreign language offered in many school districts, offers great professional potential; there is an abundance of jobs right here in America requiring Spanish language proficiency. But it is hardly the only one and even proficient native English speakers of Spanish are going to be competing against hundreds of true bilinguals. NSEP, a major Federal initiative designed to build a broader and more qualified pool of U.S. citizens with foreign language and international skills, lists more than 70 languages as "critical" with Arabic, Chinese, Hindi, Indonesian, Korean, Russian, and Turkish in particular demand. All represent significant and growing opportunities in business, intelligence, and cultural and governmental exchange. So, too, albeit to a lesser degree, do less commonly taught languages from Albanian to Swahili.

## Learning Mode Options

What is the best way to learn a second language? Traditional classroom learning is always preferable if it's available. But there are also both alternatives and supplements to regular, structured classes:

- **Language clubs.** Informal groups meet in cultural centers, parks, and faith-based institutions in the local communities and on the Internet.

- **Language-learning self-study books, software, and apps.** Many adults have acquired various levels of ability using commercial learning programs such as Rosetta Stone®, Berlitz®, and Pimsleur®. These programs also generally have versions aimed at school-age children. And while studies give the nod to classroom-based lessons over software for language learning at all levels, school children in particular do seem to be able to make significant progress learning languages using age-appropriate software, apparently because of the "fun" and novelty of using the technology.

- **Private tutoring.** One-on-one tutoring can be expensive, but amazingly effective. And sometimes, it can come free—as part of playgroups designed for native speakers, and/or in exchange for one-on-one tutoring in English. Check out bulletin boards, real and virtual, to find potential language study buddies. As in all situations involving introducing your children to strangers, however, be careful about safety.

- **Immersion programs.** For older children and teens, immersion study— where everything is done in the target language—can help make the leap from novice to intermediate, or intermediate to fluent, in an accelerated period of time. Immersion programs are available during the school year and over the summer, one-on-one and for groups, in the United States and around the world, sometimes with cultural activities and home-stays. Some have been around for decades and others are new, so be sure to check out references. Programs and policies on receiving academic credit for participating vary, so if that is a factor, be sure you coordinate beforehand with your children's schools.

As your child grows, you can help her improve her language learning whether it's in a structured classroom or via an alternative method:

- **Invest the time.** The more time children spend engaged with the language they are learning—and it doesn't have to just be in formal study, but can include music, movies, and television programs, and live cultural activities— the faster they will learn. But patience is still required: remember those 50+ exposures needed with every new word in every form (reading, writing, speaking, listening) before it really sticks. It takes time to really connect with a second language.

- **Focus on "communicative competence."** Don't have your child just memorize words and phrases. Language communicates—so let them communicate! Take them to ethnic restaurants and have them order in the language they are learning, visit ethnic grocery stores and have them talk to the merchants, or attend local cultural fairs, events, or performances in that language and have them engage. Make sure, however, they use dictionaries to learn key words correctly.

- **Let them explore.** Children have to want to do it to succeed. Let them follow their curiosity and learn the words and phrases that interest or stimulate them. Let them set their own goals and work to achieve them.

- **Enjoy it!** Remember that the more fun children have when learning a language, the quicker they are likely to learn it. Make it as enjoyable for them as possible.

*My husband and I grew up speaking Hindi and Malayalam, the local dialect in Kerala. But it is a constant struggle to try to teach our children these languages now that the United States is our home. We've managed to do so by speaking mostly Hindi in the house. When we travel to India, which we do every year or so, my children will try to speak and don't get embarrassed or give up when they make mistakes, since that's the best way to learn. It makes me feel so proud that our son tries to speak Hindi.*

Indira Pulliadath, pharmacoeconomist and mother

## Heritage Language Learners in Schools

America is filled with heritage language learners, those studying a language in which they have some proficiency or a cultural connection. As we face a critical shortage of adults with foreign language proficiency, we need to cultivate this rich linguistic resource. It is critical that these students be able to continue to develop their heritage linguistic and cultural skills in order to become fully bilingual and biliterate. By doing so, they will be well-positioned to live and work in an increasingly multilingual environment in the United States. Heritage speakers benefit from instruction that draws on and enhances their native/heritage language skills and cultural knowledge. In addition, research has shown that continuing to learn their native/heritage language benefits them in their acquisition of English language proficiency. ACTFL encourages language programs to ensure the academic success of heritage and native speakers by providing:

- Curriculum design that reflects the fact that the needs of native speakers and heritage students are often significantly different from non-native and non-heritage speakers;

- Challenging curriculum that builds upon the existing linguistic skills and the cultural heritage and knowledge of the students;

- Assessments that integrate language, culture, and literature for all students pre-K through 16;

- Opportunities for heritage and native speakers to become involved in their language communities beyond the classroom; and

- Systems to award credit or appropriate placement for oral and written proficiency and prior learning for native and heritage speakers.

*One hundred and eighty-nine languages are spoken throughout the New York City public school system. For the benefit of teachers and parents alike, we need innovative strategies to highlight this rich source of native language speakers while enhancing students' language learning and cultural understanding. Clearly, this is becoming a new normal for cities and towns with immigrant populations across the United States.*

Dr. Frank D. Sanchez, college administrator

# If Your Child Is Not Learning a Second Language

Becoming proficient in a second language is a long-term goal. So, too, is improving the educational system which needs to be at the heart of the language acquisition process, and is now woefully inadequate in giving our children the foundation they need to have a chance at becoming proficient. As a result, it cannot be expected that all American children will become proficient in a second (much less a third) language by the time they graduate from high school.

But all is not lost. Statistics show that approximately 50% of the rest of the world's children are not proficient in a second language. Moreover, many globally successful adults today have become that way with little or no foreign language skills. But the world is rapidly changing and if American graduates are to be able to compete with their counterparts from around the world who are proficient—or even fluent—in one or more foreign languages, we must improve as a nation. Getting from where we are to where we need to be will take time, effort, money, and lots of political will.

In the meantime, however, there is still much to be gained from striving, even knowing that our efforts—both individually and collectively—are destined to fall short of the objective of actual foreign language proficiency. Beginning to learn, or being exposed to, another language at least allows children to appreciate how difficult it is and to respect those who have mastered it. It also gives them something to build on and aspire to later in life. Moreover, it exposes them to other cultures and ways of thinking, which are, after all, the foundation stones of a global mindset. The point, therefore, is not for parents to stress out if they can't find the time or resources to get their children early second language exposure or to materially advance them along the road once they have started in a classroom environment. Speaking another language is a great advantage in developing a global mindset, but it is only one of a number of such assets. At least as important is an open-minded approach to learning about other cultures and perspectives, a topic which will be discussed in the following chapter.

# Real Stories from Real People

### Mackenzie Abate, *undergraduate student*

In the summer of 2012, I had the opportunity to take a three-week introductory Hindi class taught at the University of Pennsylvania through a program called STARTALK. This program is known throughout the United States for teaching languages not commonly taught such as Hindi, Urdu, and Arabic. Most of the classes are even offered for free, as long as the student does not request academic credit. The programs include not only lessons in the language, but also lessons in the culture of the native speakers of the language. The experience was a memorable one that taught me a lot about the Hindi language and culture in a fun and engaging way.

Although I had been taking Spanish in high school—I even went on an exchange to Spain my junior year—I signed up for the class primarily because I believed it would look good on my college application, which is probably true. I also thought that it would involve three weeks of goofing off on a beautiful campus with my best friend. Within a few days, however, I realized that it would be much more than that, and I was excited and ready for the challenge.

We began the class the way that most other language classes that one might take begin: We learned how to say "hello" and how to introduce ourselves. Then we learned how to exchange general pleasantries, such as asking each other how he or she is doing. Every other day we did yoga, which is a very important and even religious practice in the Hindu culture, in the park next to our building. By the end of the first week we were challenged to issue commands to the class on which yoga poses to do next. We also had to present mini-projects to our class, which could involve anything from introducing our family members to acting out a scene at fruit or vegetable market.

One day we took a field trip to a local Indian community where we visited sari shops and food markets. Included on the excursion were a little jewelry store and a video store where I bought two great Bollywood films that we had previously watched in class. These movies are usually in Hindi with an English word or two here and there, so it's pretty cool that I can now understand some of the conversation. For all that I don't, there are still the English subtitles.

My STARTALK Hindi class opened me up to a language and culture that I had little knowledge of before. Penn's libraries and computer labs allowed all of us taking the class to efficiently learn how to read, write, and speak Hindi even though we never imagined ourselves doing so. I'm lucky to have had this opportunity because I do not know another place where I would have gotten such an enriching experience. In showing me such a different culture, this class has increased my desire to learn more about other cultures. I learned how differently people live in another part of the world and how many of them bring that culture to the United States with them. I now have a much better appreciation and understanding of a culture and language so different from my own, and I think that appreciation and understanding is exactly what we all need to become more tolerant and accepting. This Hindi class opened my eyes and mind to a whole new world that I will never forget, and for that I am grateful.

### Angela Jackson, *leader in global education*

I founded the Global Language Project (GLP) in 2009 on the premise that you could transform the professional and educational prospects—and thus the life—of a child from an underserved and under-resourced background by exposing them to world languages and cultures. My own life story suggested that this could be done. I was raised by my blue-collar grandparents who could not afford vacations and most certainly had not spent any time outside the country. As fate would have it, I found myself working for the multinational company Nokia in a position where I interfaced with colleagues from around the world in multiple time zones and languages. I was astounded by the extent to which knowledge of another language enhanced both company and individual employee success. This experience enabled me to see that the skills that students need to achieve success in our increasingly globalized world are dependent on their abilities to communicate across borders and cultures.

As a result of this experience, I felt compelled to found GLP, whose mission it is to equip elementary school students with skills in a second language. You can't turn on the television or open a newspaper without hearing about the global economy. I thought everyone would understand why students with the least access and exposure would need language and culture skills.

However, when I approached traditional funders for feedback, I was surprised to learn that their approach to language education remained in a stagnant place. Funders would tell me that starting another language in high school and college was early enough to get students ready to stand with the competition. This idea was paired with the belief that students from underserved areas in particular should be focusing on perfecting their English, nevermind learning a foreign language. Learning a second language, they continued, was a luxury, not a priority for students from struggling communities.

I realized that GLP's mission had to take a different approach, one that was geared toward transformative change, one that linked learning another language to community empowerment and fighting systemic poverty in the lives of these students. It was then that I outlined the three pillars on which GLP's strategy has thrived:

1. Starting young;

2. Acknowledging that learning a second language is a priority, not a luxury; and

3. Focusing on underserved students and communities.

To tackle these three issues, GLP has worked closely with ACTFL to share research with prospective funders on the cognitive benefits of starting to learn a second language early. We have also built strong and enduring partnerships with private corporations for whom language and cultural competency are critical for professional mobility.

As for working with underserved students, we didn't ask for permission—we just did it. In 2009, we worked with administrators at Teachers College in New York City to identify high-need schools in Harlem that were committed to excellence and would benefit from community-based partners. After 4 years, we found that the students at our founding school, P.S. 368, were able to acquire the target language they were learning at the same rate—if not faster—than many of their counterparts at nearby private schools. We took this data to our corporate partners and were able to secure funding to run programs for three additional schools over the next 3 years.

The moral of GLP's story is that if the right strategy is adopted, languages can matter a lot in cultivating the new generation of professionals who are equipped with a nuanced understanding of how the world works. The other lesson we have learned is that if you have a solid and timely set of reasons backing the importance of language learning, the benefits will be undeniable to both supporters and student participants. GLP has grown from serving 30 students in one school, to now working with more than 1,000 students in six schools teaching Mandarin, Arabic, Spanish, and French. We are currently in the process of offering our unique curriculum to schools throughout the country, beginning on the East Coast. Our commitment remains stronger than ever to bringing language and culture programs to students in elementary schools nationwide.

### Bernie Lee, *tutor and father*

I was born in Hong Kong and immigrated to the United States with my family in 1972 when I was 5 years old. I grew up speaking Chinese with my parents, but English with everybody else. My Chinese-American upbringing was quite typical of Asian immigrants of my era; my parents were strict and expected me to study hard and earn good grades. However, nearly all of my classmates and friends were American-born and White. I grew up straddling both worlds, learning to bridge both languages and cultures. As such, I don't consider myself Chinese or American, but rather somewhere in-between. I'm able to see things from different perspectives and believe this upbringing made me a much more flexible person and provided a broader and more empathetic view of the world. It also gave me a lifelong preference for things that are different.

Languages came naturally to me and after studying French in high school, I decided to study and then major in Russian in college. I was intrigued by Mikhail Gorbachev's *perestroika*, the political liberalization of the former Soviet Union's one-party communist state, and the career opportunities it might offer someone like me. After graduation I parlayed my Russian language skills into a job as a contractor with the U.S. State Department in Moscow where I lived for 2 years, excited to be living in a country going through massive historical change. I met my wife, an American who had studied Russian in college, in Moscow. She shared my passion for the Russian language and culture, as well as my appetite for international adventure. I cherished my time in Moscow because I learned to work, eat, drink, and play alongside Russians and these experiences enabled me to learn more about Russian language and culture than I could have imagined. But it was also in Moscow where those early life lessons of empathy and a willingness to understand someone else's perspective matured into a core tenet of my personality as I experienced what it was like to truly be a stranger in a foreign land.

These core values are the ones that I've impressed on my children. Whether they choose to live in Hong Kong, Russia, the United States, or anywhere else in the world, empathy goes a long way. So, too, do language skills and a sincere interest in other people and cultures. Both are studying Spanish and Russian, and in addition to learning how to conjugate verbs and decline nouns, they're exploring cultures and finding out for themselves how interesting other people can be. We try to enhance this by exposing them to a variety of foods and diverse experiences where we live. There's a sense of discovery that we've incorporated into our lives that makes life fun.

My study of foreign languages and my international experiences have certainly made life more interesting and flavorful. I continue to enjoy encountering the new, the exotic, and the out of the ordinary. I want my children to experience this same sense of exploration in their lives. I can think of no better way to embark on this journey than to start studying foreign languages and to learn about cultures from different parts of the world.

### Jennifer Maniscalco, *marketing professional and mother*

"I want to listen to French." "I'll read it to her in Spanish." "I want to go to South Africa." "That's Paris."

These are phrases I've heard from my 2-year-old and 5-year old as a result of exposing them to global cultural activities since the moment I knew they were coming into the world. They have no idea that the games we play, the music we listen to, and the events we participate in are gearing them to succeed in global situations. The short-term goal is to make learning languages, trying new cuisines, and visiting new places fun experiences that are based on exploring the unknown and becoming comfortable with it so that in the future, when a global situation presents itself, they will have the tools to approach it with confidence.

As a first generation American, I was always aware of a faraway place that was near and dear to my mother—Italy. She consistently reinforced the Mediterranean values that feel so natural for me today. And while my husband was raised in a typical Midwestern family, he must have caught a touch of the global bug because after meeting me, he obtained a passport, started eating new foods like crustaceans, and now drinks espresso. It is our common understanding of the importance of developing an international mindset for our children that fortifies our commitment to raising global children.

Our daughters are taken to Indian restaurants instead of burger joints. Thanks to my mother, or Nonna, they are constantly exposed to Italian language and culture, be it through finding children's Italian videos, using Skype with Italian family members, and preparing Italian savouries such as *focaccia* and *ciambella*. As a result, my older daughter is able to play with Italian-speaking children at ease, and my younger daughter is on a similar path of dual language abilities.

Raising global children is our lifestyle. For us, being global isn't simply speaking a foreign language or traveling to a foreign country. Rather, being global means a level of comfort and confidence in situations outside of what life brings you day-to-day. It means constantly being the parent that is thinking differently about what our children are encountering. Sometimes it feels like I am walking on my hands while every other suburban parent is walking upright. It would be a lot easier for me to just speak English and not constantly repeat terms in Italian. It would be much simpler to go to a standard American restaurant, order wings, and call it lunch. (Well, maybe not quite so easy for this vegetarian, but you get the idea). Attending foreign language classes means driving over 30 miles downtown on a Saturday morning. I could skip that gymnastics routine and sleep in after a busy workweek. We choose to execute the handstands that give our children a global perspective. And just to keep things real, there are times when they would rather listen to Disney songs, watch Doc McStuffins, and eat French fries—which is right because they need to balance their international activities with those typical for American children.

Yes, I am often walking on my hands. But I get to discover traveling overseas again through the eyes of our children. I get to reinforce my language skills and discover new languages. I meet parents who are striving to have their children become part of a better tomorrow through cross-cultural understanding, and I receive extra cardiovascular exercise by running around on my hands keeping our global girls busy.

# CHAPTER 5

# Exploring Culture:
# Having Fun with Global Food, Music, Books, and Friends

*I speak Chinese, I lived in China for 12 years, and I had brought my daughter Sarah along twice on business trips to China. But only when a hip, young Chinese teacher did a homestay with us did China become "real" for Sarah. Somehow watching Mommy negotiate with other "old fogies" lacked the fascination of watching lovely teacher Jin Skype with her Beijing family and play Angry Birds in Chinese. It's all about finding the connection that motivates your kids. Bringing culture into your home may be what provides that connection.*

Rebecca **Weiner**, entrepreneur, author, and mother

If foreign languages open doors for children, then exposure to the broader cultures from which those languages spring fills the worlds beyond those doors with real people. The rich excitement of new cultures—the smells and tastes of foods, the colors and drama of art, the shapes of stories, and rhythms of music—engage children's senses. And those fulfilling sensual encounters teach children that the new and different can be wonderful, rather than scary and strange. In turn, such happy experiences build curiosity and appetite for other cross-cultural experiences and adventures, the cumulative effect of which is that the child is eventually able to function fearlessly as a global adult. In fact, "expose children to other cultures through music, visual arts, dance, film, books/literature, museum exhibits" was rated the number one factor in developing a global mindset in children by our survey respondents.

But cultural exposure doesn't happen in a vacuum. To be truly authentic, it needs to be incorporated into an individual's lifestyle, mindset, and belief system. In all societies, parents, teachers, caregivers, and friends surround children and help craft their beliefs and values from an early age. But unless the child is also exposed to people of other cultures, he or she will grow up to be a product of only his or her native culture, a perfectly acceptable result from time immemorial, but a demonstrable liability in today's increasingly global society. Continuing these early childhood experiences into pre-teen and teenage years builds on the foundation and enables the next generation of emerging independent thinkers to more readily accept people who are "different." Moreover, they will have a much more expansive definition of different, one that allows them to become both more reflective of their own culture and more appreciative of what other cultures have to offer. In time, this openness to different approaches will help them become better problem-solvers and team players, as well as prepare them as high school and college students for global adventures such as exchange and study abroad programs. In the long run, this early cross-cultural exposure will foster the cross-cultural competency skills that today's employers are increasingly seeking. And it all begins with childhood basics: food, music, movies, art, toys, games, and books.

## Fun with Food

We first experience the world through our mouths. To the consternation of parents and older siblings everywhere, babies stuff whatever they can reach into their maws, then lick, gum, or chew, experiencing all kinds of flavors, textures, and shapes, before spitting or swallowing as they wish. We begin as oral explorers, and parents can take advantage of that by providing their children with richly varied tastes.

In an ideal world, this variety should start with mother's milk. We know that "breast is best" for many reasons, including weight control, mother–child interaction, support for intelligence, and the transfer of antibodies to prevent disease. A less well-known advantage is flavor variety. Breast milk varies tremendously in consistency and taste by the season, time of day, and especially with what the mother eats. Scientific studies have confirmed what curious parents have always known: breast milk carries flavors, from sweet to salty, spicy to garlicky. If mom has Indian food one day and Mexican the next, the nursing baby does too. And studies have shown that tastes transmitted through breast milk translate into preferences for those flavors in toddlerhood and beyond. Such variety helps a child grow up accustomed to enjoying different cuisines. By contrast, formula is formula: Parents who taste to make sure the mix is right know one batch tastes just the same as the next.

Continuing with solid food, savvy parents have long advised against an overreliance on commercial baby and especially toddler foods, which tend toward soft blandness and hence discourage the development of adventurous palates. Instead, while still following all the schedules for introducing new foods recommended by pediatricians, parents can feed babies chopped or ground versions of all the foods they themselves eat—to the benefit of the baby's health and tastebuds, not to mention their parents' wallets. By toddler age, kids can eat most of what the rest of their family eats, just chopped smaller and without the spiciest of spices.

*As a child, I learned best about other cultures through food. Global education doesn't have to be something formal or solely academic. We can learn about each other on a human level through sharing of culture.*

survey respondent

*I am amazed how many parents get lured into relying on commercial toddler "food products," as if a 3-year-old can't eat an unprocessed banana or avocado or peach. And what is the result? At age 8 or 10, kids still prefer bland processed fruit from little packages to the real thing in the fruit bowl. Baby food companies know exactly what they're doing by hooking babies and toddlers on specially processed foods. And believe me, they're not doing it for your kid's health, or for her ability to eat flexibly or travel well.*

survey respondent

Once you have a small child eating essentially the same foods as parents and older siblings, you have all the ingredients you need for family culinary adventures. Here are some tips for making your first such forays successful:

- Start with favorites and expand. If Junior already likes grilled cheese, it's a simple stretch to quesadillas. Puréed spinach and cut-up cheese isn't far from saag paneer. Spaghetti lovers will probably welcome Chinese or Japanese noodles.

- Introduce new ingredients one or two at a time so as not to overwhelm.

- Remember that young palates are delicate, so go easy on salt, hot spices, and other strong tastes.

- But do use spices, letting babies and toddlers smell them and appreciate the colors before gradually introducing them as tastes.

- Keep recipes simple at first or purposefully omit nonessential ingredients. It's often easier for kids to start with only a handful of ingredients, then work their way up to complex foods such as casseroles and stews.

- Cook together! There is nothing like putting on a chef's hat and helping mix, pound, and roll the ingredients to get a child interested in eating the end result.

- Whenever you can, secure your ingredients from a farmer's market or pick-your-own farm. Better still, grow them yourself. The more a child feels connected to where his or her food comes from, the more interesting that food will seem.

- Make new foods festive by using interesting colors, shapes, and layers. Sushi, burritos, dumplings, spring rolls, empanadas, blintzes, stuffed cabbage, and layered salads can encourage even picky eaters to try new things.

- Decorate food whenever you can. Kids can be big on presentation, which can also be a great kid activity while an adult handles the sharp knives and hot stove.

- Expand fun and learning opportunities by organizing themed evenings with food, a story, some music, and maybe a game from the same country.

- Be sure to include cuisines to which your family has a personal connection, such as special dishes from your ancestral home country or places where you have spent time, so that stories about the place can reinforce the pleasure of the new foods.

- Expand your repertoire by using global cookbooks and by searching websites for creative ideas on global cooking with kids. A few of our our favorite websites are Global Gourmet, Cooking with Kids, and Epicurious.

Restaurants can be wonderful shortcuts to culinary adventure, especially when you don't have the time to cook or just want something different. Restaurants featuring ethnic cuisines frequently offer some of the best and freshest food around, typically in settings with music, art, and other cultural artifacts that can ignite a child's imagination. But don't stress out too much about authenticity. Even jumbled exotica can offer fun and flavorful inspiration for kids.

*I like to try different kinds of foods and will try most anything. If other people eat it, it has to be good.*

**Paige,** eighth-grade student

*While growing up, my family often visited one of those "Polynesian" restaurants that served a hash of Asian cuisines. One of my favorites there was a heap of grilled appetizers with the wonderful name "Pu-pu Platter." The platter came decorated with a coconut shell and plastic flowers around a clever miniature brazier, served by waitresses with grass skirts and leis who I do not remember ever looking bored. It was all as authentically Polynesian as Santa Claus, but felt very exotic in 1960s upstate New York. When I finally visited the actual South Pacific decades later, I was a little wistful to find no Pu-pu Platters, but grateful that those coconut shells and leis helped spark an interest in the wider world that has led to a lifetime of travel.*

**Rebecca Weiner,** entrepreneur, author, and mother

Try not to let any restaurant visit deteriorate into demands for the blandest items on the menu. Gently encourage trying new things via tastes from grown-up plates or a selection of interesting, kid-friendly appetizers. Whenever possible, avoid the greasy, salty and/or over-sweetened dishes so often featured on "kid's menus."

*I never let my boys order from a children's menu. It's always the most boring, unhealthy food: fried this, overcooked that, and the other thing in syrup. It's as if restaurants are colluding to head our children toward heart disease and diabetes and taste buds that don't know how to like anything healthy, let alone varied.*

**Roya Hakakian,** journalist, author, and mother

Once you have cultivated a reasonably adventurous eater, you'll find that both family meals and travel become much easier. A child who has learned to like real food as much as—and hopefully even more than—chicken nuggets and French fries is a child prepared to explore the world.

*Rituals around the dinner table are very important in every culture. Children can learn patience, delayed gratification, and responsibility. They also have an opportunity to talk about issues of the day, big and small. I really think the dinner table is an important laboratory or proving ground for raising global children.*

**Brent Riddle,** transportation planner and father

## Music, Movies, and Art

In her groundbreaking books, *Art and Intimacy* and *What is Art For?*, the famously self-taught anthropologist Ellen Dissanayake explores the many ways that art, and especially music, are fundamental to human development. A mother singing lullabies and nursery songs to her child, Dissanayake says, teaches language, rhythm, and connection in ways that parallel the celebratory, ceremonial ways that art and music have brought us together throughout human history.

Music, movies, and art are part of how all human societies and individual people come to understand themselves. Through both "high arts"—from painting to symphonies—and "low arts"—from pinch pots to crafts—we express ourselves as individuals. Thus learning to enjoy art, music, and movies from both our own and other cultures can be enormously powerful in helping children learn about themselves and the world.

Appreciation for global art starts with appreciation for all art, and that often starts with creating art. Babies are natural music makers and artists, gurgling and cooing, banging on cans, smearing finger paint or daubing with clay. Encourage artistic exploration and creative expression in your children and it will yield dividends later on in their ability to read, write, and think independently. Keep a cupboard filled with arts and crafts supplies and a basket full of things to use as makeshift instruments so that moments of inspiration can be explored without first being delayed by visits to the crafts or music store or permission from mommy or daddy.

Studies have shown that it is a small step for children from personal creativity to appreciating the work of other artists, and from there to enjoying the arts of other cultures. Again, awareness builds outward like layers on an onion. Children should have plenty of access to the music, movies, and arts of their home country and culture. For children born in the United States, that can include anything from jazz to hip-hop, bluegrass to blues, Disney to Dior, Jasper Johns to John Philip Sousa to Jay-Jay the Jet Plane. Enjoy such cultural expressions together and talk about how the varied arts you enjoy express the values and traditions you most appreciate in your own culture.

As enjoyment of the artistic expressions of their own cultural traditions grow, children also begin to appreciate and enjoy the arts of other cultures. This will help strengthen their interest in—and curiosity about—the rest of the world. Here are some tips:

- Learn songs from around the world, then play and sing them together. Check out the website resources at World Around Songs, Songs for Teaching, and Traditional Music Library.

- Play recorded music and dance with your children to the beats of many different rhythms. For some ideas, see websites for World Music, World Music National Geographic, and Putumayo.

- Remember that music aimed specifically at children can be lovely. But it is also beneficial to introduce children to "grown-up" music from around the world in all its richness and complexity.

- Combine music with evocative visual images of the lands the music comes from. Libraries have many wonderful book/CD/MP3 packages that take children on rhythmic journeys that are intermeshed with new stories.

- Incorporate age-appropriate movies about other people, places, and cultures into your lifestyle. Good movies help transport us to places and experiences we might never have imagined. Talk about what you're watching before, during, and after the film to encourage your child to open up his or her imagination.

- Watch family-friendly foreign films together. Foreign films help viewers appreciate and care about other cultures. When children experience cultures through foreign films, they more naturally relate to the wider world and are transported to faraway lands, without even needing a passport. You can find many in libraries and on Netflix. For some ideas, see the website for Common Sense Media and PBS recommendations.

- Make art together in many different traditional styles, from Mexican paper mache piñatas to Chinese fans. Then create your own variations. For some ideas, see websites for KinderArt and Crafts for Kids.

- Display your child's artistic creations in your home in ways that show you respect and take them seriously. A child's painting, nicely displayed in a matted frame salvaged from Goodwill, can look stunning on your living room wall and will send an important message about how you view their artistic efforts. By cycling through a display of multicultural pieces your child has created, you will subtly underscore your interest in the global dimensions of art.

- Do not, however, let children dictate all the art you display. Continue to show whatever grown-up paintings or posters or prints or other art you enjoy, and tell your kids why you like them. If you enjoy artistic creations and reproductions from a variety of cultures, so much the better.

- Read books that encourage a broad understanding of what constitutes art and artistic expression. Some of our favorites include the Museum of Modern Art in New York's *Museum 1-2-3* and *Museum A-B-C* and *Seen Art?* For a wonderful list of books for introducing children to art, artists, and art around the world, see The British National Gallery of Art's website.

- Seek out art from around the world in museums or art galleries near you. Visit museums created by and about America's various ethnic groups, such as the Museum of Chinese in America or the Polish American Museum in New York City, Chinatown museums in Chicago or San Francisco, or the German-American Heritage Center in Davenport, Iowa. Children who might otherwise tune out in art galleries can focus wonderfully when given clues to find for a scavenger hunt with ice cream as the prize, or some similar incentive to really **look** around them. Many museums now have special children's maps or activities—just ask a docent or at the information desk.

- Don't forget libraries and art books as sources of artistic exposure and inspiration. Many libraries even have art loan programs that let you take home paintings or reproductions to live with for periods of time.

- Small commercial galleries can be wonderful places to discover contemporary artists in your area. Get to know your local musicians and other artists, and seek out the wonderful (often free or very low-cost) programs they have for kids in parks, libraries, schools, and neighborhood centers.

- Whenever you travel, look for new local arts, movie ideas, and music resources.

Art, movies, and music help feed global interests best when they are not separated from—but are incorporated into—daily life and other learning. Just as language lessons work better when looking at a picture book and chores are less onerous when done to music, appreciation of the images in a gallery is enhanced when the visual can be incorporated into stories, games, or other activities. Research into "visual literacy" programs demonstrates that children who learn to "read" works of art and write creatively about them fare better with academic reading and writing as well as in many other areas. But note: This advantage only seems to work when the child is actively engaged with the work of art, music, and writing. Having a child passively watch even the best-produced film with the most wonderful images and music is far less likely to encourage meaningful learning than is spending time with your child discussing the movie or making up stories to music inspired by a work of art. Ensuring that the art, movies, and music children encounter is diverse and global only broadens this learning.

*To be successful citizens of the world, children must be able to see the world through the eyes of others, and to accept and perhaps even delight in the differences in attitudes and habits. Exposure to foreign films and television shows, even if dubbed, can open their eyes to how people in other cultures have a party, dress for work, hail a cab, and eat breakfast—even seeing what they eat that's different can be surprising.*

**Patricia Guy,** international wine expert and author

## Toys and Games

After eating, playing is probably the most fundamental way that children learn about the world. Children learn basic science by manipulating blocks and simple levers, and "try on" many versions of the adults they will eventually grow up to be through dramatic play. Toys and games can also be important ways to learn about the wider world.

For one thing, many of the traditional games played around the world, which are often geared to develop specific skills of cultural importance, use few or no props, and thus stimulate the imagination. Playing such games can be a great antidote to an overly technological, electronically focused childhood. Some great examples include:

- African and South American drumming games in which children imitate increasingly complicated rhythmic patterns made by older kids or adults. These games teach listening skills, patterning, and simple logic as well as musical rhythm and eye–hand coordination.

- Various forms of tag and other running games from around the world such as China's sticky rice-cake tag (where kids who have been tagged become "sticky," and soon find themselves in tangled knots) and tiger-tail tag (where runners have cloth "tails" tucked into their pants for taggers to grab). A similar idea is the Khazak game *Bagya* ("horse-riders"), where players run in pairs: one in front as the "horse," holding hands behind his back with the "rider." These paired teams can run various sorts of races. Spanish kids have a similar game in which the tagger is called the "vampire," and lies down in a circle of children who chant the hours until the one the vampire has decided to "wake up" and chase them. In addition to providing great exercise, such games also teach cooperation and simple strategy.

- Hopscotch-type games, such as the Polish *Grawklasy*, in which squares or circles to be hopped into are broken down by categories that can be called out (names, birds, numbers, etc.), help with categorization, coordination, and other skills.

- Jacks-type games, often played with pebbles or shells, which teach counting, eye–hand coordination, and turn-taking.

- Soccer, a game the rest of the world calls "football," which is played in more than 200 countries around the world.

- For more ideas on global and intercultural traditional games, go to the websites Wilderdom, Games Kids Play, and Library Think Quest.

*With our elementary-school age son, we make the world relevant to his world. He likes Star Wars and has learned about the global, or intergalactic community. Different planets have different cultures, international politics are at play, and travel matters. His heroes travel across these very diverse places and must deal with other governments and cultures to succeed.*

**Dr. Liesl Riddle,** professor and mother

Commercial toys and games that involve geography and thinking about the wider world can also be fun and helpful in developing global skills. Among the most productive are:

- Kid-friendly, interactive globes and puzzle maps;

- Puzzles and play games that include images from around the world; and

- Puzzles and games that involve maps and other geographic information, as well as information about other cultures.

*We have a great big map on the wall and we love to look at it. It's like an old friend, comforting as we reminisce about the good times we've had and the people we've met from all over the world.*

**Michelle Morgan Knott,** mother

## Books as Magic Doors

When it comes to bringing new peoples and places to life for a child, there is nothing like curling up with a good book. Most globalists remember flying as armchair travelers on the wings of book-fed imaginations long before they boarded their first real airplane. A set of Reader's Digest Condensed Children's Classics can take your children far away to the Swiss mountains with Heidi, on Robinson Crusoe's island, at Lilliput with Gulliver, or logging 20,000 leagues under the sea with Captain Nemo. These tales haven't been classics for more than 100 years for nothing. And even in this day of routine air travel and constant electronic contact, books still have a near magical role to play in helping children connect to the world.

Research shows that reading—that is to say, reading real books, with pages to be savored and turned—has an irreplaceable role in learning. Ideally, even babies should be read to, starting with soft and indestructible books they can mouth and toss about to their hearts' content. Reading early and often with kids, and making reading time a special connection between parents (and later teachers) and children, inspires a lifelong love of reading. From the stories and images of those early-age books, children begin to people the world with their imaginations, from gingerbread boys and little red hens to Red Riding Hood and Rapunzel to Pooh and Paddington to Harry Potter and Percy Jackson. Just about any book that gets a child excited about reading and keeps him or her reading is a good book as far as we're concerned.

Not surprisingly, parents generally want to start with the books that they themselves loved as children. And there is nothing wrong with this. They might explore *The Boxcar Children, Nancy Drew, The Hardy Boys, American Girl* novels, and the *Magic Treehouse* series, as well as books about U.S. history from Native Americans to NASA, American inventions from lightning rods to the Internet, and the better angels of U.S. history from Dolley Madison to Martin Luther King, Jr. The stories that are central to your child's heritage should help shape the core of her sense of self and culture.

But as children develop as readers, we also strongly recommend turning them on to some of the hundreds of wonderful books that will help introduce the larger world, from lesser-known corners of America to the globe beyond, from myths and culture to history to science to issues of common concern such as protecting the environment. Lists of books recommended for introducing kids to world culture can be found at: Worlds of Words, Scholastic, and Association of Library Service to Children.

Just to be sure we have mentioned them, here are a few of our favorites:

- **For Babies:** *Mama, Do You Love Me?* by Babara Ann Joosse & Barbara Lavallee (ill.); *How Many Baby Pandas?* by Sandra Markle; *Ten Little Fingers and Ten Little Toes* by Mem Fox and Helen Oxenbury (ill.); *Lala Salama* by Patricia Maclachlan and Elizabeth Zunon (ill.); and *Families* by Rena D. Grossman.

- **For Toddlers:** *Chicken Man* by Michelle Edwards; *Juan Bobo Goes to Work* by Marisa Montes and Joe Cepeda; *Too Many Tamales* by Gary Soto and Ed Martinez (ill.); *Borreguita and the Coyote* by Verna Aardema and Petra Mathers (ill.); *The Singing Snake* by Stefan Czernecki and Timothy Rhodes (ill.); and the Sammy Spider series by Sylvia Rouss about Israel and Judaism.

- **For Preschoolers:** *Yoko Writes her Name* by Rosemary Wells; *In the Small, Small Night* by Jane Kurz and Rachel Isadora (ill.); *All the Way to America* by Dan Yaccarino; *The Castle on Hester Street* by Linda Heller and Boris Kulikov (ill.); *Amira's Totally Chocolate World* by J. Samia Mair; *Anansi Finds a Fool* by Verna Aardema and Bryna Waldman (ill.); *The Market Lady and the Mango Tree* by Pete and Mary Watson; *Sweet, Sweet Fig Banana* by Phillis Gershator and Fritz Millevoix (ill.); *Bread Comes to Life* by George Levenson and Schmuel Thaler (ill.); *Planting the Trees of Kenya* by Claire Nivola; *The Woman Who Outshone the Sun* by Alejandro Cruz Martinez and Fernando Olivera (ill.); and Aesop's fables.

- **For Lower Elementary Schoolers:** Fairy tales by the Brothers Grimm and Hans Christian Andersen; the original Winnie the Pooh and Paddington books; *Suriya & Roscoe* by Bhagavan Antle & Barry Bland (ill.); *Energy Island* by Allan Drummond; *Daisy Comes Home* by Jan Brett; *The Magical Starfruit Tree* by Rosalind Wang and Shao Wei Liu (ill.); *The Tooth Fairy Meets El Ratón Pérez* by René Colato Láinez and Tom Lintern (ill.); *Hanna's Cold Winter* by Trish Marx and Barbara Knutson (ill.); *Celebrate Ramadan* by Laura S. Jeffrey; *Manfish: A Story of Jacques Cousteau* by Jennifer Berne and Éric Puybaret; *D'Aulaires' Book of Greek Myths* and *D'Aulaires' Book of Norse Myths* by Ingri d'Aulaire and Edgar Parin d'Aulaire; *One World, One Day* by Barbara Kerley; *Children Just Like Me: A Unique Celebration of Children Around the World* by Anabel Kindersley, Barabas Kindersly, and UNICEF; *Just So Stories* by Rudyard Kipling; *Pinocchio* by Carlo Collodio; and *Tanglewood Tales* and *The Wonder Book* by Nathaniel Hawthorne.

- **For Upper Elementary Schoolers:** *Lost in Lexicon* by Pendred Noyce and Joan Charles (ill.); *Neo Leo* by Gene Barretta; *Where the Mountain Meets* *the Moon* by Grace Lin; *Moon Lady* by Amy Tan and Gretchen Schields; *Pippi Longstocking* by Astrid Lindgren; *The Jungle Book* by Rudyard Kipling; *The Swiss Family Robinson* by Johann Wyss; *Habibi* by Naomi Shihab Nye; and *The Whale Rider* by Witi Tame Ihimaera.

- **For Middle Schoolers:** *A Place for Delta* by Melissa Walker and Richard Walker (ill.); *City of Orphans* by Avi and Greg Ruth (ill.); *Bamboo People* by Mitali Perkins; *The Red Umbrella* by Christina Diaz Gonzales; *Shooting Kabul* by N.H. Senzai; *Before Columbus: The Americas in 1491* by Charles C. Mann; *Ask Me No Questions* by Marina Tamar Budhos; *Being Muslim* by Haroon Siddiqui; and *Kaleidoscope Eyes* by Jen Bryant.

By high school it can be difficult to make recommendations to students who can and should be making their own choices and who already have heavy school reading loads. But it can be helpful still to direct young adults toward quality reads with a global focus such as *The Kite Runner* by Khaled Hosseini; *The English Patient* by Michael Ondaatje; and *The Code Book* by Simon Singh.

In all of this, however—starting with parents reading to young children, progressing through those first attempts of a child to read to an adult, and on to school events and family evenings with dramatic retellings by ever-more fluent readers—the key is to make reading both important and fun for your child. Here are a few tips:

- Set aside dedicated reading time every day—at wake-up, at bedtime, and as often as possible in between. Limit screen time in favor of reading time.

- Set up a comfortable reading nook that your kids will come to associate with pleasant snuggling as well as with reading time.

- Find whatever sorts of books interest your child and focus on them, all while regularly adding new things.

- Remember that until your child is a fluent reader (and even after!), there is great value in having an adult or older sibling read aloud, even as the child reads better and more independently. If you have been reading to them all along, they will love being read to and stopping that could become an unintended disincentive. In addition, they can probably understand much more interesting and complex stories than they can read independently, so give them both experiences.

- Whenever possible, let your child set the pace of reading, ask questions about the text and illustrations, make comments, and initiate discussions.

Unless used as a bedtime delay tactic, this isn't interrupting at all, but a productive opportunity for your child to make connections to the words on the page.

- Set a good example by making sure that your child sees you reading for pleasure as well.

- Finally, read, read, read! Make the time, and take the time. The resulting interest in reading that it will generate will benefit your child for years to come.

# Friendships Across Cultures

Cross-cultural learning and sensitivity is all theoretical until children actually begin interacting with people from different backgrounds and with different assumptions about the world. Such interactions aren't always easy, but they are rich with possibilities for new perspectives, ideas, experiences, and awareness. The most productive of these, naturally, will be those with other children with whom they can relate on the level that comes most naturally and comfortably to them. Having play dates and caregiving swaps with children and families from different cultures often means a chance for your child to try new foods, games, and other fun activities, and hopefully is a way to avoid play dates centered around Xboxes and the classmate with the most American Girl dolls.

There are many opportunities for children to find more diverse friends. Consider for instance:

- **School.** Both public and private schools are generally more diverse and multicultural today than ever before. That is one of the great advantages of living in regions of cultural diversity. By making a point of inviting over classmates who come from different backgrounds, you will be helping both children learn that different doesn't mean wrong, just different.

- **Libraries and parks.** Local libraries and parks often host events celebrating a range of holidays relevant to various immigrant and established cultural populations in the area. These events, along with the stories read and games played there, can be great ice-breakers for building friendships. There may also be groups that meet regularly at a local park or library that focus on a certain language or culture. Ask your local librarian or park supervisor for details.

- **Faith-based groups.** Churches, synagogues, and mosques often host exchange programs with fellow members in different parts of the world. Some faith-based communities organize mission trips for young Americans, trips which can often be positively transformative.

- **Cultural festivals.** Check out community calendars, local websites, and other sources for information on ethnic festivals, holiday celebrations, and cultural activities. Attending these can be a lot of fun and offer new and interesting games, crafts, foods, and other activities to add to your family's repertoire. Ideally, you will also meet some families whose kids hit it off with yours, and who can provide your children with new ways of viewing the world.

- **Sports teams.** Depending on where you live, immigrant families may regularly get together to play their national sports. Such groups are generally welcoming to local families who want to join in. In addition to learning how to play a new sport, you are also likely to learn a good deal about the culture from which it comes.

- **Immigrant neighborhoods.** Immigrant communities typically offer ethnically focused restaurants, groceries, art galleries, craft supply stores, and other venues where it is possible to meet and get to know significantly different American families.

- **Refugee groups.** Many groups around the United States help resettle refugees who have come to our country from difficult situations in their home countries. Of course, newly arrived refugee families often still dwell emotionally in their home country crises and you will need to exercise reasonable caution in not exposing your children to too much "second-hand trauma." But children can be very resilient, and often what newly arrived refugee children most want and need is to find welcoming, new friends with no connections to the turmoil they have left behind. As a result, they can quickly become steadfast friends and playmates for U.S.-born children. Time spent with refugee children can also work wonders in helping your child focus on what is important in life, especially family, and all the fun that can be had without a lot of money or material goods. For information on volunteering as a family or otherwise helping make connections with refugee groups in your area, contact your local chapter of Integrated Refugee & Immigrant Services (IRIS).

- **Academic visitors.** Your local college or university may have a host of graduate students, post-docs, visiting scholars, and other academics who have brought along their families, and whose children are looking for friends among the local population.

- **International exchange groups.** A variety of national organizations are increasingly dedicated to helping strengthen people-to-people exchanges between Americans and the rest of the world. You can do a tremendous amount to introduce the outside world into your home via any of the many programs that bring foreign visitors to the United States for periods of time and involve home-stays. Many local chapters of the World Affairs Council, for instance, host visiting delegations through the U.S. Department of State's International Visitors Program, and many such visitors enjoy short home-stays, anything from a meal to a weekend. Hiring an au pair to care for your children is another option, and some places to look include Au Pair in America, InterExchange, and Cultural Care Au Pair.

- **Pen-pal programs.** The Internet has transformed traditional pen-pals into electronic pen-pals or "ePals." And while there will be no more exotic stamps and fascinating stationery arriving from far away, gone, too, is the necessity of waiting weeks for a response. Parents should exercise caution and focus on sites that do not require **any** personal information from your child, and monitor with whom they email or chat. But having said that, there are still many rewarding sites worth looking at, including Students of the World, ePals Global Community, and A Girl's World.

- **Meet-up groups.** The Internet can be a rich source of information on groups organized around any number of topics, including those focused on language or cultural exchange. As mentioned before, just be sure to exercise caution when meeting up with people you don't know, especially when children are involved. Choose a public place for first meetings.

If you can't find a group to join in your area that is dedicated to international and cross-cultural exchange, consider starting one!

*We've created a family dinner club in our neighborhood, a southern suburb, to celebrate different cultures through cooking and conversation among our diverse families. We've built relationships with each other, one of the most powerful means of connecting across cultures.*

José D. González, professor and father

*My parents set a good example of enjoying different cultures, teaching us history, and constantly taking us to historical/cultural sites, talking to us about what was going on in the news, and expecting us to know what was going on in the world around us.*

survey respondent

Of course, friendships must be natural and not forced. But if your lifestyle permits, try stretching yourself and encouraging your children to add more diverse and multicultural friendships to their existing mix. Your children can learn many great life lessons from dealing on their own terms with children from radically different cultures and backgrounds, whether they are kids from faraway places or kids who look and act differently and yet live in the same town.

*Befriending people of different cultures and nationalities is the most important aspect of developing a global mind.*

survey respondent

## Hosting an Exchange Student

Opening up your home to a foreign student is one of the best and most cost-efficient ways to learn about another culture. Student exchange programs identify and pair teenagers from around the world with host families so that they can get a taste of what daily life is like in the United States. Students usually attend classes and participate in organized activities with their sponsoring group, but the host families provide a home, meals, a family, and cultural interaction. Timeframes range from two weeks to a full year. If you're interested in hosting an exchange student, some resources include Ayusa, Youth for Understanding, and CCI Greenheart.

*I grew up in Lubbock, Texas. My parents worked in local jobs and had never traveled outside the United States, but they thought it was important for us gain a better understanding of the world. After my sister had excelled in Spanish for a few years in junior high school, they decided to host Spanish exchange students so she could practice. They turned to Youth for Understanding and ended up hosting 10 exchange students—each who stayed 1 year—from all around the globe and even kept it up after we graduated high school. We learned so much about other people and cultures through these exchanges. It inspired me to want to study other languages and explore the world.*

**Brent Riddle,** transportation planner and father

*Exchange students can bring the world into your home. We've had a Chinese researcher stay with us for 2 years while she studied at Georgetown University. We hosted a group of high school kids from Norway as part of the Norwegian Young Life group. We also had a group of four Chinese middle schoolers come for 10 days as part of a summer ESOL program. Our kids can see for themselves that although people have different backgrounds and cultures, we're also a lot alike.*

**Michelle Morgan Knott,** mother

*It's challenging to host an exchange student, and you have to be really open-minded because of the differences you encounter daily. For example, they want to experience everything and think everyday normal things are cool. But a family learns to adjust and, as my family did, embrace the experience wholeheartedly. I know it broadened my whole family's horizons, and that's a good thing.*

**Mackenzie Abate,** undergraduate student

## Schools Play an Important Role

As parents, there is a great deal that you can do at home for your own children. But you can also have a large impact on many other children by advocating for global education at your children's school. It's important to note that we're not recommending overhauling the entire education system here, but rather supporting ways for teachers to look for opportunities to broaden the scope of their teaching to include other cultures, economies, and geographic regions. Teachers do not need to rewrite their curricula; they need to think about the connections and then help their students think about them as well. They need to deepen and broaden their curricula so that appropriate global understandings and connections are a part of as many lesson plans as possible. All subjects can be taught through a global lens. In many ways, the students, because of their experience with the Internet, are already aware of global connections and can bring some of that interconnectedness to class. But it will be up to the teachers to do the rest. Global education gives them a framework for teaching children the responsibilities of being a world citizen, including accepting differences among cultures and peoples. It should not be an add-on activity or a once-a-year event, but one that integrates international themes into the daily curriculum. For more details on parents and teachers working together, see Chapter 8.

*We've moved away from multiculturalism to a much more natural mindset in truly allowing children to explore what they like. For example, if we're reading a book about Asian elephants, it leads us to explore where they live and allows us to learn about other cultures and different parts of the world. We use our SMART Boards to look up information, and the multi-media images are incredible. They really captivate young learners in a way that a teacher reading just can't. And to think that I'm able to do it with 5-year-olds; they'll know so much more at 15.*

**Kindergarten teacher** in Oklahoma City

*We chose an elementary school before buying a house. Our school district is diverse and our son is in the minority as a Caucasian. Many of his friends are the children of immigrants. His multicultural class is representative of the world and so when the class talks about history, religions, and social customs, he participates in a broad discussion with many perspectives. He experiences the same with friends and at sleepovers. He's getting a global perspective without having to leave the United States because he has learned to see and understand the world through the eyes of immigrants.*

**Dr. Liesl Riddle,** professor and mother

## Local Global Adventures

Food, music, art, movies, games, and books are excellent means to bring the world into our children's lives from the toddler through the teenage years. But combining multiple elements to create a local global adventure is even more powerful. To be sure, local global adventures come in all shapes and sizes and do not have to be expensive. In fact, they don't have to cost much at all thanks to your local public library. What you will need, however, is a healthy dose of curiosity and initiative.

Local global adventures can last anywhere from an afternoon to a few weeks. It can be a theme over the summer or an exploration of another culture over the holidays. You might consider it as prelude to an international destination you're planning on visiting someday, or the next best thing to actually going there if financial or logistical reasons make that impossible. It's important that you create local global adventures that you and your children want to experience and that you do so within your own means. The overarching point in exploring another culture is to open your children's minds to the beauty and validity of other people and places. Here's a detailed example of a local global adventure to Egypt:

Most large city or university art museums have at least a few permanent Egyptology exhibits, while many others occasionally host traveling ones. (The Metropolitan Museum of Art in New York City, the Institute of Art and Archaeology in Memphis, and the Smithsonian's Freer and Sackler Galleries of Asian Art in Washington, D.C., all have large, permanent exhibits.) First, since geography matters, find Egypt on a map. Trace the Nile River and explore its important role in Egyptian society. Research the country's extensive history. Find and play popular Egyptian music. Study hieroglyphics, check out modern Arabic, look at beautiful picture books found in the library, watch the movies *Cleopatra* or *The Ten Commandments*, and learn about mummification. Then visit the exhibit and try to find a restaurant nearby that serves Egyptian or Middle Eastern food where you can discuss what you saw. Depending on the age of your children, read about contemporary Egypt in the newspaper. Explore the topics of democracy and Islam and the effects that the recent "Muslim Spring" have had on Egypt and the region. In short, bring the exhibit to life and up-to-date through an expanded exploration of Egyptian culture.

And of course, Egypt is just one example. The whole world is open to a local global adventure with you and your children as the tour directors. Perhaps a movie, a magazine, a travel article, or a lifelong dream to visit a place or see a particular sight will spark some ideas. Creating a local global adventure takes both imagination and organization, but the preparation is a large part of the experience—and the fun. To be sure, each adventure is inherently different, but by following a loose framework, you can keep yourself focused and the adventure age-appropriate.

- **Pick a country, a culture, or a region that interests you.** Build your adventure around a cultural event, such as a local festival or museum exhibit, a particular landmark, music, or food. Examples include choosing the Great Wall of China, the Taj Mahal, Machu Picchu, the Eiffel Tower, or the Pyramids of Giza, and learning about its origins and the various roles that it has played over time. Use a book to inspire an adventure, such as Mark Twain's *Following the Equator*, any of Charles Dickens's Victorian novels, or Rudyard Kipling's tales of India.

- **Find it on a map together.** How close or faraway is the country from the United States? What do you know about it or any of its neighbors? Just seeing the country on a map allows you to begin to deduce basic characteristics. Note: One of the best investments for armchair globetrotting is a large world map displayed prominently in an easily accessible, common room where it can be referred to quickly. Explore the capitals of the European Union by first mapping out a Eurail itinerary followed by visiting museums, trying different foods, and listening to music.

- **Use food to stimulate learning.** Go on a culinary adventure that incorporates geography, culture, and history. For example, explore differences among Chinese, Japanese, and Korean foods and cultures by starting with a map to locate the countries. Go to the library to check out books, including travel guides, and take a virtual sightseeing tour of each country before you sample their cuisines at local restaurants.

- **Seek out background information for context.** Get a sense of the country by learning about population, languages spoken, historical facts of interest, and current events. The Country Studies Series produced by the Federal Research Division of the U.S. Library of Congress or CIA World Factbook online both have a tremendous amount of interesting information. Among other things, you can listen to the national anthem, learn the head of state's name and title, find the name of the current U.S. ambassador, read interesting demographic statistics, and understand what drives the national economy. Search through kid-friendly sites such as Kids National Geographic for simple country overviews. Spend time at your local library looking for age-appropriate literature, picture books, travel books, magazines, movies, and music.

- **Learn about current events.** Research what is happening in the location or to its people. Discuss what relevance these events have to the United States. Keep tabs on your destination after the adventure is over.

- **Seek out interactive information, crafts, and puzzles.** Numerous online sites offer a variety of downloadable crafts and coloring pictures. The National Geographic "Atlas Puzzle" pages offer online virtual puzzles.

- **Build curiosity and appetite about the country through food.** Find a restaurant in your area that offers authentic cuisine from that country and encourage your kids to sample a wide range of native dishes. Or better yet, try making your own together. Look for recipes to learn about ingredients, whether you plan to follow them or not; the BBC site or Epicurious "Around the World in 80 Dishes" have some great recipes, with the latter having the added benefit of a Culinary Institute of America chef doing a video demonstration.

- **Use music and rich visual images to bring culture to life.** Search for music on Amazon, iTunes, or in the library, as well as look for art books, "coffee table" photo books, back issues of *National Geographic* magazine, and travel videos in the library, online, or on cable channels. Seek out national art in museums or art galleries near you.

- **Be curious about the language.** Visit Ethnologue online for a quick survey of the languages spoken there and to learn a bit about them. Then go in search of free language examples on either Hello-Hello, Live Mocha, or the Peace Corps Multimedia Language among others. Practice a few expressions you might use, such as common greetings and phrases (e.g., "Hello, how are you?" "I'm fine, thank you, and you?" "please," and "you're welcome"). Make flash cards to practice and use them with each other during the course of the adventure.

- **Prepare to discuss culture.** Culture is a system of shared values, attitudes, and beliefs. Food, music, and art are just the surface manifestations of culture, and it's important to teach children this point. Be open to exploring the culture—both the different and similar ways of doing things—and be prepared to reflect on your own culture in light of the alternative perspectives that you will encounter. Be open yourself and your children will learn to be the same.

Once you've gathered all of this information, begin planning your adventure. Create an itinerary that incorporates as many elements from your research as you can into your adventure. But keep in mind that your learning does not have to end when the adventure itself is over; you can keep it going for weeks and even months by continuing to play the music, eat the food, and use the language. The world is an interesting place with so much to learn and enjoy, and a local global adventure is a great way to get your children started exploring it.

## Real Stories from Real People

### Betty Berdan, *eighth-grade student*

I'm a foodie—a global foodie would probably be more accurate. I've grown up eating food from all around the world on a regular basis. Middle Eastern, Latin American, Asian, and European: You name it, I've probably had it. Roughly three or four times a week our meals at home have an international element. And I love it. I have nothing against (most) good ole' American food, but broadening your palate can help you become globally aware as well as develop a curiosity for foreign places. What could be more important in the world we live in today?

There is so much in the world to discover, and foods have shown me how unique and special a country can be. I can see how some people might find a new culture and food experience daunting. Unrecognizable smells, weird textures, strange combinations of ingredients, and difficult (if not impossible) pronunciations are what many people may fear. Plus cooking such dishes may seem like a lot of work. But cooking globally as I've experienced it isn't actually all that hard. You can find many recipes online or in cookbooks at the library. The ingredients are mostly familiar, just prepared differently and combined in unusual—at least to us—ways. It is very easy for people to make international dishes at home if they have the desire and dedication.

Some of my favorites include Thai coconut curry, which combines ginger (one of my favorite flavors), spicy chili peppers, and coconut milk into a thick broth to which you can add whatever you like—green beans, peas, carrots, mushrooms, onions—and serve over rice. Middle Eastern shish kebabs are similar to hamburgers, but prepared differently. You take ground beef and add garlic, tomatoes, parsley, and cayenne pepper, grill them on skewers and serve them with falafel, pita bread, and humus. I also like an assortment of traditional Chinese dishes such as peanut chicken, snap peas and pork, and corn with pine nuts, which are all included in a cookbook we love, *The Cultural Revolution Cookbook*, most of whose recipes are simple enough for kids to make, and I do help. We eat this dinner "Chinese style." All the dishes are in large bowls in the center of the table, and we each take small portions and put them on top of our individual bowls of steaming rice to eat with chop sticks.

By preparing these meals in our own kitchen, I've also learned a great deal about other cultures. For example, a large portion of the Chinese population is lactose intolerant which is why Chinese dishes contain very little or no dairy products. In addition, I've experienced the Lebanese, Egyptian, and Middle Eastern custom of using a great deal of spices, particularly cumin, which we use large amounts of when making homemade falafel. When you learn these little facts about another culture, it makes you think about the people, their background, and their daily lives.

This connection to other people can really be felt when you eat dishes while traveling. When we traveled through Nicaragua, Costa Rica, and Panama, for example, every morning we would eat the typical rice and beans dish called *gallo pinto*. But each country's version tasted slightly different. We liked the Nicaraguan version the best, so when we came home, I found a similar recipe and have made it every now and then. From Peru we brought back a fondness for quinoa (an Incan grain, food of the ancient gods), from France *steak frites* and *tarte aux pommes* (apple tart), and a multitude of pasta dishes from Italy, many from my Mom's best friend, Eleonora, who lives in Rome. Most of the other international dishes we eat originate from countries and places my parents traveled to before I was born. Just by eating and absolutely loving all of the Indian food we make at home and have enjoyed at restaurants and at Indian friends' homes, I have become inspired to travel there some day.

People are often surprised by what I've eaten, and the foods I like. I've found foods are an interesting and fun way to learn about other cultures and delicious, too!

### Patricia Guy, *international wine expert and author*

Verona, where I have made my home for over 20 years, is 75 miles from Venice, 100 miles from Milan, and light years from El Dorado, Kansas, where I grew up reading *Black Arrow, Nancy Drew*, and *The Three Musketeers*. I would climb right down inside each story and live within it. They offered me windows on worlds that I could not actually see from my vantage point on the Great Plains, where the only sound was the relentless wind sweeping uninterrupted across the fields and the view consisted of a flat yellow line of golden wheat crisply abutting a cloudless blue sky.

When I decided to see Europe for myself—and not through the eyes of Frances Hodgson Burnett, Arthur Conan Doyle, or Victor Hugo—I was ready. My childhood reading had prepared me. Novels had shown me other ways of approaching life, of making decisions, of assessing the world around me.

Charles Dickens, Mark Twain, and R.L. Stevenson showed me wickedness and taught me to keep my eyes open for both evil and good. Ray Bradbury and T. H. White reinforced in me a delicious sense of being alive in a world filled with wonders. Novels are where children learn to solve problems and sympathize with people unlike themselves. They also learn that there exist different sets of manners and attitudes from those in their own home. These are fundamental characteristics for a person who wants to live in a world beyond narrow national borders.

A well-written novel allows a child to live in the skin of another person—the hero—and to thereby understand heroic behavior: defending the weak, forgiving the foolish, having the confidence to take that first daring step into the world alone. In short: to grow up. To recognize that the world isn't either black or white: it is in fact in glorious Technicolor.

## Tammy Dann, *teacher and mother*

We work hard to create a bilingual home that also incorporates other cultures into our everyday life because raising our daughter to be a global citizen is a priority. Since we want to delay traveling abroad until she is old enough to remember it, we look for other ways to learn about a variety of cultures in the middle of Iowa. One of the biggest challenges is making experiences meaningful and concrete enough for a child younger than five years old. Trying foods from other cultures is one solution that works.

Eating foods from other cultures has presented us with opportunities to learn new words in different languages. I am not content to just point at a word or picture on a menu; I want to learn how to say it correctly. It often takes many attempts, but eventually we learn how to say the names of the foods we are trying. Once those are mastered, we expand our vocabulary to other food-related words.

It is important to me that we not only eat foods from other cultures, but also consume them the same way as someone from that culture. One of my daughter's favorite foods is pho, a Vietnamese noodle soup. She knows that it is served in a large bowl and that she must use chopsticks and a special spoon when eating it. Child-friendly chopsticks foster successful eating since eating with a fork is not an option. When we eat *gazpacho*, a tomato and cucumber soup served cold, we drink it out of a glass instead of using a bowl and spoon because the family I lived with in Spain always ate gazpacho this way.

Food is a central part of holidays and celebrations. We eat moon cakes during the Chinese Mid-Autumn Festival and *turrón* (Spanish nougat candy) during Christmas time, as the Spaniards do. *Poffertjes* and Dutch letters are a special favorite during the Dutch spring festival called Tulip Time. The CelebrAsian Heritage Festival here in Des Moines gives us the opportunity to try foods from many countries and cultures in one place while also teaching us something about the games, music, art, and traditions of those places. We can either choose to make a meal from only one country or from a variety of countries.

We let our noses help us decide where to eat. The other heritage festivals celebrated throughout the year provide us with more opportunities to try new foods.

Because our daughter is not always excited about trying new foods, we turn it into a game. When we go to an ethnic restaurant, we order a variety of dishes that we all share. Everyone must try one bite of each new food, even if they think they will not like it. As we sample, we talk about what we like and dislike about the dishes. Larger portions are served next, with our daughter choosing first. At the end of the meal, we figure out the number of new foods we tried and total how many of those foods each of us liked. The person that liked the most is the winner!

One year during spring break, we had food from a different country for supper the entire week. We ate *bouillabaisse* from France, *albondigas* from Spain, *pho* from Vietnam, *poutine* from Canada, *Zvrkovi* from Bosnia, enchiladas from Mexico, and sushi from Japan. For some of the meals we used recipes we already have in our repertoire, for some we used recipes I found online, and for some meals we ate in restaurants. Several meals presented opportunities to share photos and travel experiences with our daughter.

As our daughter matures, we will expand the cultural experiences and resources we use to improve her understanding of the world and her role in it. In the meantime, our international food adventures will continue.

### Brent Riddle, *transportation planner and father*

At the dinner table one night when I was 14, Carmen, our very first exchange student from Spain, began discussing something she had read in history class that day in school. The class was learning about the Spanish-American War and the textbook had presented some information that conflicted sharply with what Spanish students learn about Spain's involvement in that conflict. I don't remember the precise issue, but I remember clearly the larger discussion that ensued as the conversation went beyond the details of the Spanish-American War (which I barely knew anyway) to how the United States is perceived by Spaniards, Europeans, and the rest of the world. As Carmen explained, the United States is not always regarded as a force for good. In fact, students in history classes in other countries are exposed to a more critical version of the United States' role in world affairs. This came as a huge shock for me. Eventually though, I had to acknowledge that we had our moments of shame (e.g., the treatment of Native Americans and slavery). Still, I argued to the best of my 14-year-old ability that although we may have our faults, Americans are continually improving, thanks to our Constitution and the diversity of peoples who call themselves American. I was not as eloquent as MLK's, "the arc of moral universe is long, but it bends toward justice," but I thought I had won the debate. Carmen looked at me with a polite smile and finished the debate for the evening, "Don't be so naïve, Brent!" That was truly the beginning of my education about the world beyond Lubbock, Texas.

Our next student, Ulf from Denmark, was a staunch 17-year-old socialist. In Lubbock, he was a total fish out of water. But he was a deep thinker with a generous and kind spirit. Everyone he met loved him. And although we did not agree about many things, Ulf and I became brothers. He taught me how to appreciate and understand others' views, even if I didn't agree. I learned from Ulf that most people come by their views honestly and based on personal experiences—either individually or collectively. It is a lesson that I have carried with me throughout life. Being aware of or having the capacity to understand where others are coming from is important in an international career, but it has been equally important for me domestically. To be effective in my job, it is critical that I take the time to listen and to understand what other people think or believe.

This ability to understand where people are coming from, their experiences and backgrounds, and how those things influence decisions and actions comprises a critical set of skills that I wish to pass along to my children. In an increasingly global world, it is more imperative than ever to have and hone these skills. By exposing our children at an early age to international experiences (people, places, language, and culture), my wife and I believe we are giving them a substantial head start for wherever life takes them.

### Jen Stassen, *tutor and mother*

Each time we welcome a new foreign exchange student or teacher into our home, we are reminded by the course leaders that they have signed up to immerse themselves in a different culture and are looking forward to practicing their English while experiencing life in a typical American family. Although we are happy to help them with their journey, we wonder if they know how much we gain from them during their stay.

Over the past 3 years, our family of five has welcomed visitors from China, France, Italy, and Hong Kong. While they are absorbing our culture, they are also bringing to us a little of their own as well as a greater appreciation for the differences in the world. Some of our most memorable visitors were the Chinese teachers who came to America to observe our schools. They spoke virtually no English, so my children learned how to lead them around by the hand. As long as they had a smile on their face, the teachers were happy to follow them just about anywhere. Thankfully, a smile is universal because that was almost the only way we could communicate. Our kids watched as the teachers took pictures of our dishes and explored our dishwasher, which was clearly a novelty to them. Our children quickly learned that the rest of the world does not live like we do. We have tried to emphasize that our way of life is not necessarily better. Our kids seem to have learned that lesson because they are quick to remind us that although our dumplings are good, nothing is better than the dumplings the Chinese teachers made while huddled over a pot on the kitchen floor. We had no idea what they were saying, but that experience is one of our favorite memories and they certainly were the best dumplings we have ever had. We felt as if they had brought China right into our kitchen.

In fact we feel as though we have been to China, Italy, France, and Hong Kong, which is good because we can't afford international travel. But with exchange students, these cultures come to us. For example, a teenage boy from Italy asked if he could make dinner for us using his grandmother's recipe. We spent the afternoon in the grocery store searching for just the right ingredients. We were all surprised that we could not find some of things he needed. When we returned home, our son and our visitor spent an hour cooking a pasta dish together. They sometimes had a difficult time communicating, but with patience and lots of translating on the computer, they prepared a fantastic dinner. We still cook that dish and think of the Italian grandmother somewhere in Rome that helped bring two teenage boys closer together.

Our most recent visitor was a 15-year old young man from a very small village in France. He was rather shy and probably a little overwhelmed when he arrived. We taught him how to play baseball and the correct way to throw a spiral in football. We talked about the courage it took for him to leave his village and travel to a foreign country to live with someone he had only met over the Internet. He was so excited to experience the American way of life, and we were happy to practice a little of our French.

Ultimately, we think our children have learned that people from around the world may have different faces, clothes, languages, cultures, and foods, but that inside they have similar values, hopes, fears, and dreams.

# CHAPTER 6

# Learning Through Travel:
# Broadening Minds At Home and Abroad

---

*Hang a world map up on your wall and talk about the places you want to visit, as well as what's happening in the world so they have some familiarity. Put pins in the places where you have gone, domestically and internationally. But don't think you can't travel internationally just because you have children. Find a way to do it for it enriches all of your lives manifold.*

**Jennifer Maniscalco,** marketing professional and mother

Books, movies, television programs, documentaries, and even Internet downloads are all beneficial to introducing your child to the big, wide world that lies beyond the confines of his or her family, school, and neighborhood. But as long as it is only on a page or on screen, it can be turned off and put away on a shelf of the mind where it may never be referred to again. Anything significantly impressive experienced in person, however, gels in a multi-sensual way that is difficult for a young mind to forget, especially if it is radically different from anything else experienced before. While the specifics may dim over time—especially if overlaid with subsequent experiences of a similar nature—there will be no shrinking of what the mind remembers once it has been expanded to the realization that there is so much more than just one's own hometown, state, and country.

So if your objective is to develop a permanent global mindset in your children, there is no substitute for travel. This point has been confirmed by our survey respondents: 96% agreed that international travel and 85% agreed that domestic travel contribute to instilling children with a global mindset. When we asked teachers the same question, the number was similar for international travel at 97%, but significantly higher for travel within the United States at 94%. And it's not just the complete experience of seeing, hearing, smelling, and touching everything with their own eyes, ears, nose, and hands. What is just as important—and absolutely beyond replication by any current technology—is the fact that when they are there in person, they control the manner and sequence of the experience. They're not just seeing what the person controlling the camera has decided to show them, but whatever they want to see, for whatever length of time, and in whatever order they choose. That makes them the directors of their own travel documentaries and the resulting imagery their own personal video archives, starring them. And nothing locks in the inevitable mind-expanding experiences of travel more than that kind of ownership.

## Going Beyond Your Community

Given the limited vacation time that most families have and the increasingly high costs of travel, we recognize that many families are unable or unwilling to travel overseas. And although there are some very effective ways to minimize costs, which we detail later in this chapter, international travel will inevitably cost more than a vacation by car to a favorite mountain lake or beach. Fortunately, America is a very big country with plenty of its own nooks and crannies to explore, many of which come complete with their own global flavor. What is important, therefore, is that you explore beyond your own backyard and a handful of favorite non-local destinations. For example, if your annual vacation is always to a campsite or lodge on the coast of Maine, consider instead visiting a national park such as Yellowstone or Glacier. If you take a Disneyworld or Disneyland trip every year or so, calculate your costs and compare a trip to Washington, D.C., (where most of the museums and monuments are free) to take in our nation's history. Having a sense of the world and of America's place in it can begin right here at home. It's all about attitude—being a traveler instead of a tourist.

> One of the best things parents can do for their children is travel, and it doesn't have to be abroad. The United States is quite diverse and traveling takes you out of your element. You have to deal with people you've never met. Everything you're experiencing—culture, foods, architecture, sounds, smells—stimulates thinking, creativity, and wonder in an all-encompassing and powerful way.
>
> **Brent Riddle,** transportation planner and father

> I attribute my global mindset to lots of travel with my family. Since my mother won't fly in an airplane, we drove all over the United States and Canada. I think that knowledge of the diversity of cultures within the United States is essential to having a global mindset.
>
> **survey respondent**

## Domestic Global Experiences

Given the great cultural diversity that can be found here in the United States, it's not absolutely necessary to go overseas to have an authentic global experience. Any number of American cities can provide a legitimate partial immersion experience, especially those with geographically concentrated, historically established, residential immigrant communities. Many of these continue to be known as some nation or other "_____-town" or "Little _____", followed by the name of the country, or its capital or largest city. To be sure, many of the more well-known of these communities, such as Little Italy in New York and Koreatown in Los Angeles, have long since ceased being particularly Italian or Korean respectively as third, fourth, fifth, and even sixth generation members have moved into mainstream America and out of the immigrant neighborhoods in which their ancestors were once effectively confined. The restaurants and shops that are left are as much for tourists as they are for what remains of the original ethnic community.

But newer and much more culturally genuine communities can still be found throughout the United States. Generally speaking, the larger and more cohesive the community and the higher the percentage of recent immigrants, the more authentic the mini-immersion it offers outsiders. In good-sized ones, storefront after storefront cater primarily to members of that culture, with not only products and services from that culture, but signage and most conversation taking place in that language as well. At the largest of them, you can attend regular cultural events—not just once-a-year fairs or festivals—and even spend the night in a culturally authentic hotel, be it in terms of décor and menu, or a true *ryoken*-style room complete with futons and tatami mats as can be found in San Francisco's Japantown.

Even in the most ethnically authentic enclaves or communities, however, there will always be those who speak English, street signs and other public information will be in English, and by walking just a few blocks, you can quickly return to more typical American neighborhoods. Nor is the climate or topography likely to fool you into thinking that you are actually in that particular country.

Still, you will be amazed at how much of an authentic global experience you can have without leaving the country and for generally only a fraction of the price. In the case of a few particularly diverse cities, you can even string together several such enclaves into a multi-country "tour." Perhaps best of all, you can incorporate one of these domestic "global" destinations into a trip that you were already planning on taking anyway, be it a fun-oriented family vacation or a visit with far-flung friends or relatives. A short detour of just a couple of hours or a day can introduce your children to a culture that they might know very little about and would probably not have the opportunity to experience firsthand otherwise.

So, where to go? Not surprisingly considering our location in North America, the most numerous ethnic communities are those populated by our Latin American neighbors to the south. Almost any big city in the Southwest has a large Mexican population and finding a vibrant and authentic Mexican neighborhood there is relatively easy. Among the largest and most cohesive of these are the ones found in Dallas, Houston, San Antonio, Albuquerque, Phoenix, Tucson, San Diego, and Los Angeles—which also has sizeable populations of Salvadorans and Guatemalans. Other Latin American nationalities, especially Cubans, Nicaraguans, and Venezuelans, have established their own cultural enclaves in the Miami area, while there is another large Salvadoran community in Washington, D.C., and a significant Brazilian community in Newark, New Jersey. Not too far behind are East Asians whose most vital communities are found on the West Coast. Los Angeles, for example, has a prominent Little Tokyo and Little Cambodia while San Francisco, in addition to its well-known Chinatown, also has a prominent Japanese community, and San Jose has the nation's largest Vietnamese population.

But the East and Midwest regions are not without authentic cultural pockets of their own, many of which are little known outside their own immediate area. The Detroit suburb of Dearborn, for example, has the largest Arab and Middle Eastern population in the country (more than 40%). St. Paul, Minnesota, has the country's largest Hmong (Laotian) community, and Milbourne, Pennsylvania (suburban Philadelphia), the highest concentration of Indian Americans. Of course, you can find just about any nationality you care to look for in New York City, which makes it a perfect "around-the-world-in-just-a-few-days" destination. Among the more expansively authentic of its many contemporary immigrant neighborhoods are Flushing (Chinese and Korean), Greenpoint (Polish), Brighton Beach (Russian), Elmhurst (Colombian), and Flatlands (Jamaican).

Finally, no discussion of mini "global" experiences would be complete without mentioning America's handful of international theme towns. To be sure, these are mostly tourist destinations based loosely on old (and generally atrophied) historical roots and not authentic, contemporary cultural communities. But they can still give first-timers a glimpse, albeit generally a stereotypical one, into a culture that has otherwise long since been assimilated into the American melting pot. Among those worth seeking out in this capacity are Frankenmuth, Michigan, and New Braunfels, Texas (both German); New Glarus, Wisconsin, (Swiss); Holland, Michigan (Dutch); and Solvang, California (Danish). The "natives" you meet there will be as American as you are, but the taste you will get of their ancestral homeland will undoubtedly be the most authentic one you can get short of visiting the original.

## Creating a Traveler's Mindset

It started off as a *New Yorker* cartoon, became a documentary, a feature movie, and is now an established cliché: "If it's Tuesday, this must be Belgium." It is, of course, a satire—and an uncannily accurate one—of what travel, and especially foreign travel, often means to Americans. That is to say, a two-week, rapid-fire sequence of big cities and famous landmarks whose only lingering benefit seems to be that years later the participant can claim at a party or around the office, "Oh, I've been there."

There is much to be said for seeing the greatest and most revered testaments of human ingenuity, creativity, and sense of beauty, places like the Gateway Arch in St. Louis, the Golden Gate Bridge in San Francisco, Notre Dame Cathedral in Paris, the Great Sphinx of Giza in Egypt, or the Taj Mahal in India. See them once and you will forever be enriched. But travel, and especially travel for children, is much more than just a mental checklist à la *1,000 Places to See Before You Die*, the juvenile spin-off of which, *500 Places to Take Your Kids Before They Grow Up*, came out in 2006. Sure, they will remember their ears popping as they ride two separate elevators up to the 102nd floor of the Empire State Building in New York City, chasing the cats around the Colosseum in Rome, racing down the Great Wall of China, or petting the llamas that roam around Machu Picchu in Peru. But how much of the history and nature of the civilizations that spawned them will they absorb? Certainly, the older they are, the more they have had the opportunity to learn about these places in school, but it might be a lot to expect young kids to take in everything.

*As a business executive and former U.S. ambassador who has lived and worked around the world, I have seen no small number of tourists who have left the United States for a vacation, but who still insist on re-creating overseas the day-to-day experiences of life back home, be it regularly dining at U.S. fast food restaurants or searching out the latest U.S. coffee franchise to open in town. In contrast, there are also people*

*back in the United States who have never had the opportunity to travel
overseas but who are more open—and more willing—to explore the
new and the different.*

**Curtis S. Chin,** international business executive and former U.S. ambassador

The point here is that travel, and particularly travel with elementary-school age children or younger, is just as much about the journey itself as it is the physical destination. This is especially true when the object is to begin to create a global mindset. What is important is that your child begins to see the big-picture reality that the world is made up of many different people, speaking many different languages, practicing many different religions, and doing common, everyday things—eating, working, socializing—in many different ways. And this applies to travel within the United States, too, albeit not as dramatically. Consider it not so much as an education itself, but as an introduction to learning. What's more, if effectively initiated, that learning will continue throughout their lifetime.

Seen in that light, the sooner a child gets his or her exposure to the great big classroom that is the world, the better. No one expects a 6-year–old to appreciate (or even enjoy) an afternoon in the Prado or a 10-year-old to "get" the architecture and history of the Alhambra. But they will come away from a trip to Spain with an understanding of the fact that the locals speak a different language, eat different foods and at different hours, rely more upon public transportation, tend to live in urban apartments, and are fanatic about soccer, to name just a few things. The older the children are, the more they will be able to understand a bit about why the Spaniards are the way they are, and by extension, why Americans are the way we are. In the meantime, they will be learning the most fundamental and important of global mindset lessons: the world is a very large place populated by people who often look and act very differently, but who, upon closer inspection and reflection are, in fact, much more similar than different.

*Teach your child to be a traveler, not a tourist. Travel with them but as a
local and not high-end.*

**survey respondent**

*I will never forget the joy of sitting in a snooty restaurant in Paris and
watching a well-dressed matron pushing a piece of bread around her
plate to sop up the delicious sauce. In my Kansas childhood my mother
would dive on me like a shrike if I did this. "It's bad manners!" she*

*would say. That moment in the Paris restaurant was pivotal. I realized that good manners are fluid and the only universal rule is that you should try to make everyone around you feel comfortable—that was the essence of good manners. It was liberating.*

**Patrica Guy,** international wine expert and author

## The Beginning of a Lifelong Journey

While just one trip can start them down the road to becoming 21st-century global citizens, the more such experiences they have—and especially the more divergent such experiences—the better. Nothing reinforces the understanding that there are different ways of doing things more than seeing them done in a true multiplicity of approaches. This can begin with an exploration of some aspect of the United States that is different from where you live: Go to Boston if you live in the Midwest, New Orleans if you live in the Pacific Northwest, or Chicago if you live in the Southeast. For the vast majority of Americans, a first trip beyond our borders to Québec City in Canada can be followed up by another "Western culture" such as Europe or Latin America, for example, or by one to Asia or the Middle East where the differences will be even more pronounced. Just as in construction, the broader the base, the more stable the structure that can eventually be built on it. This journey does not have to be completed before your child turns 18. It can happen over his or her entire lifetime, beginning with you on family trips, expanding as he or she decides to study abroad in college, and reaching fulfillment by exploring the world on his or her own as an adult.

Just as seeing for themselves how things really are can amend the incorrect impressions that children get from animation and computer-generated imagery, so, too, will it rectify many of the dangerous prejudices and stereotypes that American children grow up with even today. One day spent in Mexico City, for example, will demonstrate to your son that not all Mexicans wear ponchos, sandals, and sombreros, eat only tacos and enchiladas, and listen to mariachi music all day—stereotypes that are all too easy to develop thanks to those ubiquitous "authentic" Mexican restaurants here in the United States.

This benefit can be preventative as well as prescriptive. That is to say, an exposure to foreign lands can prevent other, perhaps even more corrosive, prejudices or stereotypes from taking root later on. For example, your teenage daughter is less likely to fall prey to ill-informed cultural stereotypes later in life after having seen for herself what daily life in modern China is really like.

*It's important to expose young children to international environments and encourage cross-cultural interaction. Doing so makes it more difficult for them to dehumanize others by providing opportunities to socialize and appreciate and understand each other. The mind of an 8- to 15-year-old, in particular, is very sensitive to understanding social situations. This can develop into empathy and compassion, critical components to global awareness.*

**Dr. Liesl Riddle,** professor and mother

*Bring your children up with a love of learning about the world—not just school curriculum—and talk about the world using maps, games, puzzles, and airplane tickets.*

**survey respondent**

A more positive and more quickly realized personal growth benefit is in finding out that there is nothing inherently scary about traveling abroad and that your kids can not only do it, but in fact enjoy it. For many children, and especially younger children or even older children from more homogenous and isolated environments, venturing beyond the familiar can be extremely intimidating, especially if it also involves losing their ability to communicate freely and easily with anyone they meet. Getting over this fear takes time and experience, and there is no better time for them to get that experience than while they are with their trusted and comforting parents. How quickly and how effectively it happens will depend on many factors, but eventually it will occur, and no doubt it is better that it happens sooner rather than later.

Once they have gotten over whatever initial fear of the unfamiliar they may have, it is just a matter of time before young people become positively comfortable in the new situation. This, however, generally takes a bit longer in that it requires the accumulation of positive experiences and not just the negation of fear. How soon a sense of comfort comes will depend on how old and experienced your child is, how outgoing she is by nature, and how easy it is for him to become comfortable in the immediate situation. A teenager experiencing London, for example, is much more likely to become quickly confident of his adaptive abilities than the same one in Lima. True comfort in a foreign setting, however, may take several exposures and additional maturity. The sooner your child gets started on the learning curve, the sooner she arrives at the ultimate destination. Furthermore, having gotten there more quickly can make a significant difference when he or she has the opportunity to study abroad in college or receives a job offer that requires working internationally.

Last, but hardly least, children are naturally curious creatures and cannot help but find things on overseas trips that appeal to their developing intellectual tastes or interests. A fascination with mythology may be the result of a trip to Greece, while a snorkeling excursion in Panama can lead to an interest in marine biology. Any child will find something of compelling personal interest just about anywhere you take him, though it may not be the interest that you expect. In some cases, that interest will run its course and wither away. In others, it may burn slowly and steadily for years, if not for an entire lifetime. And in others still, it may develop into a rewarding and satisfying career.

Whatever his or her personal interests might be, time spent in a place where English is not spoken or widely understood generally results in a child's desire to learn a foreign language—not necessarily the language that is spoken there, but some language. This is a natural and logical consequence of a young person's initially finding herself unable to communicate, but eventually acquiring a few words or phrases to make herself understood in certain limited ways such as finding out if the bathroom is occupied, how much a desired souvenir costs, or ordering a treat at a pastry shop. Even only a week or so will generally convince someone that he or she can learn another language after all, and that the rewards of doing so in terms of human interaction are worth the effort. If he has already learned some of that language in school, he will generally return home convinced that the time spent in the classroom, at the language lab, and doing homework was worth it and will be inspired not only to keep it up, but actually to increase his efforts. As we saw in Chapter 4, no single thing is more integral to becoming a true global citizen than mastering a second language.

*I was so surprised at how quickly I picked up the language while in Spain. Being immersed in it helped, but so did the complete experience of food, culture, and lifestyle. It's like nothing I ever experienced before.*

**Mackenzie Abate,** undergraduate student

*Our daughters have taken Spanish since the first grade. So three times in the past few years, we've taken family vacations in Spanish-speaking destinations to help them improve conversationally. We were amazed at how well they were able to use their Spanish, especially how quickly they picked up on local accents and vocabulary despite how fast the natives spoke. They were conversing with taxi drivers, wait staff, and museum attendants in no time!*

**Mike Perry,** engineer and father

There is nothing more fundamental, therefore, to raising global children than getting them out there observing and experiencing the world for themselves. But there are other benefits of travel beyond expanding their minds. Our survey data highlighted the following:

- Appreciation for different cultures;
- Correcting misimpressions or stereotypes;
- Countering or preventing prejudices;
- Gaining confidence in their abilities to handle new situations;
- Stimulating lifetime interests, possibly even career ones;
- Boosting self-awareness, independence, and patience;
- Strengthening adaptability, communications, and problem-solving skills;
- Learning that different isn't bad, just different;
- Heightened sense of curiosity;
- Increased interpersonal awareness and empathy;
- Experiential learning;
- Inspiration to learn another language; and
- Overcoming the fear of travel or foreign lands.

In order to streamline the discussion, we have focused the rest of the chapter on specific advice for international travel. To be sure, many of these tips can be applied to U.S. travel as well. But it can be a bit confusing advising Americans on different places to go within the United States when many readers will invariably already be living in these locations or know them well. Therefore, the focus here is on travel beyond our borders.

*The opportunity to be able to travel beyond my Midwest hometown, first beyond my state and then eventually overseas, at a fairly early age, enabled me to develop a global mindset.*

**survey respondent**

*I think it's important to expose children to many different places and
families in the United States and beyond, if possible, in order to inspire
curiosity and acceptance of others.*

survey respondent

*We consider traveling with our kids to be a necessary part of their
education. We don't have the Ritz-Carlton experience, but rather travel
as an adventure and make it fun. We assign the kids, who are 6, 8, and
11, tasks as we travel, such as packing and planning, airport navigation,
and menu interpretation as we take on the world together as a family.*

Michele Morgan Knott, mother

# Planning Your Trip

To be sure, there are few things more enjoyable to veteran travelers than picking up an atlas with the purpose of finding where in the world you want to go
next, or, if it is your first overseas trip, where you want to go. As such, it is not
likely to be a task to which you will give short shrift. But there is more to it than
just deciding which of the many places that you have always wanted to visit
is the single most desirable. Taking your children abroad involves much more
than just wish fulfillment. It is a complex practical equation, one involving many
variables, the value of each only you and your family can determine. It is also
one for which there can be no objectively correct answer. What is right is what
is best for your family and your family's unique circumstances and dynamics.

Some of the most important factors that any family should take into consideration must include the following:

- **The amount of time you have.** Generally speaking, the best results come
from spending as much time on the ground as you possibly can. Ten days
to two weeks would seem to be a reasonable minimum, but smaller destinations closer to home (e.g., Québec, Caribbean islands, and Central
America) can certainly be done in one week, and of course should be if
that is the only option. It is important that you pick a country or region that
can be reasonably "done" in the amount of time allotted—or else limit your
scope to a suitably manageable portion of that country or region. You could
spend two months in China, for example, and still only see a small portion
of the country. So if China is your choice and you only have two weeks, limit
your trip to a handful of reasonably contiguous areas rather than small bits

of several disparate parts. You will want to maximize your time experiencing, not traveling, especially if that travel requires airplanes. And wherever you go, remember to allow for jetlag. At its worst (across eight or more time zones), jet lag can take a full week to recover from completely, with the first day often a total waste.

- **The ages and interests of your children.** Just as books and movies are appropriate for specific ages, so, too, are trips. While many destinations lend themselves to being worthwhile educationally for all ages, those reasons are not going to be the same for all ages. In general, the more intellectual or culturally sophisticated the destination, the less it is going to appeal to younger children. For example, 7- and 8-year-olds are likely to be much better suited temperamentally to spending a week in a tropical rainforest with its animals, lush vegetation, and outdoor activities than they are to a week in Madrid with a focus on palaces, museums, and café and restaurant life. So while that doesn't mean you can't take your 9-year-old to Vienna, for example, make sure that if you do, you also include stops at pastry shops, rides on trams, and a spin or two on the Giant Ferris Wheel at the Prater. And, of course, your children may be of divergent enough ages that you need to find a happy medium anyway.

- **Expenses.** Rare indeed is the family for whom money is no object. What your trip is going to cost is much more likely to be a factor limiting just where you can go and for how long, and quite probably eliminating some places you would have liked to have gone. It's going to be up to you to determine how much is too much. The problem is that it is often difficult to accurately estimate the total cost of your trip. Yes, airfare and hotel costs can be known precisely, and a current guidebook (or its online version) can give you reliable tour and admission costs. Food, drink, and guides, however, are variables that cannot be fully known until you are actually on the ground, as is the cost of gifts and souvenirs. But there are other costs as well, and some of them can be quite significant.

  - **Budget busters.** Some of the most commonly overlooked expenses are the cost of a visa (some countries charge well over $100 per person); tourist taxes (generally added right onto the cost of hotel rooms, restaurant bills, and occasionally services); booking fees; transportation surcharges in the form of landing, docking, and bus terminal use fees; and departure taxes. Then there is always the unforeseeable expense of medicine or toiletries and replacing anything that you brought that gets lost or broken. Even the most thorough readers of small print are likely to overlook some of these charges, so a good rule of thumb is to round up your total estimated cost by 25%. That way, if you are surprised, it is probably going to be pleasantly.

- **Ways to save.** There are ways that you can economize so as to make a trip that at first might seem beyond your budget, actually fit. This is especially true with airfare, where significant savings can be realized by buying well in advance and booking through reputable Internet services, and hotel rooms, which can also be booked online often at significant discounts, but typically either only far in advance or immediately preceding your arrival. Another good place to look, especially for local discounts, are official national or regional tourism websites. In addition, discounts for children are often available when purchasing bus, train, and airline tickets. Paying in cash for most items can save money as well. But the biggest savings of all can generally be realized by traveling during the local off-season, whenever that might be, and by bargaining, assuming that is an accepted part of the country's culture and the conditions are conducive. Bargaining, however, can usually only be done once you are on the ground, not in advance. See the discussion below on "to plan or not to plan."

*We found modest places to stay, walked, took mass transit, and took carry-on luggage that each of our two teenage daughters managed herself the entire trip. We ate at markets and local, out-of-the-way places, using a variety of travel websites and books we brought with us to find them. We visited museums and historical sites at reduced rate times. We also found that just wandering through a local store was often as entertaining and educational as a museum or historical site.*

Laura Perry, nurse and mother

- **Weather and season.** Remember: what counts is not the weather at home, but the weather at your destination. Travel guides are filled with cautionary tales of someone who forgot that summer vacation in North America corresponds with wintertime in Australia. Or who forgot to ascertain that January through March is the rainy season in Peru and were thus prevented from going to Machu Picchu. Adults have a hard enough time dealing with this kind of disappointment, but for children it can be devastating, particularly if what they end up not being able to do was the one thing they most wanted to. It is important, therefore, that you know both what is going to be impossible to do at the time of year that you are traveling and what has the possibility of becoming too difficult. For example, May and June are months when Europe is generally subject to its most devastating floods. Summer is typhoon season in East Asia and—although it doesn't happen very often—February is the heart of fire season in Australia. Knowing what can happen and having a Plan B ready to execute can help to salvage a potentially bad situation. Fortunately, no matter what time of year you plan on traveling, there will always be plenty of destinations where the weather is going to be ideal— and an even larger number for which the weather is going to be perfectly acceptable, especially if it also comes with fewer crowds and lower prices. Summer may be the best time weather-wise to go to Europe, but you might only be able to afford it in April or September. Over Christmas can actually be a wonderful time to visit Southeast Asia or Latin America.

- **Safety.** No one wants to have their big trip compromised and possibly even derailed by having their money or passports stolen. Or to have to forsake a major part of it because someone becomes too ill to travel—or even worse, ends up in a hospital. But this happens all the time. And just as important as staying healthy is staying safe. Concerns about both are likely to affect the choices you make of where to go, though not in a positive way. That is to say, you aren't likely to choose to go to one country because it is safe or healthy, but rather to choose not to go to one you otherwise would like to visit because it is perceived as being unacceptably dangerous or unhealthy. And while there is often validity to these concerns, they can also be grossly (and unfairly) exaggerated. That is because crime and disease statistics are almost always given for the overall population, not for the small subset that is most important to you—tourists. The differences are usually enormous. For example, as a country, Mexico has a murder rate that is four times that of the United States. But a little scrutiny will show that the vast majority of those crimes take place in border towns and involve professional drug traffickers fighting for turf and money. Parts of Mexico City are certainly dangerous (the same can be said for New York, Chicago, and Washington, D.C.), but generally speaking, the rest of the country is relatively safe. Not surprisingly, tourism authorities are reluctant to publish statistics that they feel will deter potential visitors from coming unless they can easily add—and document—"yes, but this doesn't affect tourists." Commercial travel guides are generally better, but they, too, can gloss over the issues or not be on top of recent developments, especially disease outbreaks or the civil unrest that has been surfacing in many emerging democracies or in once comfortable countries now facing economic decline. Your best source of information is the U.S. State Department's series of country-specific travel advisories, which not only give detailed and specific information about health and safety issues, but the absolute latest on conditions on the ground. Of course, it is important to remember that there are bad actors everywhere and that there is no such thing as a completely safe destination, be it abroad or in the United States. And while some criminals do prey specifically on tourists, the vast majority of travelers have no or only minorly unpleasant experiences. Don't forsake common-sense safety practices, but do consider leaving your assumptions about "certain people" at home.

- **Health concerns.** The federal government puts out a series of health warnings and advisories, including current alerts, through the Department of Health and Human Service's Center for Disease Control and Prevention. Information can also be found there about any required or advised immunizations, including the time frame for getting them, and what precautions you can take to avoid exposing yourself to potentially dangerous situations. If immunizations are required, you will want to discuss them with your family doctor or pediatrician, first to see if there are any compelling reasons why you shouldn't get them (the CDC site contains a "Who should not be vaccinated" section) and thus decide to go somewhere else. If all is fine, you'll need to make arrangements for getting the necessary shots which, since most family doctors don't stock travel vaccines, generally involves going to a nearby travel clinic.

- **The type of vacation you prefer.** Some children and their parents are just naturally more oriented towards outdoor adventure, while others prefer culture and manmade attractions. Obviously you should make sure that you include your children's interests, since you don't want to end up just dragging bored kids along from reluctant activity to reluctant activity. Such an experience could turn them off on travel for years. But it is also important to maximize their exposure to the foundation stones of a global mindset. A balance must be found, therefore, between your children's initial enjoyment and local culture and lifestyle. In any case, the two are not mutually exclusive. The balance is frequently found by having a little of both: a week sailing though the Galapagos Islands combined with several days in Ecuador's capital city of Quito; or a beach resort in the Dominican Republic combined with a stay in the 16th-century heart of Santo Domingo.

- **Guided tour or going on your own.** Generally speaking, the more that you and your family are able to interact directly with local people and local cultural institutions when you travel, the better for the development of your children's global mindset. Having said that, there are also some locales where finding hotels, ordering in restaurants, and trying to figure out where you are going is just too difficult or time-consuming or where the uncertainty of communication is too nerve-wracking for comfort. Such situations typically result when the language is difficult (think Arabic or Vietnamese) or where the tourism infrastructure is poorly developed. And it isn't only non-European countries where language problems can become overwhelming. Places that don't use the Roman alphabet, such as Greece and Russia, can be equally disorienting. The expression, "It's all Greek to me!" is as much about frustration as it is confusion. Sometimes it is just best to let others do the heavy lifting for you by taking a guided tour, be it for the whole trip or just that part that might cause the most trouble. You might, for example, feel perfectly comfortable finding your way through Bangkok and central Thailand on your own, but would prefer to let a professional tour company show you Angkor Wat.

- If you do decide to go it on your own, your next decision is whether to preplan or "wing it," (i.e., travel with only a general itinerary and few, if any, hotel or transportation reservations). The advantage of winging it is flexibility. You can stay longer somewhere if it proves to be more extensive or appealing than you anticipated, or compensate for inclement weather or some other calamity (e.g., a missed train or bus, a strike, or debilitating short-term sickness) that prevented you from experiencing a true highlight. Likewise, you can speed up or substitute activities if something planned turns out to be less enjoyable than anticipated or is actually impossible to do. Winging it also allows you to bargain, provided you are not traveling in prime season and this is an accepted part of the culture. But there are also disadvantages—the amount of time you have to spend each day finding accommodations or arranging outward travel, for example, although these days that can be significantly reduced by traveling with a smartphone. Moreover, winging it can be risky. You could arrive at your destination late at night and not be able to find any place to stay, or find that all the trains to your next destination have been booked because of a major sporting or cultural event or a previous disruption of service.

- Pre-planning, on the other hand, is generally best if you are traveling to popular destinations in high season where there is a good chance that the hotel (or the type of room) that you have selected is not going to be available or where transportation options are limited. It can also save the day when it comes to popular cultural or sporting events that are likely to sell out or tourist attractions that have daily maximum admittance policies. And, of course, some people just like to plan everything because it relieves them from worry. Most trips end up being a mixture of the two, but novice travelers are well advised to err on the side of planning in advance.

- **Comfort level.** When you go abroad, you not only land in a different country, you enter another culture. In addition to the more obvious manifestations such as dress, food, accommodations, and lifestyle, culture also has an intangible aspect that can only be felt or sensed. Culture encompasses values, behaviors, beliefs, and attitudes shared and shaped by an environment. Together, these elements can be a profoundly disorienting combination, the result of which is often referred to as "culture shock." Fortunately, culture shock is not something that affects casual travelers as much as freshly settled new residents. Still, all overseas travel involves a certain level of potentially uncomfortable disorientation as a result of cultural differences. The issue then becomes how productively you and your children will react. The two most important things to do are (1) to commit to modeling behavior that is curious and accepting of other cultures, despite the differences, and (2) avoid getting yourself into more discomfort than you can handle gracefully. Not only could it ruin your vacation if you decide to leave early or stay holed up in a hotel because everything is too "strange," it could reinforce stereotypes rather than dispel them. As a parent, only you can assess just how much difference your children can tolerate (i.e., the point where neat and fascinating become weird and even creepy). Fortunately, most children do find most things fascinating. They usually haven't had the time to register stereotypes yet and so they may be more accepting than you expect—perhaps even more than you are.

The other type of discomfort is primarily physical in nature. With the possible exception of high-end, fully escorted tours, all travel involves some discomfort, be it in the standard of accommodations, the perceived edibility of the food, or the quality and safety of local transportation. This is especially true of overseas travel where the standards can be lower. And no matter how prepared you are, some things are always destined to fall short of desires or expectations. The question then becomes how well you personally accept the situation and "roll with the punches." Everyone has their own personal tolerance level, but if the normal ups-and-downs of travel affect you more than most, you would be wise to avoid them as much as possible. In practical terms this generally translates into staying at international-style hotels, dealing with more upscale tour operators, or even avoiding those countries where the standards of the travel industry are not particularly high. If carried to an extreme, however, you will end up isolating yourself from the very culture you seek to experience. But if done in moderation, you can end up with only a slightly removed experience from a destination that otherwise has a lot to offer.

- **Special needs.** In addition to all the other considerations, parents of children with special needs will need to make sure that the proposed destination will not present any trouble with respect to their child. And, of course, it all depends on what their special needs are and where you are going. Children who suffer from asthma, for example, will probably have no problem with Western Europe, but find their condition exacerbated by big cities in Asia and Latin America, with some even being potentially dangerous. Food allergies will be a cause of concern in those countries where you can't read labels, and allergic reactions to insect bites or stings can be a real problem in tropical countries. A particularly important consideration for those going to mountainous countries is altitude sickness. Unless you have been at those elevations before, you cannot predict how or if it will affect you or your children. Before you go, check with your doctor, as well as websites such as the Centers for Disease Control and Prevention (CDC) and Mobility International USA.

*Our family vacation to Belize when I was in fifth grade was a lot different than previous ones. We combined small resort living with traveling out into the rainforest, exploring the ocean, horseback riding to waterfalls, and watching glow worms off the coast from a boat. I don't remember much of what our local tour guides told us about the country, but what I do remember—my sister eating termites, my dad confusing Spanish and Italian, my brother being scared of the ocean's creatures—made the trip unforgettable. It was the first time I had explored someplace outside of the United States (beach resorts don't count), and it certainly won't be my last.*

**Morgan Abate,** undergraduate student

# Creative Alternatives

## Volunteer Vacations

One alternative to the standard tourist vacation is to go as a volunteer in which you and your family become participants in an established or ongoing charitable or service project. The primary benefit of a volunteer vacation is that it allows you to actually make a meaningful, tangible contribution to the present and future well-being of the country, and not just insert your tourist dollars into the local economy. Projects can include wildlife and forest care and restoration, cultural and archeological preservation work, and working with refugee populations. By their very nature, volunteer vacations will expose you to a part of the local culture that you will not see as a tourist, and by doing so for a longer period of time, allow you to gain much deeper insights and appreciation. They can also save you a good deal of money, especially if food and board are provided.

The downside is that they are generally quite limiting in time and space and will thus prevent you from seeing and experiencing many of the things that might interest you. (Some programs address this shortfall by providing a few days of sightseeing at the end.) They are also hard work, which may not be what your children had in mind for their trip to an exciting overseas destination. Moreover, they tend to be populated by other overseas volunteers, so though you may end up making friends with people from a variety of different nationalities, you will probably only get to know a few locals, particularly the in-country supervisors. But if you are planning to be gone for a longer period of time, and will still have ample time to travel about the country on your own as well, a volunteer vacation could prove to be a rewarding experience, especially if it instills a new—or furthers an existing—intellectual or emotional interest in your child.

## House Swapping

For those who feel comfortable letting strangers stay unsupervised in their home, house swapping offers an economical way to spend a protracted period of time in someplace of particular interest, perhaps so that your child can take a course (language, history, culture) at a local educational institution or indulge in some extracurricular interest such as sports or crafts, without having to become long-term hotel residents or pay rent. You get to stay in the more comfortable and spacious surroundings of someone's home, and you gain the micro-level cultural experience that comes with living in a residential neighborhood.

## Global Mindset Destinations

As stated earlier, every family has to set its own weight and priority on each of the factors noted above, plus any others that may be of consideration to them, such as the appeal of pursuing their own cultural heritage or the presence of friends or relatives with whom they could stay or who might show them around. As a result, no two families will rank these considerations in the exact same way. But when taken together, they should make some countries obvious contenders while effectively disqualifying others, even some that might have seemed compelling at first.

However everything sorts itself out, remember that it's not the destination as much as the journey and that the overall objective is to give your children a truly eye-opening global experience, one that will be as intellectually rewarding as it is sensually appealing. To that end, you must figure out what works best for your family. For more specific ideas, consider these broad category suggestions:

- **English-speaking countries.** Not being able to understand the language can be a significant challenge for some adults and children, whereas being able to speak the local tongue fluently invariably opens doors. Certainly there is a lot to see and do in the United Kingdom, Ireland, Australia, New Zealand, Canada, and South Africa. But there are also more exotic places where English is commonplace like former British colonies, including Jamaica and Barbados in the Caribbean; Belize in Central America; Sri Lanka, Nepal, and India; and the Philippines (a former American colony) in Asia. It bears noting that in none of these countries is the English exactly the same as we speak in the United States. Vocabulary, sentence structure, and especially accent can be quite different, thus demonstrating to children that there are viable cultural differences at play even in speaking what they have probably always considered to be "their" language.

- **Beach vacations with a twist.** Another effective way to introduce a child not otherwise ready for a full cultural immersion is by expanding something that you know that he or she would enjoy, such as a beach vacation, especially if it is just as appealing to you. To do that, simply forsake traditional domestic destinations in favor of an overseas one, such as a Caribbean island, Mexico, Central America, the Mediterranean, or even Bali, and then wander away from the hotel or resort, either on daily excursions or for a few days afterwards. Your children will still be having their fun and you can control the length and level of your cultural exposure. The best destinations for accomplishing this are those where the local culture really does begin right across from the resort and not miles away.

- **Popular continental European destinations.** Austria, the Benelux Countries, France, Germany, Greece, Italy, Portugal, Scandinavia, Spain, and Switzerland make for ideal introductory trips. In none of them is English the national language, but as long-standing democracies with extensive tourist infrastructure, English will be spoken, at least enough to allow your children to make themselves understood. What these popular European destinations offer in abundance is easy access to different cultures; numerous historic and cultural sites and activities; and an extensive, high-quality tourism infrastructure.

- **Countries where they speak the language your child is already learning.** If your child is already making good progress in a second language, a logical choice would be a visit to a country where that language is spoken, not simply to practice and improve skills, but to gain a toehold of cultural understanding. Nothing is more conducive to becoming a true global citizen than to begin to be able to communicate effectively in another language, and few things inspire children to continue language study more than their own positive experiences with practical application. Through the open door of language—regardless if it is only a crack or completely ajar—they will be able to see their way through to the possibility of effectively participating in that culture. Since many American students are learning Spanish, this makes Spain and all of Latin America (with the exception of Belize and Brazil) appealing destinations. Your kids will be able to read many of the signs and be able to both initiate and respond to basic conversations. And though the number of options for those learning French is less, there is still France, Belgium, and former colonies such as Morocco, Quebec, the Caribbean islands of Martinique and Guadeloupe, and the more westernized destinations in Africa, such as Senegal and the Seychelles.

- **Ecotourism/adventure.** Most kids naturally love animals and outdoor adventures, and are fascinated by climates and topographies that are different from their own. This makes ecotourism and adventure travel destinations a much more likely winner in the "fun" category than centuries-old capitals and cultural centers, no matter how attractive their setting and architecture. One problem with major eco-adventure destinations such as Costa Rica, Ecuador (for the Galapagos islands), Brazil, East Africa, Australia, New Zealand, or Iceland is that the focus on wildlife or adventure generally means prolonged stays in areas isolated from the mainstream culture, though in some cases that will be countered by exposure to indigenous ones. A practical suggestion, therefore, is to divide your time between the different destination types, alternating a week on Australia's Great Barrier Reef with stays in Sydney, Melbourne, and Alice Springs, for example.

- **Heritage trips.** In the melting pot that is the United States of America, we (or our close ancestors) all came from somewhere else—unless we are Native Americans. Whether or not we retain much connection to that "somewhere else" depends in large part on how long ago our ancestors arrived and how tightly they held on to their original cultural heritage. For some, the connection has faded to almost nothing over the generations or been diluted through frequent mixing with other cultural heritages. For others, the connection is only one immigrant grandparent—or even parent—away. But the strength of the pull of one's ancestral culture is determined by the one being pulled, and so if making that long-lost cultural connection (be it in Eastern Europe, East Asia, or Latin America, or elsewhere), is one of your child's motivating factors for seeing the world, by all means indulge it. Nothing promotes identification with the world at large for an American quite like being connected to some far-off part of it. Every child will relate to some degree to the village of his ancestors and his cultural roots; it is, after all, all about his or her own identity.

- **Great sites.** Most people have their hearts set on eventually seeing certain famous and truly unforgettable sights such as Machu Picchu, the Taj Mahal, the Great Pyramid of Giza, the Roman Colosseum, the archeological city of Petra, the Great Wall of China, and Angkor Wat. Visiting these is a lifetime goal and one that your children will appreciate for the rest of their lives as well. Fortunately, they all tend to be located in countries or areas that are also rich culturally, thus allowing for a very fulfilling complete trip, not just a fly-in, fly-out experience. So if one such place is calling you, go ahead and answer it—just make sure you do so in a way that gives your children the context in which to appreciate it themselves.

- **Rising global economies.** So far the operating principle we have offered here has been that all countries and cultures have values to impart, and that what is important is that your child gets a productive and meaningful exposure to one or more of them. While that is true, it is also true that exposure to some places are more likely to pay long-term dividends in terms of an international career. These would be the BRIC countries (i.e., the rising economic powerhouses of Brazil, Russia, India, and China), as well as Mexico, Indonesia and Turkey, which also have fast-growing economies. Exposure to or experience in any of these will be helpful in fostering a global mindset. But as these countries are expected to drive global economic expansion in the coming decades, they may also prove most worthwhile later from a professional/career standpoint. This is not to say that you should decide to go somewhere solely for the sake of studying the economy. But if you do go, make sure that your child gets plenty of exposure to contemporary life, and not just focus on ancient monuments, historic sites, and scenic wonders.

- **The whole nine yards.** By virtue of their location and geographical nature, some destinations present a complete smorgasbord of cultural differences, everything from language to religion to food to history to interpersonal norms. Throw in a still vibrant indigenous culture, and you've got it all! As such, these destinations effectively constitute graduate school for children learning the variety and degrees of cultural diversity. But they could be overwhelming for many, so if there is any serious doubt that your children or you can handle it, wait until you all have a few more trips under your belts. But if you are convinced they can take it on now, what they will experience and absorb will be well worth the extra time, effort, and often cost involved. Among the developing nation members of this elite group are Morocco, Indonesia, Vietnam, Thailand, Ecuador, Peru, Nepal, and India. Destinations like Japan, Korea, Russia, and China also fit the bill, but as more sophisticated members.

# Preliminary Planning

Once you have some idea(s) of where you might want to go, it's time to assess how well these preliminary destinations are really going to work. (It's worth noting here that this type of planning is just as important for domestic as well as international travel.) To do that, you will need to acquire a more in-depth knowledge of your destination to ensure that you not only know all that it has to offer, but also how to access it. Doing that will require more than just a superficial knowledge of geography, climate, history, culture, religion, current events, and pop culture. What will be needed is a solid understanding of the mechanics and logistics of local travel. Lacking that, you are likely to make any number of "rookie mistakes." In most cases, these will be just minor miscalculations resulting in equally minor inconveniences. But if the remedies are not easily applied—which they often aren't in developing countries—the consequences could be more serious. Most importantly, you may discover that you are biting off more than you can chew, a realization that is much better to make at home, when you can still switch destinations.

The more you know beforehand, therefore, the better prepared you'll be to accomplish your objectives and to take advantage of any unexpected opportunities that may arise. In any case, the more you study possible places to go and see, the more your own knowledge about the world will expand, even if you don't end up going to those specific places.

## Travel Guides

Travel guides are an indispensable source of information and are equally useful before, during, and even after your trip. Moreover, there is now a plethora of them on the market and the coverage is no longer limited to just all-purpose, country-by-country accounts. These days you can find a travel guide for just about every genre of travel and activity that you can imagine, including traveling with children. Because of their ubiquity and comprehensiveness—collectively rather than individually—travel guides are a natural and logical place to start. Any good guide will tell you not just about the sights to see and things to do, but about the people and culture. You'll also find practical tips on taking local transportation, the location of good, cheap food, and the names of books, music, and apps that will enhance your time in the country. Many guides also include a few pages on key phrases in the local language to get you started with basic greetings and vital travel-related questions.

You will also learn some important information that you wouldn't think to look for. Did you know, for example, that in many developing countries, the sewage system cannot handle toilet tissue, and that it must be put in a wastebasket? Or that in Muslim countries it's considered an insult to eat with your left hand? (The left hand is used for hygiene and considered unclean.) Or that giving the thumbs-up or the "OK" sign are considered obscene gestures in some cultures? Or that blowing your nose is considered rude in some countries, yet belching after a meal is a compliment?

So, travel guides are a great place to begin your research. But make sure that you avail yourself of a variety of them and don't rely upon just one, even if it is the brand that you prefer and have found to be most helpful before. Each has a slightly different focus and point of view and hence covers different material or the same material in different ways. Reading several thoroughly can give a much fuller perspective on the overall subject. Even if you end up reading about the same aspects three or more times, you are only reinforcing your bedrock knowledge.

## U.S. Department of State

All prospective international travelers should spend time on the State Department website's section on "International Travel," which provides information on every country in the world, the location of the U.S. embassy and any consular offices, visa requirements, crime and security information, health and medical conditions, localized hot spots, the name of the U.S. ambassador, and a fact sheet on bilateral relations. This is important information to know and something that is often overlooked in traditional travel guides. In addition, the Department of State, which isn't trying to persuade you to go to any particular site or even destination, tells it like it is, not as the commercial tourism industry wants you to see it.

## Central Intelligence Agency (CIA) World Factbook

The CIA World Factbook is a treasure trove of information. Included for each country are brief summaries of the history and people, including language, religion, literacy rates, and demographic statistics. In addition, there is basic geographical information, including country and regional maps for context, climate, and terrain. You can find information on government structure, the legal system, national holidays, a description and picture of the national flag, the national symbol, and even the words to the national anthem. The economic overview provides a concise description, followed by hallmark statistics such as GDP, unemployment, taxes, imports and exports, and currency exchange rates. Also included is information on transportation, energy, communications, military, and all transnational issues relevant to the United States.

## Word-of-Mouth from Trusted Relatives, Friends, or Colleagues

There is nothing like someone's firsthand experience, and especially a recent one, to provide an important reality check. If you are already leaning towards going to a particular country, this can often help you resolve many practical considerations such as where you should go and how long you should plan on staying in each place. If you are just considering a specific country, it can help resolve any qualms or concerns you might have about whether something will work out, especially if your circumstances or situation are unique and not addressed well in any guidebook. It is, of course, imperative that you consider the source. You may believe that your own family, close friends, and neighbors are reliable sources, but you shouldn't rely exclusively upon their opinions. Finding another person who has actually been to Tibet, for example, can provide just the reassurance that you need to go there—or conversely tell you that you are probably making a big mistake. But whatever they have to say needs to be assessed in terms of its recency and relevance to what you are thinking about doing. Their three-day trek around sacred Mount Kailash, for example, will not really be relevant to your state tourism board's bus tour of Lhasa in Yarlung Zangbo Valley.

## Involving Your Kids in the Process

Nothing serves to get your children actively engaged and looking forward to the trip like involving them in the planning process. Their input should actively be solicited as it will demonstrate that the trip is largely for them and their benefit. Obviously, the older and more travelwise your children are, the more helpful they can be since they are more likely to be able to read a map and utilize the practical information contained in guidebooks. But even younger children should be included in the process, even if it means creating the illusion that they are making decisions when in fact those decisions will be made by you or have even already been made.

The most productive place for this to happen is in the selection of things to see or do. Your children will either already have some ideas based upon what they have been exposed to in school or from various media, or will acquire some from guidebooks, picture books, travel videos, or other sources subsequent to being informed where the family is planning to go. Most children, and especially younger ones, aren't going to be able to sit down and pore through most practical travel books, but those with lots of pictures should get them to spend some time at least. Fortunately, there are overview books written for just about every age group, kid-friendly websites such as National Geographic Kids, and travel videos. With a little luck, they will focus on the most well-known sites and activities, ones that you already had every intention of seeing and doing.

Unfortunately, they might also come up with selections—and occasionally impassioned ones—that are neither convenient nor feasible for your family. Getting your kids' hearts set on seeing Komodo dragons in the wild during a two-week trip to the main Indonesian islands of Java and Bali, for example, is probably going to be a difficult wish to grant. Or if they decide that they most want to see Italy's Mount Etna erupting—which it may or may not be doing anyway—when you were planning on going no further south than Rome, may present a problem. In these situations, a straightforward explanation or gentle redirection will usually work to start them down more productive avenues.

While nothing is going to be quite as compelling to a child as what he is going to see and where he will be going, it is arguably even more important for your children to learn as much about the background culture of your destination as they can absorb. This serves two valuable purposes. First, the more familiar they are in terms of what to expect before they arrive, the less likely they are to be overwhelmed when they actually do and are no longer able to close the book, turn off the video, or withdraw into their room.

> *When we travel we do research before we go to learn as much about the country's history, political system, economy, and culture. Then once we're on the ground, we try to explore what we've learned and talk to local people. It makes the experience so much richer and more rewarding.*
>
> **Kristi Vitelli,** lawyer and mother

Second, the more they know, the more likely they are to step forward and embrace the culture rather than have to be gradually or even reluctantly coaxed into it. Rare is the child who, after having seen travel videos, looked through picture books, and visited cultural websites, won't have a handful of new things they really want to experience for themselves, especially in the realm of foods and unusual (to them) cultural practices—be it a wurst stand in Germany, a crêperie in France, or sleeping on the floor on rice mats in Japan. And while your children may find out about these things for themselves, ultimately it will be up to you to draw them to their attention through your own research or personal experience. Only you know the kinds of things most likely to appeal—and conversely the things most likely to repel—which you can either downplay as warranted or ignore altogether. Cuisine in particular can even be experienced firsthand before you go by visiting reasonably authentic local ethnic restaurants. Likewise for music, although unless your community has a viable population of that nationality, it will have to be at home via the Internet or CDs checked out from the library. For more specific information on how to involve your kids in the process, see Chapter 5; the same steps detailed there on how to create a local, global adventure can be applied to your real-life global adventure.

# Secondary (or Advanced) Planning

Actually finalizing your travel plans can be a long, drawn-out process with many steps and many potential missteps. Walking you through that entire process is beyond the scope of this discussion. Instead, our purpose is to give you a general idea of the main steps involved in making your proposed trip happen.

## Secure Necessary Documentation

In order to travel outside the United States, you need to have a valid passport. Depending on where you are going, you may also need a visa. Passports are issued by the country of which you are a citizen, and are the only document universally recognized as verification of your citizenship. U.S. passports expire after 10 years if issued at the age of 16 or older, but after only 5 years if issued before age 16. An often overlooked "catch," however, is that your passport generally must be valid for at least six months beyond the date of your projected return. If it is not, you will need to get a new one.

- **Applying for a Passport.** Getting a passport is probably easier than you think, but it takes time and you must be in possession of certain documents, such as proof of citizenship or a birth certificate and photos of the specified size and nature. In addition, it may take longer to get your passport closer to the summer when more people travel and may realize they need to get (or renew their current) one. Should you need your passport sooner than the standard four to eight weeks, an expedited service is available (for an additional fee) that reduces the delivery time to five working days. Overnight delivery charges will also cost more, but are recommended to ensure timely delivery if you're not able to pick up your passport in person. For detailed instructions and information, go to the U.S. Department of State's website on passports. By the way, you can also use travel documents as tools for teaching your children about the whole process. Air tickets, passports, and visas provide the opportunity to discuss international borders, immigration restrictions, and customs.

- **Getting a Visa.** A visa is an official stamp, seal, or document affixed in your passport that allows you to enter a foreign country for a certain amount of time and for a specific purpose such as tourism, study, business, or cultural exchange. You can determine if you need a visa by going to the website of the country you're visiting (invariably this information will be offered in English), or by going to the U.S. State Department's website and clicking on "Country Specific Information." In most developed countries that have good relations with the United States, tourist visas are typically stamped in your passport upon arrival. But never assume that you can get one when you arrive. If obtaining a visa before departure is required, it's up to you to obtain it. Depending on the country and your access to one of its consulates, this may take anywhere between a week and several months, and can sometimes be a tedious process. Moreover, you must already have a valid passport before you can apply for a visa. To apply, you must complete that country's application form, supplying all requested information, required photos, and occasionally even presenting a copy of a roundtrip air ticket.

## Review Health and Medical Information on the Centers for Disease Control (CDC) and Prevention Website

The CDC website offers comprehensive health and medical information for travelers. It provides great tips on staying healthy abroad, as well as information on what to do if you become ill or injured. You're probably aware that the United States has among the world's highest standards of disease prevention and medical care; diseases such as malaria, dengue fever, cholera, and diphtheria have been eradicated or are extremely uncommon. But these diseases still exist in many parts of the developing world. It is critically important, therefore, that you research disease prevalence in the countries you'll be visiting, and take the appropriate preventative care. Using the CDC site is easy; it's broken down into the following sections:

- **Destinations:** an interactive world map that shows health information for travel to more than 200 destinations and includes the sites of recent disease outbreaks;

- **Vaccinations:** an overview of the types of vaccinations required and/or recommended and the necessary timeframe for getting them;

- **Travel Clinics:** state-by-state listings of travel clinics, as well as recommendations for private travel medical clinics;

- **Ill or Injured Abroad:** detailed information on what steps to take and who to contact in case of a medical emergency; and

- **Stay Healthy and Safe:** tips on being proactive, prepared, and protected while abroad.

## U.S. State Department's Smart Traveler Enrollment Program (STEP)

At least two to three weeks before you leave, register for the Smart Traveler Enrollment Program (STEP) on the U.S. State Department website. It's easy to do: simply fill in your name, where you're going and for how long, and your contact information. The State Department will use this information to send you important security or emergency messages, whenever warranted. These could include safety alerts (e.g., strikes, civil disturbances, protests), health warnings (e.g., disease outbreaks), and significant changes in bilateral relations. You can also download the free "Smart Traveler" app at the State Department website.

## Consider Finances

Everyone manages finances differently, so we've created a short list of financial tips to consider when traveling outside the United States.

- **Set a budget.** Create a budget for yourself in the currency of the host country and monitor your spending as you go. Be careful not to fall into the trap that many do: spending more money than you realize because the currency is unfamiliar and it somehow seems less like "real money."

- **Get to know the currency.** Familiarize yourself with how much the local currency is worth in relation to the U.S. dollar. Learn how to say monetary amounts, and take the time to get a feel for approximately how much certain benchmark amounts (e.g., $1, $10, $25, $50, $100) are worth. Sites like Oanda and XE offer quick currency conversion, or X-Rates can help with quick comparison calculations.

- **Use cash whenever possible.** Cash is king in most of the world, and as such, it gives you greater bargaining power and frees you from having to pay any financial service charges. If using U.S. dollars, be sure to have small bills, and carry local currency in small denominations as well. Also be aware that in many countries, U.S. bills perceived to be too well worn or with a minor imperfection such as a tear or corner missing might not be accepted, even if they are perfectly good and would be accepted anywhere in the United States.

- **Use ATMs wisely.** Let your bank (and your credit card issuers) know before-hand of your impending travels so they don't suspect fraud and freeze your accounts. Also inquire about limits and fees before you leave. Use your ATM inside banks or in secure areas as much as possible (be on the lookout for cameras trained on you and the keypad). Refrain from using them at all after dark unless absolutely necessary.

- **Make sure your plastic will work in your destination.** Many European countries accept only credit cards that have an embedded microchip, which most U.S.-issued cards don't have.

- **Use credit cards wisely.** Although safer overall than carrying cash, using a credit card often incurs additional fees. Find out about international trans-action fees. Keep in mind that many merchants abroad pass on their credit card fee to you by charging an additional 2–4% on top of your purchase. Be sure to ask.

- **Do not keep all your cash or credit cards on you.** Use a hotel safe when-ever possible and store cash in various places on your person, including in a secure wallet or small purse tied around your neck or in a money belt. To avoid flashing money in public places, stuff a few small bills/coins in your front pockets or use a change purse for small, quick purchases, such as food from street vendors or bus and taxi fares.

## Using Mobile Phones Abroad

Mobile phones are common all over the world and having one makes sense for emergencies and confirming local plans. Explore all options to determine which phone will work best for you based on the amount of time you will be abroad, where you will be, and the amount of money you are willing to spend. If you have a U.S. cell phone, most providers offer supplemental services and plans so that you are able to use your phone abroad. But it can be quite expensive and may not work if it isn't compatible with foreign networks. Another option is to buy a local SIM card to use in your U.S. phone, but this will only work if you have an unlocked tri-band or quad-band U.S. phone.

## Map Out a Tentative Itinerary

Once you feel you have a solid grasp of the country (or region) and all its possibilities, it's time to start mapping out a preliminary itinerary. "Preliminary" is the key word here as you will want to keep it loose, both for the sake of maintaining your mental flexibility so as to be able to see alternative routings, and to allow for the inevitable late addition to the "must see" list. This could be something that you had overlooked altogether or something you had initially ruled out only to have it reinstated based on new information, typically a glowing recommendation from someone who has been there recently. The last thing you want to do is find out about a very compelling sight that is close to your projected route after you have already made a binding reservation that locks it out.

Begin with what you have determined are the top-priority sights that first attracted you to the country and that you wouldn't want to return home without having seen. For example, no one would think of taking children to China without visiting the Forbidden City and the Great Wall. But after that, then what? Explore Shanghai and up the Yangtze? The old capital of Nanjing? The terra cotta warriors in Xian? All the way down to cosmopolitan Hong Kong or incredibly scenic Guilin? Naturally, tastes, abilities, and previous experiences with similar opportunities vary, so every family will have a different hierarchy of preferences. But choices must be made, and the sooner you start making them, the sooner you will have an itinerary with which you are completely comfortable.

Getting to that level of comfort generally involves revisions, and it is only by putting the pieces that you have in place that you can begin to see what doesn't really fit and why. Sometimes the solution will be obvious and easily done; other times it will be difficult and require extensive rethinking or even rerouting. And other times still, it will be completely unresolvable, requiring a fresh start altogether. The point is that the only way you can know is to go ahead and try to assemble all the pieces, then double-check your work to make sure that it all fits, most importantly by going back and ensuring that the sights you want to see are indeed open on the days you plan on being there and that the modes of transportation that you plan to use are indeed operating that day. This not only takes time, but generally requires a fresh look that can only come by getting away from it for a few days. The end product, however, will be an itinerary that is destined to work well barring any inherently unforeseeable situations such as strikes and natural disasters.

# Making the Most of the Trip for Your Kids

As mentioned above, a tentative itinerary is just that—tentative. And one of the things that you'll want to do before you finalize it is to make sure that it best serves not only your overall goals and logistical needs, but your children's educational and enjoyment needs as well. A brief checklist of some of the things that you will want to consider is given below.

- **Start off with something big.** Children need something to keep them eager before departure and then to re-energize them once they are there. To that end, it is wise to have one of your bigger attractions early on so as to pull them forward through any last-minute anxieties or reluctance. However, this shouldn't be your absolute biggest bang or you risk making the rest of the trip all seem anti-climactic.

- **Save something really big for near the end.** Enthusiasm or just plain endurance can wane on any trip, no matter how inherently exciting or interesting the destination. To counter that, it is wise to have something that they are really looking forward to—including the single most anticipated highlight if feasible schedulewise— near the end to keep them going. You may also want to hold one or two secret options in reserve, either as an emergency reviver or as a reward for cooperative behavior.

- **Keep it interesting.** Some segments of your itinerary are destined to be more intrinsically appealing to your children than others. It is important, therefore, to keep those "others" as appealing as possible by including—or offsetting them with—a smattering of activities or diversions that will revive them. The opportunity to go swimming, for example, or to a local amusement park, will go a long way to counterbalance an afternoon spent at a museum.

- **Enable interaction.** Without the opportunity to interact with locals themselves—and not just those in the tourism trade—your children won't be able to develop a particularly deep or nuanced understanding of the country. To that end—but only as it is practical and safe—you should stay in local hotels rather than international ones, eat at local restaurants instead of tourist ones, and take local public transportation. Not only will they gain much greater insight into local ways of doing things, you'll be amazed at all the small, quirky things that they observe even if primarily for their own amusement.

- **Provide opportunities for them to explore on their own.** While your objective is to maximize the quality and quantity of your children's international exposure, traveling invariably also includes an element of emotional growth. Going out on their own will teach them that they can do it and give them a sense of accomplishment, one that could well be determinative later on when faced with the opportunity to study abroad in college or accept a work assignment overseas. Just how much of this you will feel comfortable with will depend upon the age and maturity of your children and where you happen to be, with safety, ability to communicate, and the ability to get in touch with you being the preeminent concerns. And it certainly doesn't have to be anything major—just going down the street to a park or a nearby ice cream store that you have already scoped out will suffice to give them more confidence.

*My husband and I do not speak Spanish, so when we went to Spain, we were truly dependent on our teenage daughters, especially for things such as interpreting menus, reading train schedules, or deciphering museum policies. They also helped plan various outings, navigate to and from places, and manage money. This was very empowering for them, and I feel we were able to teach them the valuable skill of how to travel safely in a foreign country, while seeking out experiences that make the destination special.*

**Laura Perry,** nurse and mother

*Food is a big part of culture, so when we travel, we go local. It helps to get kids prepared by trying things at home before you leave, or better yet, incorporating a variety of foods on a regular basis.*

**Kristi Vitelli,** lawyer and mother

## Maximizing Their Participation

In addition to whatever you have worked into the itinerary for their benefit are the things that your children can do themselves to get more out of their trip, both during and after.

- Give them age-appropriate jobs to do such as navigating around the airport, figuring out how to get from your hotel to the sight or restaurant that you have selected, or interpreting menus, even if you have every intention of backstopping them. Kids need to feel that they are in charge of something (even if they really aren't) and that they are contributing to the group effort.

- Pack or acquire books, games, and other things to amuse kids on longer plane, train, or bus rides, some of which can be quite tedious and boring.

- Have them document their experiences:

  - Photos. Children will naturally want to share their experiences—and especially the most unusual or entertaining of them—with friends or relatives upon returning home. That is good. Whatever keeps the trip going for them only reinforces the learning experience and builds the global mindset. More important, however, is what they keep for their own post-trip pleasure and edification. So bring a camera and, if it's practical, hand it to them every now and then so the trip can be captured through everyone's eyes. Consider bringing a few disposable cameras, including an underwater camera if appropriate.

  - Journals. Regardless of whether they keep a journal at home, you should encourage your children to keep one while traveling since they will experience many new feelings; have many new experiences; make many observations; and begin to realize many things about life, themselves, and the world. With all the technical wizardry available today, they may think they will be able to remember everything that happens in the course of two weeks, but they really won't. And what they do remember is destined to fade with time, especially their initial reactions to brand new things. You never get a second chance to record a first impression. It is only through writing down their thoughts, impressions, or reactions as they happen that your children will be able to bring them back months and especially years later when they have become more accustomed to and accepting of all the diversity out there. And it is only by bringing them back to those initial reactions that they will be able to appreciate just how far they have come. In the shorter term, keeping a journal will also prove valuable in the numerous school projects or papers that could be generated by (or the subject of) their experiences over the rest of their pre-college academic career.

- Buy souvenirs or small artifacts. Nothing helps a child remember a trip like a variety of small reminders placed about his or her room or in equally frequented family spaces in the house. They don't have to be anything big or expensive, but they should be able to immediately trigger fond or otherwise meaningful memories, something that clearly reminds them of what they saw and learned. Such items also subconsciously reinforce the lesson of how wide the world is and how populated it is by many other cultures. In that regard, the best items tend to be indigenous handicrafts and other items not found in the United States.

## Keeping the Trip Fresh After Your Return

Since your trip was taken for the primary purpose of expanding your child's world view, one that you hope will only grow and expand over a lifetime, the worst thing that you can do is to just put it behind you as "done" upon your return and move on to whatever comes next in your child's life, generally completing the current academic year or moving on to the next one. A truly successful international experience is one that continues to resonate long after your return. Moreover, it should also continue to develop after your return. All children in general, and especially younger ones, are not able to understand all that they have experienced in the moment. Only time will bring out additional meanings and relevancies to their experiences, and even those can sometimes only be triggered by later experiences in their lives back at home. The important thing for parents to do, therefore, is to facilitate the opportunity for that post-experience learning and reflection. Whatever you do, avoid sending the unintended message that comes from putting all the photos, travel materials, and souvenirs away in a box and not looking at them again for months. Instead, try to extend the trip by incorporating these elements into your life:

- Create a photo book together, preferably one that also includes textual commentary, not just identification;

- Enlarge a special photo or two and place it in a common room of the home to show that you value the experience you had together;

- Encourage them to present the trip to classmates at school;

- Allow them to take the lead in describing the trip to grandparents and family members;

- Find a few recipes of foods you enjoyed and try to make them at home;

- Talk about the trip, not only the incredible sights, but also the people you met, the differences you encountered, and how these experiences relate to everyday events; and

- Follow up, if possible, with visits to museum exhibits, traveling performances, and restaurants from that particular country so as to rekindle the memory.

# Real Stories from Real People

### Connie Berdan, *eighth-grade student*

My family travels a lot. This year, instead of our usual moving around every few days to explore a region or country, we stayed 10 full days in a very nice house in the Mexican town of San Miguel de Allende. Altogether, it was very pleasant and much more relaxing, except for the neighborhood rooster that insisted on crowing at 5:45 every morning. People are very quiet in Mexico in the mornings, as opposed to the evenings when they play music, have conversations, and even buy items from the wandering salesmen calling out their wares every evening— "*elotes!*" (corn-on-the-cob)—sometimes as late as 9:30 p.m.!

We really got to experience what it was like to "live" in another country because every morning for five days we went to a Spanish language school for foreigners. We were in a class of five including kids from the Bahamas. Our teacher's name was Sara. In addition to improving our Spanish—we learned many irregular verbs and all 20 different tenses—the program included field trips to San Miguel's gigantic Tuesday "everything" market and the local university where students in the last two years of high school and first year of college practiced their English with us. Each day, we walked the six blocks to school, stopping at the nearby *tienda* (store) on the way home for snacks and cold drinks. (The Coca-Cola® brand sodas made in Mexico use real cane sugar instead of high fructose corn syrup and so taste much better.)

Within just a few days, we began to fall into the Mexican routine for meals: pastries and fruit in the morning, a large, late lunch after school around 1 or 2 p.m., and then a light dinner, for which we went three times to neighborhood taco stands. Sometimes we even skipped dinner if we were full from lunch and went straight to our favorite churro maker around the corner from San Miguel's central plaza, where we watched the parade of people and listened to the strolling mariachis. One night, there was even a fashion show.

We walked to restaurants and shops in the center of town. We went to the same *panederia*, or bakery, so frequently that the owners got to know us and let us choose our own donuts and buns from behind the counter. And they were so cheap! We'd leave the bakery with a bag filled with freshly baked sweets for only a dollar or two. Since our family loves guacamole, we had fun comparing several restaurants' guacamole. After many samples, we came to the conclusion that the winner was the small, neighborhood place just up the street,

Rinconcito. We did the same with our two neighborhood taco stands where you paid by the taco for *bistec* (beef), *chorizo* (sausage) and *pollo* (chicken).

Staying in one place for so long also gave us enough time to take day trips to nearby towns as well as going horseback riding in a nearby canyon—twice. If you want to really get a feel for how the people there live, I would definitely recommend staying put for at least a week.

### Chris Page, *winemaker and father*

It had been almost 2 years since we returned from a three-month trip to Europe and my family (with kids aged 10 and 6) were itching for another global adventure. We chose Peru as our destination mostly based on recommendations from friends. Despite our previous experience learning what works and what causes meltdowns when traveling with kids, Peru would be different. I was forging ahead alone with my 10-year-old son for a month and a half before my wife and daughter would join us in Cusco. A month before our departure, I had a dream that I lost my son in the wilds of Peru. From then on, I was nervous about the trip.

The decision to leave early was driven by the desire to have intensive Spanish lessons for my son, who needed a little push in his second tongue. I, too, wanted to practice my Spanish, so I found a language school that had options for lessons and homestays throughout Peru. The homestays included three square meals and a bed for around $160 each, depending on the city. With the one-on-one lessons, which were 3–4 hours a day for five days, the total came to around $650 per week for the two of us.

From the beginning, things did not go as planned. We missed our connection in Houston by SIX MINUTES! We were rerouted through Mexico City and because the official transportation was closed for the night, our only option was to catch a ride to the next terminal with a friend of a security guard. After talking to him and sizing him up, I sat in the front seat the whole way, ready to react, if necessary. We survived the ride and made it to the terminal only to have my son develop a massive headache. Finally we arrived in Lima. Exhausted, we waited for the pre-arranged van to our hostel, which took an age, all the while my son laid himself down on the floor with our luggage next to a cell phone kiosk and fell asleep with the bustle of the airport racing by. We stayed a day and a half in Lima before making our way to Trujillo by overnight bus for our first homestay. While on route, my son lost his *chifa* (Chinese take-out, Peruvian style) all over an unsuspecting passenger. So why do we bother traveling to a faraway place with our children when so many things can—and do—go wrong? There are several main reasons.

First of all, the good moments always outweigh the bad. We've had the privilege of seeing some amazing sites like Machu Picchu, Andean Condors soaring above Colca Canyon, and fireworks over Arequipa in every direction on Christmas Eve just to name a few. Nothing brings your family together more than surviving the trials of travel and enjoying the wonders of the world together. It's the ultimate team-building experience.

The way we choose to travel, staying a longer time in one area rather than hopping from place to place, gives us time to fully take in our new environment, letting what were originally foreign sights and sounds become familiar and eventually comfortable. In all, we spent two weeks just in Cusco, right in the center of the old city. While we visited a few of the historic sites and museums, our main accomplishments were finding our favorite walking routes; passing familiar popcorn vendors on our way to the open air market; and braving a ride in a tiny taxi up a steep hill to the best *cuyeria* to enjoy deep-fried and surprisingly delicious guinea pig. This is when we connected with people, locals, and fellow travelers alike. The family at the first homestay in Trujillo became so precious to my son that at the bus terminal not one of us had a dry eye. The teenage son whispered in my son's ear that he was like the little brother he never had. All over Peru, my wife and I noticed that the amount of attention and help we received from strangers because we were with kids was much greater than as adults traveling alone. Our children learned about the kindness of strangers everywhere. Our daughter spent hours on a bus tour with a Brazilian girl communicating solely with smiles and giggles.

We like traveling with our kids because they help us notice things we otherwise would not. Guided by our children, we explored the sea life in Paracas National Reserve, browsed comic book stands, and sampled local candy. After we had returned home, my son had a writing assignment where he had to imagine he was the teacher for the day. He gave a stunningly detailed account of how he took the class on a field trip to Machu Picchu, putting to rest any lingering doubts whether the trip was worth it.

Beyond the memories themselves, our children now see the world as theirs to explore. They have both suggested future travel destinations just as other kids might choose a restaurant for dinner. They are not only curious about how people live in other parts of the world, they are also empathetic to the many immigrants in our hometown trying to adjust to a new language and culture because they understand firsthand the challenges and rewards of embracing a new country.

### Michelle Morgan Knott, *mother*

Early in our marriage, my husband and I asked our family members to share their top three experiences from growing up. In almost every instance, they mentioned a trip. Their stories of hitting the road and visiting new places reminded us that travel changes people. It inspires and shapes the traveler. One is never the same after being somewhere new. Realizing this, we decided that we would try to take our children overseas every year until they graduate from high school. Six years later, we have visited Italy, France, Switzerland, Canada, Slovenia, Croatia, Bosnia, China, Israel, and Jordan. It helps that we homeschool our kids . . . we are able to travel in the shoulder seasons, save money, and visit sites when they are less crowded. It also helps that we are able to instill a broad worldview every day through their education. In fact, rather than homeschool, we prefer to say we globalschool our kids.

A few years ago, I suggested we sign up for Couchsurfing, an online network of travelers who stay in people's homes for free. At first, my husband thought I was crazy. "Do you realize we have young children?!" he asked exasperatedly. I actually was aware of that. But I thought we could give these said children unparalleled experiences if we hosted international people in our home. Plus, it would help keep our homeschooled kids from being sheltered, "bubble-boy" types. My husband relented, and so began a most surprising and wonderful cross-cultural adventure for our family.

In the past 4 years, we have hosted individuals and families from China, Norway, France, Sweden, Vietnam, Thailand, Slovenia, Germany, Holland, and Switzerland. A Chinese researcher came for two weeks and ended up staying for 2 years. We tried to meet up in Israel with a French family who stayed with us. Three years after Slovenians came to our house, we ended up staying with them in their country. The bonds formed make these travelers feel much more like family than the strangers who initially walk in our front door. Our minds grow as we learn about their countries; our hearts grow as we get to know them as individuals. My kids are so accustomed to this way of life that my daughter said last year, "Mom, it wouldn't be Christmas without at least one Chinese person!" So we found a young couchsurfer from Beijing who stayed with us Christmas week.

If this sounds kind of unusual, I would agree. Many of our friends think we are nuts. Remember, even my husband thought it was crazy to begin with. But ask him now, and he beams as he describes the rich, beautiful experiences our family is sharing. Our children love the world. They love visiting it. They love hosting people from all over. Our lives will forever be shaped by having been exposed to people from other cultures here and abroad.

### Jennifer M. Olshan, *mother and family traveler*

"Grazie," my 10-year-old daughter said automatically as the waiter handed her the food. My husband, seated across from me in a small piazza in Lucca, Italy, caught my eye and smiled. This was exactly the sort of thing we were hoping for from our trip: Getting our children to feel comfortable attempting a foreign language.

International travel has long been important to us and in the early years of our marriage, my husband and I traveled often and easily. Then came the birth of our first child. Suddenly, we questioned if we could continue traveling overseas with children. After much debate, we decided to try. As I sat completely covered in a white sheet balancing my 4-month old son on my lap for his first passport photo, I wondered if we were crazy.

It turns out that we weren't.

Over the years we have taken a number of trips and our varied experiences have shaped the way we think about family travel. Our children have had to develop valuable skills on these trips. They have had to work on their communication when they (and we) can't rely on speaking English. They have had to learn flexibility—not every country eats, sleeps, and thinks like we do. They have also had to learn acceptance: The world is a large place made up of vastly different people and ideas.

We decided early on that our primary goal in family travel is to get the children *engaged*.

When the kids were young we would hunt out playgrounds and parks and watch them communicate with foreign children through play rather than language. We traveled like the locals would: picnicking in public squares or eating in "beer gardens" behind pubs. When we wanted to see an art museum, we would have the kids search the paintings for a specific color or object; or—better yet—hit the gift shop first and buy postcards of famous artworks and "hunt" for them together. While pushing our stroller through the crowds in Rome we would encourage our 4-year-old to say, "Mi scusi, mi scusi!" We sought out engaging ways for our kids to enjoy their travel experiences.

As our children have gotten older, we have had to come up with more stimulating games. We prepare travel journals. We filled them with writing paper, plastic sheet protectors for all the brochures and ticket stubs they collect, and pockets to stash local currency. We create "scavenger hunt" lists of things for them to find and do: Find *five* angel statues in Florence. Try *four* flavors of gelato. Eat *seven* Irish foods. Learn *ten* French words. We make up games as we go along: Who can spot the most pairs of red shoes? Finally, on the plane ride home we create "scorecards" to review the trip and vote on the best sights, local foods, and experiences. We want our kids to take away important observations and ideas from their travels, but also to have fun.

The best part of family travel is seeing these countries through our children's eyes. It's been wonderful watching them flourish as "global citizens." Their travels make them much more tolerant of differences, more open to new ideas, and more comfortable in their own skins.

On our last trip, we watched our 14-year-old son negotiating with an Italian vendor through exaggerated body motions and limited language. After he paid for his goods in Euros and came bounding back to us proudly beaming with success, my husband and I just smiled at one another. That is exactly what global family travel is all about.

### Elizabeth Shutt, *high school freshman*

For years I have been begging my parents to go traveling abroad. At the beginning of eighth grade, my mom said, "Alright, if you get straight A's this year, we will go on a trip outside the United States as a graduation present." We began planning a family trip to Costa Rica, but one day I came home telling my mom about a friend's plan to go to Africa. We joked around about my going with them. My parents could see how much I wanted to go and said my eyes lit up as we discussed it as a real possibility. When I told my friend, he got excited and said he would ask his parents if I could join them. It took about a week to find out if there was room on the safari, in the hotels, and on the airplane for me. When news came back that there was, my parents were pleased—until they saw how much it would cost! Surprisingly, they both agreed that it was a trip of a lifetime and that they would figure out the finances.

I was fortunate to travel with my friend and his family, who I have known since kindergarten and already traveled with on long weekends. I felt safe with them.

They chose Tanzania because of the diversity it had to offer with wildlife and culture. Ironically, Moshi, Tanzania, is the "sister city" for Delray Beach, the town right next to mine, which I learned when I won $100 in an art contest put on by the Sister Cities organization in Delray. (I put the winnings toward my trip.)

We were all excited and a little nervous about traveling, but we did our best to prepare. We went to Passport Health where they explained all the dangers involved in traveling to Tanzania, including sicknesses that we had to prepare for by getting several shots. I also had to take medicine to prevent getting malaria. I read up on the places we were going to visit, and it really helped prepare me for the culture and sights. It was exciting to fly from Miami to London and London to Nairobi, Kenya, where we spent the night before traveling to Tanzania.

Although I had heard about the poverty and AIDS epidemic in Africa, it is quite a different experience to see it firsthand and listen to the AIDS training and education prevention in schools. I saw people who have very few material goods, but are extremely happy and so connected as a community. Everyone was so friendly and welcoming to us with big smiles on their faces! All of us enjoyed visiting the schools and playing with the children. We brought books, supplies, and soccer balls to several schools. We barely had any cell signal, so our phones didn't work. This allowed us to live in the moment and enjoy the trip more fully. I also learned about myself. I'm confident, adventurous, and have a strong desire to be with animals in their natural habitat. On our nighttime safari, I was the least scared and got the closest to the lions and their cubs to take photos from our open jeep. A highlight of my trip was photographing my favorite animal, the cheetah, in the wild.

Although my parents sent me with the thought that they would never go themselves, I am hoping to return with my entire family because it is such a special place. I would never have guessed that my first real adventure outside the United States would be Africa at 14, and so who knows what my next opportunity to travel will be? I'd like to visit Europe, Costa Rica, Bali, and India.

I hope my experience helps parents to be open to travel opportunities for their children because I think this trip has broadened my perspective of people and the world and has given me greater courage to do things out of my comfort zone. My trip to Tanzania was an amazing, unforgettable experience.

### Steve Finikiotis, *business leader, emerging markets*

The word "transformative" is over-used these days, but I'd make an exception for a 10-day holiday to Cairo, when I was in my 20s, that caused me to follow a different path. That sensory and cultural experience inspired my approach to working with businesses since launching my company over a decade ago.

Today, I enjoy the privilege of working in Africa and the Middle East, regions that have captivated me since visiting Egypt in the '80s. That's when I began exploring cities, delving into the architecture, art, music, food and, most importantly, the people.

My first impression flying into Cairo was of its breathtaking scale. The city's sprawling boundaries pushed far beyond the verdant Nile Valley and into the desert engulfing the pyramids in Giza.

For much of its two-thousand-year history, Cairo has been the world's biggest metropolis. In the modern era, it has been the largest city in the Arab world, Africa, and the Mediterranean. Bedouins, Nubians and Hamitic Arabs flock to the cultural capital of a region that extends from the Atlantic Ocean to the Gulf of Oman.

My most lasting impression of Cairo was its humanity. I'd never before been any place where strangers, men and women alike, not only made eye contact, but they sometimes held my gaze disarmingly. Men and boys gave a palm-up salute of respect popularized by Egypt's beloved Anwar Sadat who'd died only a few years earlier.

Hence, I found it easy to engage people regardless of their age or gender, something I'd not known in travels to Western Europe or the United States. And, the prospect of encountering new people was compelling.

I quickly became what Baudelaire called "a flâneur"—someone who walks the city in order to experience it. Each morning, after a breakfast of mashed fava beans drenched with olive oil known as *fūl*, and spicy scrambled eggs with strong coffee, I wandered through Cairo's neighborhoods, affluent and squalid and everything in-between. Though many parts of the city are frayed, Cairo has world-class splendor on par with Paris and Istanbul. A succession of conquering powers has left their imprint on Khedivial Cairo, the central corridor. Medieval Ayyubid and Mamluk minarets stand by stately Belle Epoch buildings of the 19th century marking the city's reawakening after several centuries of slow decline.

If history has taught us anything, it's that Cairo ultimately prevails. Conquering nations have come and gone over millennia, and their remnants are now enshrined in the city's archive. That history is best understood by exploring its neighborhoods on foot, from lush garden homes in the Zamaleck neighborhood on Gezira Island to the commercial district of Tahrir Square at the city's core. To the east, in the core of the Islamic quarter, are Midan Ataba and the bustling Khan al-Khalili bazaar.

Cairo has many charms, but user-friendliness is not one of them. The ceaseless din of traffic, torrid summer heat, and the cloud of impenetrable haze infused with sand mercilessly assault the senses. At sunset, exhausted, I'd return to my hotel at the Nile Corniche, the city's focal point. Graceful felucca boats gliding along the river were a reminder that Cairo's true source lies deep in the heart of Africa.

Looking back to that trip, I discovered that I had the temperament and fascination for exploring Africa and the Middle East. That insight informed my thinking and provided the intellectual grounding to embark on a new career.

I've since visited the Egyptian capital often, watching it locked in an epic struggle between modernity and religious extremism, and hoping it would one day live up to its preternatural promise. Today, as Egypt suffers political and economic hardship, it's reassuring to know that Cairo has always staged a comeback. *Insh'allah* (God willing), it will, yet again.

"He who has not seen Cairo has not seen the world," observed a character in *One Thousand and One Nights*, the medieval Arabic tales. I'm fortunate and grateful to have seen both.

# CHAPTER 7

# Helping Teens Further Their Global Mindset

*There's a practical case for having a global view. It enables you to see more than one side of an issue and to get comfortable with the reality that there aren't right and wrong answers and life isn't black and white. You learn to deal with ambiguity.*

**Therese Miranda-Blackney,** graduate student

By the time children reach the age of 13 or 14, they have begun looking for ways to express themselves as individuals and figure out their place in the world. At the same time, they are also increasingly making more of their own decisions about everything from friends to clothes to lifestyle choices. Parents, teachers, and guidance counselors, however, can still play an important role in helping them make the best choices, even if that means—as it eventually will—going beyond their comfort zones. Part of that, of course, is inherent in growing up. We've done the best we can to nurture and mold them, and although we are still here to guide them, they are beginning to fly on their own, and will soon enough be leaving the nest altogether—be it to head off to college or to enter the workforce.

And since we know that global awareness and a global mindset are important tools that they will need wherever they go, helping them to enhance their global persona now will eventually enable them to fly farther and higher than they might otherwise. Seen in that light, it is part of our parental responsibility to continue to foster the expansion of a global mindset as they proceed through high school and their teenage years.

International skills, however, are helpful not only in the workplace and the business world. Learning another's language and culture reminds Americans that we are not alone. We share the world and its problems, and we have neither the ability nor the moral authority to solve them all on our own. Global problems require the international exchange of knowledge to forge solutions through dialogue and collaboration. Global awareness and international experience will help enable today's teens to become the global citizens and leaders that the 21st century requires.

Many young Americans are already cognizant of the need for global awareness. They recognize that the ability to work globally and cross-culturally may
make the difference between a satisfying career of progressive successes and
an ongoing struggle. A September 2012 study of 18- to 24-year-old American
high school graduates commissioned by the education nonprofit World Savvy,
with support from the International Baccalaureate Organization, shows a desire
among young people to learn more about global topics:[1]

- 80% of those surveyed believe that jobs are becoming increasingly international in nature.

- 60% say they would be better employees if they had a better understanding
of different world cultures.

- 86% agree that a solid foundation in world history and events is crucial to
coming up with solutions to the problems of the world today.

- 90% believe that developments abroad can have significant implications on
the U.S. economy.

- 79% say that it is important in today's world to be comfortable interacting
with people of different cultural backgrounds, a percentage commensurate
with the perceived importance of writing skills (78%), technical skills (76%),
and math skills (77%).

Respondents noted, however, that global issues are not taught or discussed
nearly as much as they should be in school:

- While the vast majority of respondents see the importance of global literacy,
48% actively disagree with the statement that their education in Grades
6–12 included instruction that helped them understand the roots of those
global issues that affect their lives today.

- 63% indicated that they did not discuss world events in their high school
classes.

- Only 54% thought that their high school teachers incorporated a global perspective into their curricula.

Clearly then, teenagers who have explored other cultures and are already comfortable in intercultural situations have a significant head start when they enter
the new global workplace. Moreover, they are in a stronger position to teach
others such as parents, younger children, and fellow students, that the actions

or non-actions of one person or a small group of political leaders do not necessarily reflect the sentiment of an entire community or people.

Now, you may think that we're getting ahead of ourselves by talking about
global jobs and diplomatic roles while your child may still be in middle school.
But we all know how quickly they grow up! Before you know it, your child will
be heading off to college and your opportunity to help him or her prepare for the
world will be effectively over. There truly is, therefore, no time like the present to
begin preparing your child for a global lifestyle.

In Chapter 3 we identified five important life skills to instill in young children to
help them become global thinkers. Not surprisingly, these five carry through the
teenage years, so we are listing them here again:

- Patience,

- Careful listening and observation,

- Curiosity, questioning, and analysis,

- Independence (and avoiding the over-protection trap), and

- Openness to new experiences.

What was only a seedling of receptiveness in a 6-year-old, however, should
be a healthy and thriving sapling for a 16-year-old, one that is growing straight
and true, and has proven to be immune to disease. That is to say, it is no longer sufficient that they be just open to new experiences and ideas, they must
actually be soliciting and embracing them and demonstrating the effects in the
form of increased understanding of—and receptiveness to—the world and all
its cultural and societal diversity. It is never too late to pick up a good habit, but
it should be noted that the later in life a child does so, the less he or she will be
able to profit from it.

Naturally, the degree to which any teenager will have grown in these life skills
depends significantly upon the social and academic environment in which he or
she is planted. A 13-year-old from the rural Midwest, for example, may not have
the ability to branch out as much as her counterpart from a multicultural, cosmopolitan city. But certain tell-tale signs should be observable nonetheless, especially in terms of her circle of friends (diverse or homogenous) and her choice
of activities and interests (wide-ranging or narrow along traditional, provincial
lines). If the desired global awareness appears to be taking hold, applaud it
and continue to foster it. If not, then perhaps some more active intervention
will help. It bears remembering that the mere presence of open doors doesn't

mean that someone is going to walk through them. Never underestimate the power of inertia or the role that peer pressure can play in influencing kids to do what is popularly deemed to be cool at the moment instead of what is in their long-term interest.

*Expose children to lots of different kinds of people in very different kinds of environments and then discuss at length their impressions and yours. Tell them that it is important to try to make some kind of contribution to society, or to humanity, but that it doesn't matter what they do if it is done with passion, compassion, and integrity.*

**survey respondent**

# Master English

In a world of 140-character tweets and OMG! texting abbreviations, communicating well in English, both written and spoken, seems to be a dying art. But it is an important skill for just about every career, and so teens must develop the ability to speak, write, and present logically, persuasively, and succinctly in their native language. If they need practice speaking, encourage them to join their school's debate team or a local chapter of Toastmasters International's Youth Leadership program, and seek out those academic courses that will give them the best opportunities to hone their rhetorical skills through oral presentations. If they need to sharpen their expository writing skills, have them take elective courses in subjects such as world literature, history, or political science that will both further their analytic skills through the writing of research papers and expose them more to the world beyond our borders.

*More important than mastering any specific foreign language is mastering how to communicate well in any language, including one's own. Being able to speak English does not necessarily translate into being able to write a business letter, fill out a job application, or make a compelling presentation. Strong English communications skills need to be nurtured if one is to compete in this global world of ours.*

**Curtis S. Chin,** international business executive and former U.S. ambassador

# Technology

One thing working in favor of instilling a global awareness among today's teenagers is the pervasive and ubiquitous presence of technology in their lives. Today's teens are much more tech savvy than their parents since they have grown up with computers, smartphones, and social media. They know how to do everything from taking and editing photos to posting on Facebook and Instagram. While much of a teenager's use of technology is for personal entertainment and extended interaction within their social circles, that same technology also allows them to connect to everything and everyone any time they want. So while you may deplore the seemingly endless hours they spend texting or instant messaging with their friends, this mode of interaction also enables them to expand their circle of contacts to include new friends they meet on vacation abroad, on an educational excursion, or even through some approved online introduction (e.g., an e-pal).

Technology also gives teens an advantage that previous generations lacked in that they can see and observe so much of the world with just a few keystrokes on their computer or touches on their iPad screen. Invariably, this starts with the latest pop culture sensation, be it the most popular YouTube videos or an international film star. Soccer stars Pelé and Maradona were giants on and off the field in their days, but Lionel Messi, the Argentinian who plays for FC Barcelona, claims almost 50 million fans on Facebook, while Real Madrid's Cristiano Ronaldo has more than 20 million followers on Twitter.

But it's more than just pop culture. Technology has changed our lives and brought us closer to each other than ever before. It has expanded our individual and collective world views and made us more aware of both small and large events taking place all over the world.

Technology can also serve as a strong force for good in the development of global awareness in teens. Teens can learn about actual ways to make the world a better place by getting involved in service efforts and social change campaigns around the world. Sometimes they get more of their information on peer-to-peer platforms such as Facebook and Twitter than they do from parents or teachers. Groups dedicated to reducing hunger and poverty, protecting human rights, and supporting environmental efforts around the world are just a few of the many causes teens are embracing. These passions can inspire a desire to learn about a cause, a culture, and a country. Young people are educating themselves about issues abroad and questioning their own country on their terms using their favorite tech tools. Many find they can help implement change without having to leave their country, state, or even their homes.

According to a new study conducted online by Harris Interactive on behalf of World Vision in 2013, more than half of teens (56%) say social media sites such as Facebook and Twitter have made them more aware of the needs of others. This is a significant increase from 2011, when just 44% said their use of social media made them more aware.

Parents don't need to throw up their hands in surrender to the prevalence of social media in their teens' lives. But they do need to get involved. If your child is using social media, so should you, if for no other reason than to inform yourself of what's going on in the world through at least some of their channels and to monitor their individual progress. Teens are much more likely to stay involved with such causes if they are supported by their families.

## Global Growth Right Here at Home

As anyone who has been there will tell you, raising teens requires tact and creativity, especially when it comes to getting them to do something that they are not naturally inclined to do. Fortunately, there are many ways to gradually (and painlessly) foster greater global awareness in your teen. In Chapter 2, we introduced the importance of developing a global mindset—the ability to work successfully across cultures, including but not necessarily in another country— to best prepare your teen to operate in the world. In essence, a global mindset is an open-minded perspective on the world and its people, places, ideas, and events. It's not just about thinking big thoughts in the classroom; it's also about actively investigating new cultures, practicing a language, and being curious about new people and places. Here are some tips for teens to follow to enhance their global awareness. Practically speaking, these suggestions fall into two categories: physical activities that can be performed and mental aptitudes that must be developed. By doing the first, the second should follow.

### Physical Activities

- Follow the news online for world events, but also specific countries and cultures of interest.
- Study U.S. history.
- Learn or practice a second language.

- Join local and virtual international clubs.

- Seek out and embrace diverse friends.

- Explore global food, music, movies, dance, and art.

- Use technology to pursue intellectual and emotional interests.

- Explore pop culture at home and in other parts of the world.

- Explore the world through books.

- Learn to read a map and do it regularly.

> *I have an obsession with historical fiction. It transports me to times and places from before I was born. These books and novels give me a better understanding of how the world works and—more importantly— paint pictures of cultures, religions, and societies that I will never be able to experience physically, but feel as though I already have.*
>
> **Morgan Abate,** undergraduate student

> *Just because you can't travel doesn't mean you can't learn about the world. Read the news, listen to NPR [National Public Radio] because as you do, you'll become invested in it. Once you tie yourself to it, you can fully experience it as opposed to it being just "over there" remote and impersonal.*
>
> **Jeanette Miranda,** undergraduate student

## Mental Aptitudes

- Learn to think globally and cross-culturally.

- Cultivate listening skills and other personal skills that enhance cross-cultural interaction.

- Free yourself from rigid thinking and media-fed stereotypes.

- Challenge your prejudices.

- Think for yourself; don't let others dictate your opinions.

In addition to these open-ended mental activities, which can be done sporadically or as time and opportunity allow, are a number of finite and focused programs designed specifically for teenagers. Some have been around for decades, while others are relatively new. But they all foster the growth of global awareness and will no doubt prove worthwhile in channeling your teenager's interests and perspectives.

*I have found that my knowledge of U.S. society, politics, culture, etc. has actually been one of my greatest assets in international affairs. I've met my share of people who are very immersed in other countries, but they don't know anything about America which renders them useless as cross-cultural interlocutors for Americans and foreigners alike.*

**Mitchell Polman,** public diplomacy specialist

## Community Service

One of the easiest and most effective ways of introducing the concept of global awareness to teens is via local community service. Community service is usually of great personal benefit to those who perform it, especially teens whose knowledge of and exposure to the "real" world is generally limited. Whenever and however it is performed, community service is a means to develop key life skills such as empathy, compassion, negotiation skills, team-building, and communication.

Community service can allow teenagers to experience situations and interactions with people they most likely wouldn't otherwise meet. Service anywhere—in a food pantry, at a local Boys and Girls Club, for a local chapter of Habitat for Humanity—will expose them to conditions and hardships they would have a hard time imagining or appreciating without witnessing firsthand. Once teens experience the realities of hunger, homelessness, and poverty in their own communities, they can begin to understand those conditions elsewhere in the world. Working to lessen or eradicate those situations at home generally gives them a sense of empowerment as they come to learn that they can make a difference, first at home, and then by extension, throughout the world.

For a parent or teen who has never been involved in community service, finding a suitable program for which to volunteer can be a daunting task. The problem is not that there are so few, but that there are so many. The best place to start, therefore, would be with a charity, service organization, or place of worship with which a person is already affiliated in some way or knows people who are. Most of these will have ongoing community service programs of their own or will be able to recommend others. Other places to check for this information are local newspapers, libraries, and hospitals. Smaller towns may also have newsletters with volunteer opportunities.

*I think that community service is quite possibly more important to developing a global mindset than traveling. You cross cultural boundaries, and ones that are even more problematic because they're present in your own culture. It's important to realize and accept that poverty and other hardships exist in your own community. They're problems that can't be forgotten about when you leave a country. And they're problems that force you to ask, "Why is this happening to them and not me?"*

**Jeanette Miranda**, undergraduate student

*An advantage of going to a Catholic school was that there were always service opportunities. I used those opportunities to figure out which kinds of service made me uncomfortable. That's what service is for me: leaving your comfort zone. Once you break those barriers down, you start to learn about the world around you. After that, there's nothing you can't do.*

**Morgan Abate**, undergraduate student

*Domestic mission trips have given our teenage girls the opportunity to get out of their comfort zones, yet still be in a safe environment. They've spent time in several inner cities in the United States and have witnessed firsthand what poverty is and how privileged and lucky they truly are. They've learned how important compassion is, that every human being counts, and that everyone can make a difference.*

**Mike Perry**, engineer and father

And of course, there is always the Internet. Numerous websites exist to help individuals find local community service opportunities. One such website that is fairly easy to use is Volunteer Match as it allows you to locate volunteer opportunities on a geographic basis. Once the results come up, filters such as age and cause allow you to further narrow your search. The Corporation for National and Community Service also maintains a national server that directs you to many other sites.

If your teen has a particular interest that relates to service, then contacting groups devoted to that cause is probably the best way to go. There are quite a few national organizations with chapters in every part of the country. Among the more well-known of these are:

- Habitat for Humanity,

- Girl Up,

- Boys and Girls Club of America,

- YMCA,

- Feeding America,

- Salvation Army, and

- ASPCA.

## Participate in Model United Nations/Global Classrooms

The Model United Nations (also known as Model UN or MUN)—an academic simulation of the United Nations whose purpose is to educate participants about current events, topics in international relations, diplomacy, and the UN itself—began shortly after the organization's founding in the 1940s. Participants role-play as diplomats representing a nation or NGO in a simulated session of a committee of the United Nations, such as the Security Council or the General Assembly, that investigates, debates, deliberates, and then develops consensus solutions to global problems such as climate change, sustainable agriculture, and nuclear proliferation.

In its most common form, Model UN clubs are part of the academic structure of the individual high school where they are used in the social studies curriculum or as an elective leadership opportunity. Some international not-for-profit organizations, however, also organize and host local Model UN conferences during the summer by bringing together students from numerous school districts. Find out what's available in your area, and if your teen's school doesn't have its own Model UN chapter, consider starting one with the help of a faculty member or other adult adviser.

An outgrowth of the Model UN program, *Global Classrooms* has set up Model UN conferences in 10 major metropolitan areas (Atlanta, Boston, Chicago, Houston, Los Angeles, Miami, Minneapolis-St. Paul, New York, Tampa Bay, and Washington, D.C.) in an attempt to bridge the gap between experienced programs and traditionally underserved public schools or schools new to Model

UN. *Global Classrooms* highlights critical thinking, conflict resolution, and communication skills.

---

## For Teachers

*Global Classrooms* offers a variety of curricular units dealing with issues such as peacekeeping, human rights, sustainable development, and the economics of globalization. Each unit deals with specific issues that have been at the forefront of important debates in global affairs. At the heart of each curriculum unit are step-by-step lesson plans that begin with an introduction to the United Nations and culminate in a simulation of the Security Council, Commission on Sustainable Development, or Commission on Human Rights. All lessons are aligned with standards in:

- Social studies (from the National Council for Social Studies),

- English language arts (from the International Reading Association/ National Council for Teachers of English),

- Geography (from the National Geography Content Standards), and

- Civics and government (from the U.S. Department of Education).

Lesson plans incorporate instructional strategies based on best practice methodologies in teaching social studies and literacy. More information on how to use Model UN *Global Classrooms* in your classroom is on the website.

---

# Exchange Programs, Cultural Excursions, and Mission Trips

Outside the classroom, the most common way for American teenagers to explore the world is through family travel, the basic parameters of which are discussed in Chapter 6. But work, other responsibilities and commitments, and overall expense often make it impossible for parents to be able take their teenager on an overseas trip even during the summer months. Fortunately, there are still plenty of opportunities for teens to start to explore the world without their parents under the supervision of an established and reputable academic or religious organization.

*Make sure your child is ready for both the separation and the cross-cultural experience of an international adventure without you. My daughter was ready and not nervous. The separation was much harder on me; she was living in the moment and loving it. I was nervous and missed her very much.*

**Kristi Vitelli,** lawyer and mother

*Living in another country with a family you don't know speaking a second language is a real challenge. I was way outside my comfort zone but had to adjust. I learned a lot about myself and pushed myself to overcome the challenges I faced. I learned a lot about who I am as a person that I otherwise might not have learned for a while, if ever.*

**Mackenzie Abate,** undergraduate student

Generally speaking, these teen programs can be divided into three major categories: exchange programs, cultural excursions, and mission trips. In addition to enhancing their global awareness, participants benefit from exploring the world with other teens, and have the opportunity to learn valuable life skills. If your child is open and receptive—and you can afford the often hefty price tag or find other ways to raise the funds—any of these international excursions will provide valuable and educational experience.

- **Exchange programs** come in many different forms. Some allow students to swap places with a contemporary from another country for as little as two weeks or as long as a full year. Others have the students switch at different times, or just one of them completes the exchange. Participating students live with host families in order to better learn the language and experience the culture. Experiencing another place firsthand cultivates respect, understanding, and open-mindedness, especially insofar as they will be doing it in the familiar context of being a teenager in a family and thus have a large arena in which to make direct comparisons.

- **Cultural excursions** are typically organized and run by an outside cultural or educational group as a way of promoting knowledge and stimulating interest in their particular subject matter, be it national culture or history, ethnic heritage or language, or sport. Examples include: a tour of the highlights of ancient Italy, exploring the diverse ecosystems of Costa Rica, or studying the government system in Australia. Cultural excursions tend to be led by experts in the subject matter and involve frequent changes of venue, thus resulting in a broader, but perhaps more superficial acquisition of global perspective. In addition to what they will learn and experience about the subject matter itself, these excursions allow teens to get to know others with similar interests.

- **Mission trips** are typically organized and run by religious or other charitable service organizations whose objective is to make life materially better for a specific disadvantaged community. Those that allow teenagers to participate generally restrict their activity to unskilled or semi-skilled physical labor such as agricultural work and basic construction. Mission trips, which can be anywhere in the world, but tend to restrict themselves to nearby developing countries so as to limit overhead, usually last anywhere from a week to several months. Participants may be obliged to pay their own expenses, but often those expenses are raised by the congregation or covered by the sponsoring organization out of contributions. While typically limited to a single village or community, mission trips do allow for an in-depth exposure to the basic culture and language as participants live and work side-by-side with the people they are benefiting.

*My mom taught me that anything was possible, so at age 19 I signed up with a church we weren't affiliated with and became the first member of my family to leave the country (I went on a mission trip). I wouldn't have been able to do so without help fundraising from that church community. I now have so much experience traveling and interacting with other cultures that I was able to turn it into a career recruiting international students for a U.S. university.*

survey respondent

## Benefits of International Excursions

Spending time abroad inevitably expands personal horizons, especially for those teens who are just beginning to venture beyond the confines of their own local community. If done well, it could be a transformational experience resulting in new perspectives on the world and what it means to be a global citizen. By traveling to a new country, experiencing a new culture, customs, and language, your teen's understanding of today's social, political, and economic issues will be significantly enhanced if not actually multiplied. Teens learn to appreciate other cultures by operating in an environment different from what they're used to. Spending time in a foreign country helps open their eyes to the wider world, especially different ways of doing the everyday things that they take for granted. At the most basic level, they will see that people pray and worship in different ways and on different days. They'll meet people who shake hands, bow, or kiss each other on the cheek to say hello, and who have very different concepts of being "on time." But they'll also learn firsthand about stereotypes and see that while there can be grains of truth in some, most are off-base and counterproductive.

Spending time abroad also facilitates personal growth and development. Most teenagers return home not only with radically expanded ideas about other people and cultures, but also with new perspectives on themselves and their own lives. They develop more self-confidence, even after having been abroad for only a few weeks. They will navigate public transportation systems, use foreign currency, interpret maps and schedules not always in English, and quite possibly at some point, have to ask for help from strangers. All this they will have done on their own or with peers, but without their parents' help. These experiences not only can make our teens feel good about themselves, they also result in an improved sense of maturity and independence. Such can-do confidence is critical to future success, first in academics and later in the workplace.

Teens who participate in international excursions will also make new friends, ones typically from different backgrounds. Hopefully they will stay in touch, because the friends they make, whether they're fellow Americans, other international students, or locals, are an important part of their overall experience. They will learn from one another, have formative experiences together, and forge bonds that can be some of the strongest they'll ever make. International excursions tend to bind people together much faster and much more closely because of the intensity of the experience.

*I went on several People to People programs in my teens—to Australia, Spain, France, and Italy. Then I got involved with the People to People headquarters and local student chapters, as well as the Global Youth Forum (GYF). It was a pivotal moment for me when I attended my first GYF and was surrounded by other people who were also passionate about changing the world for the better. The people I met there are still some of my best friends today—many of them even came to my wedding almost 10 years later. Getting together with them always brings back the inspiration, passion, and even obligation we felt to make a difference—and reminds me not to lose sight of those goals as I move through life.*

**Therese Miranda-Blackney,** graduate student

174

Listed below are the programs most frequently recommended by survey respondents:

- **The People to People Ambassador Program** grew out of President Dwight D. Eisenhower's desire to give everyday citizens of different countries the opportunity to meet and get to know one another so as to foster better mutual understanding, friendship, and lasting peace in the aftermath of World War II. The program has been providing educational travel for students in Grades 5 to 12 for more than 50 years and now boasts 500,000 alumni. Ambassadors, who are middle and high school students, travel to more than 40 countries where they participate in programs tailored specifically for that location.

- **World Savvy's American Youth Leadership Program (AYLP)** takes U.S. participants abroad for a fully funded, cross-cultural exchange. These exchanges unite U.S. high school students and educators with residents of host countries to explore one another's culture and critical global issues such as climate change and food security. The AYLP is sponsored by the U.S. State Department's Bureau of Educational and Cultural Affairs (ECA), and is administered by World Savvy.

- **Qatar Foundation International (QFI)** is a not-for-profit organization based in Washington, D.C., and a U.S.-based member of the Qatar Foundation (QF). Its stated mission is "connecting cultures and advancing global citizenship through education" and it focuses on grant-giving and programs that promote collaboration across geographical, social, and cultural boundaries. QFI implements educational and volunteer programs that seek to place young people from diverse social, economic, and cultural backgrounds into effective, collaborative, and global learning environments—inside and outside the classroom, in person, and online. Its core program areas are Arabic Language and Culture, STEAM (Science, Technology, Engineering, Arts, and Math), and Youth Engagement.

- **Rustic Pathways** provides 130 options for travel and service programs for high school students and families in more than 20 countries. Students are encouraged to combine two or more programs to create their own itinerary. Community service hours are awarded as appropriate.

- **National Geographic Student Expeditions** invite students completing grades 9–12 to get out in the field and follow in the footsteps of *National Geographic* magazine's photographers, writers, and scientists. Participants might snorkel with marine biologists in Belize, go on photo shoots in San

Francisco or Paris with a *National Geographic* photographer, or settle into a village in Ecuador to help out with a community project.

- **Lifeworks International** has been offering summer service adventure experiences in which teen ambassadors actively participate in promoting positive change in the world for the past 40 years. Its core philosophy is to combine one-on-one interaction with people in communities to affect positive change. Participants might assist low-income communities around San Jose, Costa Rica, for example, or work on construction projects in the Sacred Valley of Cuzco, Peru.

- **WWOOF International** links people who want to volunteer on organic farms or smallholdings with those looking for volunteer help. Volunteers usually live with a host family and are expected to participate in the day-to-day activities. In most countries, the exchange is based on four to six hours help— fair exchange for a full day's food and accommodations. Volunteers may be asked to help with a variety of tasks like sowing seed, making compost, gardening, planting, cutting wood, weeding, harvesting, packing, milking, feeding, fencing, making mud bricks, wine making, cheese making, and bread making. The length of stay at the farm is negotiated directly between volunteer and host, but most WWOOF visits are between one and two weeks, though some may be as short as two or three days or as long as six months.

## U.S.-Based Language/International Camps

Another productive option to explore over the summer is a language immersion camp. Arguably the two most famous of these are Concordia Language Villages, in operation for more than 50 years in Minnesota, and Middlebury Monterey Language Academy (MMLA) in Vermont. But there are also dozens of similar immersion camps popping up across the country, particularly at universities or colleges, local public schools, and private international schools. Some are relatively inexpensive, especially if they have received funding from a U.S. government STARTALK grant, while others are priced comparable to a traditional sleep-away camp. They offer anywhere from a week to a month of full language immersion, including academic and cultural instruction in the arts, sports, and local cuisine. Most camps accept beginners through advanced learners. The purpose is to be completely surrounded by the language and culture so as to accelerate language acquisition and simulate the experience of actually living in another country. Some programs even require participants to take a "no English" pledge. We've profiled the two most well-known camps below, but encourage you to investigate your local area to find out what might be available there.

- **Concordia Language Villages** provides cultural immersion programming in 15 languages for more than 10,000 language learners of all ages. Its stated mission is to prepare young people for responsible citizenship in our global community. A responsible world citizen is defined as "one who understands and appreciates cultural diversity, communicates with confidence and cultural sensitivity in more than one language, responds creatively and critically to issues which transcend national boundaries, expresses empathy for neighbors in the global village, and promotes a world view of peace, justice, and sustainability for all." Concordia maintains three campuses in Minnesota, with the main site located in Bemidji, and houses campers in "villages" — camp environments dedicated to each of the 15 different languages and cultures. Food, music, games, and sports are those of the focus culture, and the villages even include typical housing and décor. Campers turn in their U.S. dollars for local (foreign) currency and are encouraged to take the "no English" pledge, although it is not mandatory. Courses run from long weekends during the school year, and one-, two-, and four-week sessions during the summer. High school students taking the four-week session can apply for credit equal to one full year of language learning. Concordia also offers day camp family options.

- **Middlebury Monterey Language Academy (MMLA)** is a four-week summer program that has been in operation since 2008, but is built on Middlebury College's 95 years of experience in language education. The program offers five languages to students in Grades 8–12. Acceptance is competitive with rolling admissions beginning in the fall prior to the summer of attendance. All levels of language learners are accepted. MMLA uses the nationally recognized ACTFL proficiency scale to measure student growth. Students take an adaptive assessment to measure their starting and ending proficiency levels and are encouraged to share these assessments with school teachers at the beginning of the academic year back home. Each week is designed around a theme, with culture and excursions a part of the program. Participants are required to take the "The Middlebury–Monterey Language Pledge" and communicate in their target language at all times during the summer of study; beginning students take a modified pledge.

## Using Global Experiences as a Differentiator in College Applications

While the intangible, long-term intellectual and emotional benefits of an international excursion are the primary reasons for having your teenager participate, there is also a tangible, short-term benefit to be derived as well in the form of a potential differentiator in the college admissions process. Getting into the college of their choice is going to be tough enough: High grades and test scores generally won't do it alone. What college admission committees are increasingly looking for these days are more mature young people already focused on their future. Global experience, even if limited in scope and duration, indicates just that by showing that these students are self-starters who have already taken the opportunity to grow beyond their school environments and have succeeded in challenging circumstances. College admissions officers often express how cultural immersion or a demonstrated global mindset can be more valuable than an AP course or extracurricular activity. The most important global mindset traits that colleges look for include:

- Cross-cultural awareness,

- Language skills,

- Creative problem-solving in unfamiliar situations,

- Adaptability to culturally diverse groups,

- Ability to consider various perspectives: cultural, economic, and political, and

- Excellent listening and communication skills.

## Importance of Language Learning for Teens

The benefits of teens' learning a second language are immense. Most obviously, knowledge of another language enables them to communicate with speakers of that language. It also helps them to understand other cultures, since language and culture are inexorably intertwined. But there are indirect benefits as well: Studies show that learning a second language also strengthens other academic areas in that it keeps analytical senses honed and the memory active.

No matter what your teen's foreign language learning experience has been to date, if her high school offers languages, either as a requirement or an elective, encourage her to take one or more for as many years as she can. If her school doesn't, or if the language she really wants to learn and possibly has even already started learning isn't offered, seek out alternative opportunities. Learning a language should be treated as a long-term project. The following tips were included in Chapter 4, but are repeated here to be sure teens and parents are aware of the ways teens can learn a language outside a structured classroom:

- **Take a language class somewhere else.** Find a class at another nearby school or local college. Academic credit will typically be given and your child will reap the benefits of showing initiative.

- **Join a language club.** Informal groups, generally led by native speakers and offered free-of-charge, typically meet in libraries, community centers, and faith-based facilities.

- **Take advantage of self-study books, software, and apps.** Many people have used the materials of self-study programs such as Berlitz®, Rosetta Stone®, and Pimsleur®, complemented by free online services such as Live-Mocha or Hello-Hello, to initiate or augment their knowledge of a foreign language.

- **Enlist a private tutor.** One-on-one tutoring can be expensive, but amazingly effective. And sometimes, it can be free, particularly in exchange for reciprocal one-on-one tutoring in English. Check out bulletin boards, real and virtual, to find potential language study-buddies. As in all situations when meeting strangers, just be careful about safety.

To truly and thoroughly learn a language, there is nothing like immersion. Obviously, however, this cannot usually be done during the school year, so consider an international excursion (noted above), a dedicated language camp (also noted above), and/or a study abroad term in college. For more detailed information on language learning, see Chapter 4.

*The importance of being able to communicate in Mandarin and Spanish, as well as English becomes more evident each year—as growth and opportunities in Spanish-speaking and Chinese-speaking countries abound. Whether you operate in a U.S. business or an international business, today's interconnected global economy requires a working understanding of cultural differences (or similarities).*

**Abraham Minto,** certified public accountant

## Choosing a College that Will Further Language Learning

Unless your teens are attending a dual immersion school or you speak another language regularly at home, it probably won't be possible for them to become completely fluent in a second language by graduation. At best, they will "only" be proficient. Not too long ago, a working knowledge was considered good enough when hiring; these days, however, it isn't. The new global workplace—and the employers who populate it—want proficiency. It therefore follows that they will have to continue taking language courses while in college. So when it comes time for your children to begin applying to colleges, it's important to take their ongoing language learning needs into consideration. Any institution they apply to must be able to offer the depth and selection that they will need to become truly competent.

*Language can help anyone get ahead in any career, but I know from experience that they are helpful even before then. The fact that I was taking more than one foreign language looked good on my college application, and knowledge of a so-called critical language, like Russian, is sought after. I feel that the number of languages and the length of time I have studied them was a factor in getting into my first choice college.*

Beth Cubanski, undergraduate student

*Looking back, learning languages was probably **the** most important part of my high school career. Whether it was using grammar in French to help understand grammar in English, or learning about other cultures because I wanted to travel to different countries, languages were a huge part of my learning process. In addition, I used my languages to help decide which university I wanted to attend. I knew that I wanted a school with great domestic international program, and great study abroad programs as well.*

Ben Pauker, undergraduate student

ACTFL [The American Council on the Teaching of Foreign Languages] encourages prospective students and parents to do the following:

- Check not only language offerings but levels as well. Many universities offer majors in some languages but not others; languages such as Chinese and Arabic may only be available at the introductory or intermediate levels.

- Check language offerings for alignment with career interests. If upper-level courses focus only on literature, it may not be possible to become proficient in the subject matter of science, technology, and other modern disciplines; look for expanded language offerings that go beyond just literature.

- Check the availability of options to study abroad and find out how credits are transferred from study abroad programs. A college or university that is preparing students to live and work in a global environment will invariably encourage students to study abroad and participate in international internships.

- Check faculty backgrounds. Faculty members should reflect a diverse background and areas of expertise, again not just in literature.

**When it comes time to interview on campus, be sure to:**

- Ask about options for majoring in a language or double majoring in a language and another field. The institution should encourage students to continue to develop language proficiency through double majors/minors.

- Ask about study abroad options and scholarships. There should be a dedicated international study office with staff knowledgeable about scholarships.

- Ask about summer and academic year internships where you can use your language expertise. The institution should make an effort to place students in situations where they are able to use their language skills.

- Ask about the number of adjunct instructors in the department and the role of teaching assistants. Be wary of a significant number of adjunct instructors or too many courses taught by teaching assistants.

- Ask about faculty involvement with students outside of class and the extracurricular activities of the language department. The foreign language department should have an active presence on campus with offerings like guest lecture series, cultural activities, and service learning projects in the community.

- Ask about placement procedures and credit options for Advanced Placement (AP)/ International Baccalaureate (IB), and dual credit programs. Students should be placed appropriately in a language class so that they don't waste time reviewing materials they have already mastered or repeating coursework. The institution should also grant credits for college-level work completed in high school for AP, IB, or dual credit programs.

- Ask about language-specific residential houses or dorm floors where the language is spoken by the students. Most language programs have a designated living space for majors and interested students where they are immersed in using the language. This is an excellent opportunity to accelerate the language acquisition process.

- Ask about resources for language students. Institutions should have robust resources available to students in the target language from library holdings to magazines and videos.

- Ask to visit a language class and the language lab. Attending a class will provide you with valuable insight about how language teaching is approached at the institution and how actively engaged the students are in the learning process. It will also give you the opportunity to speak with students involved in the language program.

- If you are interested in teaching at the K–12 level, ask if there is a program that prepares you for state certification to teach languages. Also ask to speak to seniors in the program or recent graduates, especially about the student teaching experience to ensure teacher candidates are placed with highly qualified K–12 teachers.

- Ask about graduate programs and career services for students who major in languages or have a high level of language proficiency. It's important to find out the track record of the career center in placing students in positions or graduate programs where they can use their language talents.

*We need to help as many U.S. students as possible to have an international experience as part of their undergraduate education. Active engagement between U.S. and international students in American and overseas classrooms provides students with valuable skills that will enable them to collaborate across cultures and borders to address shared global challenges in the years ahead.*

**Dr. Allan E. Goodman,** leader in international education,
former dean and professor, and father

## Gap Year

A "gap year" is typically defined as the academic year between completing high school and beginning college in which a college-bound student pursues some personal or professional activity or independent—though not necessarily unstructured—course of study. As such, they come in all shapes and sizes: participating in an organized gap year program, volunteering or doing an internship with a particular organization, teaching English abroad, attending a foreign university, and even traveling the world as a tourist.

Essentially unheard of as recently as 20 years ago, gap years are now an increasingly popular option for incoming freshman to take stock of themselves or get a preliminary introduction to a career, perhaps one they would like to sample before devoting 4 years of study to it. Gap years work one of two ways: the student applies to college and then defers matriculating for a year, or else he or she simply waits a year before applying. Generally speaking, the former is the more commonly chosen route as it allows the student to go through the application and acceptance process at a more convenient time (i.e., not when he or she is preoccupied or potentially outside the country), and provides the comfort of having a pre-determined plan upon completion.

As far as a global mindset is concerned, a gap year provides students with opportunities to:

- Gain global perspective early on,

- Improve language skills,

- Develop maturity and independence,

- Participate in professional communities as a volunteer/employee,

- Pursue various interests to help define a career path, and

- Spend time abroad if study abroad during their next 4 years isn't a viable option.

*I took a gap year because I knew it was an opportunity that would never come again. I was young and able to spend a whole year of my life alone in a foreign country. I took it, despite being a die-hard math and science student on her way to becoming an engineer because I knew the math would come back, the internships would wait a year, the classes would still be there in a year, but I would never have a chance like this again.*

**Jeanette Miranda,** undergraduate student

# Start Thinking About Studying Abroad BEFORE You Go to College

Studying abroad should become an essential component of most undergraduate degrees in the United States because it's a smart way to establish international credentials before graduation. Moreover, it's a life-changing experience for most. It's important for parents to encourage their college-bound kids to start thinking about study abroad before they select their college to make sure the college has a program that will work for them. Most students who've studied abroad tend to start planning as freshmen, and many chose their college based on study abroad options. You should encourage your teen to do the same. Studying abroad takes global learning up a notch in that it requires students to get out of their comfort zones and experience another culture and education system firsthand. Studying abroad shouldn't be considered as a tangential or separate part of the college education, but as an integral part of it. This includes studying content that will offer a broad perspective, such as taking an international marketing class in Paris, a marine biology class in Costa Rica, or finance in Hong Kong. For detailed information about the study abroad process—as well as volunteering and interning abroad— check out Stacie's recently published book, *A Student Guide to Study Abroad*.[2] It offers a comprehensive overview of each step of the study abroad process, beginning with how to choose the study abroad program that is right for you and wrapping up with advice on how to leverage the study abroad experience to further a career. It's an interesting read with more than 200 personal stories and 100 tips on how to make the most of the experience.

*Study abroad programs are so valuable. Even though students study a country's economics, culture, language, and history, someone must walk them through their learning on the ground to help them process the information.*

**Liz Allred,** higher education adviser

*If I had one thing to do over again, I would study abroad. It's the easiest way to truly (and with the lowest risk) immerse yourself in a culture.*

**Adam L. Michaels,** international business executive and father

*It is imperative that higher education institutions implement strategies that allow their students to develop a global mindset. There is no better way to do that than to actually travel abroad. I have led over*

*a dozen study abroad programs and, every single time, I see the transformational impact that these programs have on our students. As I talk to my students upon graduation, every one of them tells me that a highlight of their education on our campus was the study abroad program.*

José D. González, professor and father

*Today's students will become tomorrow's global leaders. They must understand how the global economy works and learn how to participate in it—as opposed to being a victim of it.*

Steve Finikiotis, business leader, emerging markets

## Real Stories from Real People

### Morgan Abate, *undergraduate student*

I was lucky enough to have been selected by my "Main Line" high school to attend the Hugh O'Brian Youth Leadership Conference (HOBY) in North Philadelphia. It opened my eyes to a whole new world, a world where differences in schools, socioeconomic status, family background, intelligence, and talents were embraced. My perception of the world changed dramatically as I listened to people with whom I had no intimate connection talk about the various discriminations—race, ethnicity, family life, religion, sexual orientation, or personal interests —they faced in their daily lives. For the first time, I was able to understand what it is like to see the world through someone else's eyes. I learned to appreciate different points of view. I felt humbled yet also inspired by the people I met and the stories I heard. I left that four-day conference with a newfound passion for erasing stereotypes and judgment.

I believe that HOBY changed my life in the most dramatic of ways. While there, I broke out of my "Main Line" bubble. I met some of my closest, most culturally diverse friends—people who I bonded with and whose company I enjoyed instantly. I feel as though we made connections because we were all genuinely interested in each other, and we weren't judging each other. I believe this experience has helped prevent my own acceptance of common stereotypes because of the greater appreciation I have developed for the various origins, languages, and cultures of my friends. I know that this value will continue to develop as I travel to, study in, and befriend people from different parts of the world. While we may speak different languages, practice different customs, believe in different gods, and look different, at our core we are all the same: **human**.

Recognizing and accepting these differences is my definition of being a global citizen. HOBY started to teach me this, and I am forever grateful that I was selected to serve as my high school's ambassador. In the intervening 3 years, I've stayed involved in the organization and witnessed new ambassadors come to the same conclusions I did. But I've also advanced. I have found that I listen more and differently than before. I read much more beyond my culture—books by authors from Nigeria, Iran, India, China, and Sudan. And I'm much more passionate about learning languages other than the Spanish that I have been studying since high school, and about other countries and cultures.

Most importantly, I have come to believe that recognizing and accepting all people for who they are can and will change the world.

### Brenna McStravick, *high school sophomore*

Here in the United States, many people do not realize how lucky and fortunate we are. We take for granted the little things in life that can have such an impact on many less fortunate people. I used to be one of those people. Until I traveled to Cambodia and Thailand for two-and-a-half weeks with Rustic Pathways, I had never seen extreme poverty firsthand.

Although I knew a little bit about Thailand, I hadn't heard much about Cambo-dia so I had no idea what to expect. Plus I was going to be away from my family for 18 days, and I didn't know any of the other participants. What was I doing? I was embarking on something much greater than I ever could have imagined!

After more than 20 hours, I arrived in Bangkok, and took another plane to Siem Reap, Cambodia, where I met the eight other teenagers who would be a part of Floating Service Village. I made great connections with these new friends and believe I will have a bond with this group of peers for life! The first day, we visited Angkor Wat, one of the most amazing and unique things I've ever seen. We spent the evening at a local market. This market had several different vendors with mostly the same items at each one. If you liked an item, you could ask the price, but most likely be able to get it for half of what they ask for. They have such cool things there such as pictures, hammocks, chop sticks, jewelry, and more!

We then spent a few days doing service, which included painting a school and teaching English to little kids, on a riverboat gliding among the floating villages of Tonle Sap Lake. The boat was very modest and would probably be considered unsanitary in the United States, but to the people in the villages, it was huge and glamorous. We slept in a small, two-room house on the water that had a crocodile living underneath! I learned that a normal day for these Cambodian families consisted of washing their clothes, plates, and even themselves in the dirty water. Adults would sit outside their houses staring at the water, and kids would swim in the water, run around their small living spaces, or just talk with their family. Not many had electricity. It was a very sad sight to see for me, not because the people were unhappy, but because I realize that their entire life is spent on these villages, and some of the kids have probably never left their house.

After Cambodia, I headed to Thailand and an orphanage located 120 miles south of Chang Mai. The orphanage has been around for 13 years and is made of leaves and branches. Although tree leaves and branches do not sound like they make for a good house, the house was actually unbelievable. It was mostly open to the outside but the rooms were closed in. These kids seemed a lot more fortunate than in the villages of Cambodia, but it was still quite modest compared to my neighborhood. The kids would appreciate the smallest things we gave them, even if it was just a little candy bar. The kids were always happy even though their lives are so simple and they have so little. Seeing this was very eye-opening and life-changing for me because it helped me to realize that you do not need brand name items to be happy. You could be the poorest person in the world, but still be happy; it is all about attitude.

Both programs taught me very valuable lessons. First, we are so fortunate and yet often take the simplest luxuries for granted. These programs also taught me that life is about doing for others, and touching the lives of others. It is also about learning more about yourself through thinking and doing things that are "out of the ordinary." It also taught me that I can serve and do good deeds everywhere. There are plenty of less fortunate people right here in the USA, and I need to be aware and involved so that I can make a difference.

If you're looking to do service, there are definitely less rustic places to choose than the Floating Village in Cambodia and the Hill Tribe in Thailand. But I think that's what made it incredible for me. While I was in Cambodia and Thailand, I thought, "This is really hard." But the experience really helped me put things in perspective, especially to not take anything for granted and appreciate even the little things in life.

## Alex Hager, *high school junior*

Growing up in today's world, it is easy to get lost in a cycle of involuntary cultural ignorance. No child or teenager ever intends to wind up blind to the outside world, but if you do not actively pursue engagement with other cultures, there is a risk of ending up unaware not only of global diversity, but local diversity as well. In an era of omnipresent interconnectedness, young people display a paradoxically stark lack of cultural understanding. The bright side, however, is that this cycle of ignorance can be broken in the simplest of ways. Promoting human interaction amongst young people can tear down barriers of understanding in a manner that is both instantaneous and long lasting.

I actually crossed barriers of global cultural understanding before the local ones. My family promoted an awareness of world news and events, as well as international travel and educational experiences.

Yet somehow, even though I was exposed to other places, living in a "bubble" of a wealthy, somewhat insular suburb of New York, I never really learned to understand the mix and contrast of cultures that I was surrounded by. By taking just one step out of passivity, I was able to connect with a culture that existed in the very next town on a much more personal level.

I was introduced by a Spanish-speaking friend to a volunteer program that allowed me to teach English to Spanish speakers. Each week, we worked together on practical activities like practicing conversations with employers or planning meals and shopping for food. Although this sounds somewhat mundane, it was, and still is, an incredibly enriching and valuable experience. I had never been into this neighborhood, mere minutes away from my home, where the Spanish language and numerous Hispanic cultures thrived. It was eye-opening to learn about the entire network of businesses and families with a cultural dynamic so different from my own.

While volunteering there, I am able not only to learn about this community, but to actually connect with individuals. It is much more than just teaching. Using my high school level Spanish, I have been able to talk with the students as friends, improving my own language skills while helping them navigate the English vocabulary they need for their daily lives. Through my decision to help others, I have become part of a community entirely separate from my own. Despite our differences, the desires to teach, learn, and communicate are ones that transcend cultural borders. Looking back, I realize that it is not just physical distance that can block the ability to understand other cultures, but also simply an unintentional passive ignorance. By extending our willingness to help and work with others, a literal world of opportunities, learning, and understanding is opened to us.

## Amanda, *high school sophomore*

People learn a second language for many reasons: to communicate, gain knowledge, and enhance both their lives and the lives of others. Languages are the key to opening the gate that will lead a person down the path to embrace the world. Concordia Language Villages in Minnesota did this for me.

Growing up in the Midwest had narrowed my vision. I come from a family where most of my family members never live outside of their home state. My parents were inspired by the early exposure to languages and cultures that I had received in preschool in Illinois. They found Concordia and, at the age of 7, I was dropped off at El Lago del Bosque, Concordia's Spanish-speaking village. And though I might not have known it at the time, that experience would set me down a lifelong path that has enabled me to broaden my horizons and expand my knowledge of the worldwide community.

At first, I was scared and intimidated. Even though I, too, come from the Midwest, Concordia was still very far from home. But I soon came to appreciate the diversity that is found in Concordia Language Villages, which features native speakers from diverse backgrounds. I not only met but learned to relate to people that I would never have met otherwise. Concordia Language Villages helped me see what the wider world has to offer and the diversity that can be found everywhere.

Concordia teaches language through culture, with activities and classes about different countries. For example, we learned about Spain by experiencing its folk and modern dance. We also have cultural activities like painting, mosaics, and *huichol* basket weaving to help us learn about other aspects of Hispanic culture. We also learn through song, which helps us feel part of the camp community. The food is authentic, and at El Lago del Bosque, it is inspired by South America, Central America, and Spain, giving us a variety of tastes from different places. We are surrounded by counselors that speak Spanish at all times, which enables us to gain an acute understanding of the different accents and pronunciations. It is not required that you speak Spanish all the time, because some campers come with little to no knowledge of the language while others are nearly fluent. But we are constantly given the opportunity to speak in Spanish. The amount of language you learn is determined by the amount of effort you put in.

The camp village itself is architecturally inspired so you feel like you are in the represented culture. In El Lago del Bosque, we have a Spanish plaza with a fountain in the center, pathways leading to an area where cabins are inspired by colorful, Central American buildings, and another path leading to a South American courtyard. The overall effect is to engage all of your senses and make you feel like you really are living overseas, and it works.

I have attended Concordia Language Villages for 9 years now. I plan to spend one more year there as a camper and then hope to return as a counselor. The summers that I have spent there have given me worldly exposure and the confidence to venture outside my American comfort zone. Concordia has given me my passport to the future.

### Kristi Vitelli, *lawyer and mother*

When my daughter Sara was 8 years old she received an invitation from People to People to travel with one of their student programs. She was recommended to People to People by her second grade teacher. Sara was too young for the foreign travel then, but when she was 11, the Connecticut contingency was going to Australia and she was old enough to go. We knew Sara would love Australia, and we liked the fact they were traveling to an English-speaking country, so there would not be any language barriers on her first trip to a foreign country without her parents.

When we told Sara about the invitation, she was very excited and wanted to go. She applied, was interviewed, and accepted. There were several mandatory meetings to get to know the group leaders and other participants, plus online studies that had to be completed prior to departure. The online studies taught Sara about the government, culture, food, dress, animals, and indigenous people of Australia.

It was all very exciting and fast-paced. At no point did Sara waver in her interest in taking the trip despite the fact that she would be traveling with children she barely knew and away from her parents for two weeks for the first time. Sara has always been independent and mature for her age, so we were not worried about how she would handle the trip. However, as the date for departure neared, it hit me that we were sending our little girl halfway around the world with people we barely knew. Despite my anxiety, Sara had a wonderful experience and grew a lot in those two weeks. She expanded her knowledge of the world and learned how to rely upon herself away from her parents. Plus, she has fabulous memories that will last a lifetime.

Sara came home with stories about visiting the Sydney Opera House; a cave with perfect acoustics where she sang a song from Pocahontas that brought tears to the eyes of her group leaders; petting a kangaroo; holding a Koala; learning the art of throwing a boomerang and playing a didgeridoo; snorkeling in the Great Barrier Reef with the sharks; visiting government buildings, a local school, and staying at a dude ranch where they rode horses with real Australian cowboys.

We believe that it is very important for children to see the world and learn about its people. It is much easier to be accepting of differences in other cultures when you learn about them and understand them. I would recommend the People to People experience to other parents with independent children. People to People ensures that the trips educate the children about the other countries they visit, in addition to visiting some tourist types of places. Also, as part of our daughter's trip, they delivered books that they had brought with them to a school for underprivileged indigenous children. It was a nice way for them to help others. Sara loved visiting places and people that she would not have had the opportunity to experience except for the People to People program.

# CHAPTER 8

# Advocating for Raising Global Children

---

*We engaged local businesses in our school to create a career committee to discuss what our students were missing when they applied for jobs. We learned that besides soft skills, they're lacking global understanding and problem-solving skills. We adapted our curriculum, added a K–12 language instructor, and have strengthened our partnerships among the school, parents, and businesses in the community because we respected and listened to what they said.*

**Dr. Salvatore Menzo,** school superintendent

Global parenting is a mindset; it can take place anywhere and under just about any circumstances. By taking a proactive role in enhancing your child's global awareness, you can teach your child to understand and deal with the challenges of a rapidly changing world. But you shouldn't have to do it alone. As parents, we need teachers to supplement what we're doing—even lead the way in some cases—because a global education has been proven to be a better education. Well-designed global education programs enhance general education, aiding—not detracting—from the basics of literacy, numeracy, and general academic and cognitive skills. In addition, the world faces global challenges requiring global solutions. It is not enough for our schools to produce individuals who can read, write, and do math and science. We need global education, or more accurately, education infused with global learning, to empower youth by providing them with the knowledge, skills, and awareness necessary to become responsible global citizens. Education, therefore, must be transformative, changing the way children think and act. It also must fulfill a societal purpose by giving all students the opportunity to earn a living, contribute to their communities, and fulfill their potential.

Unfortunately, global education is still not a standard component of the American school curriculum. For example, despite the obvious need for cross-cultural understanding in an increasingly interconnected global world, we have no national requirement for foreign language education. For those states that do—and there are only 16 states that have any kind of foreign language requirement for graduation—it's only after age 13 or 14, precisely when research shows that the ability to learn foreign languages begins to decline. At the same time that members of Congress are appropriating billions of dollars for defense programs in the interest of national security, they also voted to cut the Foreign Language Assistance Program (FLAP), which cost the equivalent of just one nuclear submarine. As we struggle to exit Middle East wars where our troops suffered from insufficient Arabic (and other) culture and language support, we must recognize that both our linguistic gap and our lack of will to increase our linguistic capacity have contributed to failed understandings across a variety of areas, such as national security, diplomatic relations, and business opportunities, that will have long-term consequences. College administrators across the country bemoan the fact that they can't make proficiency in a second language a graduation requirement because the vast majority of students come with little or no language ability and, therefore, are unable to develop proficiency in 4 years. Even though study abroad programs enhance the language learning experience and have been proven to improve a student's cross-cultural competency, only 14% of college students actually go abroad. We just don't seem to be taking language acquisition seriously.

Although a complete national overhaul of our K–16 system to incorporate global education seems warranted, it's also not likely to happen. In fact, global education might be better served by a less contentious national debate among experts (real or self-styled), and more agreement to allow localities to implement curricula that work for their specific needs. Indeed small groups are taking action on their own. Individual school districts across the country have recognized the need to incorporate global education across the board in classes K–12, and are working to achieve that via innovative programs. These districts are taking the situation into their own hands; they know that our children can't wait and are making changes—one school district at a time.

We need to work together to create change. As parents, we must teach our children what it means to be a global citizen and how to more effectively communicate and interact with other people around the world. We must work toward more cultural education in our school systems so that our children understand and are better prepared to deal with the complexities outside our borders in whatever career they choose. We must insist upon foreign language learning in our schools by at least first grade to give our kids a fighting chance to become proficient in at least one other language. We must support teachers who embrace the importance of global education. We must work together to instill a proactive interest in the world around us. Most importantly, we need to work for change in order to: (1) raise the issue of the national need for global mindedness for all American students, and (2) empower America's families, communities, and educators to implement locally appropriate strategies toward that goal.

To those who say we can't afford the "luxury" of foreign language and global education, we say that we can't afford **not** to educate our children with the skills they need to succeed in the 21st century. Addressing these issues starts with involved parents. We must come together to help our teachers and schools incorporate global education in a way that works locally, while also advocating for change with politicians and government both statewide and nationally.

> *As a high school teacher, I witnessed a strong shift from being open to other cultures prior to 9/11 to become much insular after it. It's in our best interests as a nation to understand other cultures—not to fear them.*
>
> Claire González, teacher educator, former teacher, and mother

## Get Involved with Your Child's School

Ideally, as children begin their formal education, they should also begin to gain cross-cultural insight, be it in world history, social studies, or geography. In many U.S. schools, such classes are not available until Grades 6 or 7. Others, however, have had the foresight to begin introducing children to the wider world at a younger age. Whatever classes your school has available in global studies, world history, geography, and related topics are well worth supporting, as they instill global awareness right along with the ABCs and 1-2-3s. Introduce yourself to your child's social studies, global studies, and world language teachers, and ask how you can help them.

One of the best things that you can do to support global education at any age is to be sincerely interested in the topics yourself. When your first grader comes home to talk about the rainforest in South America, listen to him and get involved in further discussion and exploration of the topic. When your sixth grader tells you about the Geography Bee her school is having, get out the atlas and start practicing for the competition. When your teen talks about the Model UN initiative being considered as part of his high school curriculum, support it and even offer to help implement it if need be. And when your child—at any age—talks about history or current events, respond and discuss the issues together, showing him or her that knowing about the world and what's going on in it is an important part of adult life. But be mindful to do as much listening as you do talking.

> *School boards listen to parents when they advocate saving programs or starting them. In both instances, it is important to use research when presenting the case.*
>
> **Tammy Dann,** teacher and mother

> *Advocating for change within schools requires at least two things: One, a good parent/administration relationship, and two, perseverance because you'll be competing with other parents who want the fundamentals and may not appreciate the importance of a broader, global education.*
>
> **Steve Miranda,** international educator, business executive, and father

After yourself, the development of global awareness in your children depends most on the preparedness and enthusiasm of their teachers. Appropriate and effective global instruction cannot be "canned." Teachers must possess a global mindset themselves if they are to teach through a global lens and create a global classroom. Since most teachers' certification courses do not include a global perspective, they should be encouraged to sharpen their own global mindsets through training, tools, and learning experiences. Only then can they truly teach the ability to understand, appreciate, and respect cultural differences.

Fortunately, today's teachers have a wealth of readily accessible tools from which to choose, and the immense power of the Internet to bring the world into the classroom. First and foremost among these are traditional and online exchange programs that teachers can tap into, many of which are available at little or no cost. In addition, there are numerous professional enhancement programs, generally awarded on a competitive basis, some of which are also free to educators. But perhaps they're not familiar with these materials and opportunities, a detailed listing of which follows. In that case, parents can help by promoting awareness. For those that require funding, they can help raise money through the PTO/PTA with larger budget items being funded systematically over the course of several years.

## Integrating Global Topics Across the Curriculum

It's important to recognize that with the Common Core academic standards now being implemented in the vast majority of states, teachers are already beset with changing how and what they teach. It's very important, therefore, to clarify that learning and thinking with a global perspective does not mean adding another course to already heavy student loads, but rather introducing them to global issues and concepts within and throughout the subjects already being taught. Research indicates that children are most receptive to learning about other cultures between the ages of 7 and 12, before the onset of puberty when ethnocentrism and stereotypical thinking tend to increase dramatically.[1]

> *My core philosophy is to stick to your district's curriculum while also finding ways to teach what children are interested in. Young learners are interested in things that are different. Follow their natural instinct and leave it open-ended. Keep it natural.*
>
> **Kindergarten teacher** in Oklahoma City

There are some great resources online to help:

- **Facing the Future** is a nonprofit leader whose mission is to create tools for educators that equip and motivate students to develop critical thinking skills, build global awareness, and engage in positive solutions for a sustainable future.

- **Asia Society's Partnership for Global Learning (PGL)** provides leadership and structure to help move international education from the margins to the mainstream by connecting policy and practice. It offers plenty of tools to help all stakeholders work together to make their schools more global. *Going Global*, and the companion DVD, *Putting the World into World-Class Education*, are excellent starting points for sparking a community-wide conversation involving district leaders, school board members, principals, school staff, parents, and community members on the global competencies needed by high school graduates. PGL offers effective K–12 strategies for integrating international education content across the curriculum; successful approaches to creating world language programs; ways to "make the case" for global competence; policy innovations and funding resources to advance international education; and ways to harness technology and create new opportunities for international collaboration.

- **Chapman University's Global Ed Yellow Pages** is an electronic directory of global education resources for K–12 teachers and contains nearly 1,000 entries, many of which link to additional sources. These resources address issues that cut across national boundaries, and the interconnectedness of the systems involved—economic, environmental, cultural, political, and technological; and the cultivation of cross-cultural understanding, which includes development of the skill of "perspective-taking"—that is, being able to see life from someone else's point of view.

- **Globalization 101** is an online resource offered by the Levin Institute, a graduate institute of international relations associated with the State University of New York, to promote a greater understanding of globalization. It addresses the big-picture, philosophical debate about globalization by discussing polemic questions such as: Is globalization the integration of economic, political, and cultural systems across the globe or the Americanization and U.S. dominance of world affairs? Is it a force for economic growth, prosperity, and democratic freedom or a force for environmental devastation, exploitation of the developing world, and the suppression of human rights?

- **Global Teacher Education (GTE)** was established to support the internationalization of teacher preparation, and was inspired by the pioneering work of the Longview Foundation and its seminal 2008 report *Teacher Preparation for the Global Age: The Imperative for Change*. Its stated mission is to "ensure that U.S. teachers are properly trained to prepare our young people to cope and thrive in a globally-connected world."[2] The organization partners with colleges of education to support the internationalization of teacher preparation programs by connecting professionals and advancing and disseminating research and best practices. GTE invites people to get involved in its projects through building an online community to share resources and promote best practices and successes.

- **Peace Corps Coverdell World Wise Schools** programs are designed to broaden perspectives in culture and geography and to encourage service. Programs offer teachers valuable resources, including the Correspondence Match program that puts a teacher and her class in touch with a currently serving Peace Corps Volunteer; lessons about cultures and countries worldwide; and free cross-cultural publications, award-winning videos, stories, folk tales, classroom speakers, and more.

- **Oxfam** is an international confederation of 17 organizations networked together in more than 90 countries as part of a global movement to build a future free from the injustice of poverty. Oxfam Education supports active global citizenship by enabling young people to develop the core competencies which allow them to actively engage with the world and help to make it a more just and sustainable place. It offers a Learn–Think–Act process for teachers to engage students.

- **World History for Us All** is a national collaboration of K–12 teachers, collegiate instructors, and educational technology specialists. It offers a treasury of teaching units, lesson plans, and resources; presents the human past as a single story rather than unconnected stories of many civilizations; helps teachers meet state and national standards; enables teachers to survey world history without excluding major peoples, regions, or time periods; helps students understand the past by connecting specific subject matter to larger historical patterns; draws on up-to-date historical research; and may be readily adapted to a variety of world history courses. It is a project of San Diego State University in cooperation with the National Center for History in the Schools at UCLA.

## Creating Global Classrooms

A global classroom is an inclusive place where all children have an equal voice and where the music, art, and reading material reflect many cultures. Teaching materials should reflect the world's diversity, as should classroom visitors. A global classroom should:

- Encourage creative representations of the world;

- Avoid stereotypes when selecting international images;

- Create games using maps and globes;

- Play music from a variety of cultures and take time to reflect on and discuss it;

- Create a global bookshelf, including books written in other languages to show how books are physically read in other countries;

- Post and refer to the alphabets of other world languages;

- Introduce world languages via online sources, such as the one used by the Peace Corps;

- Incorporate toys/items from around the world in teaching both a subject and cultural similarities and differences; and

- Post and frequently utilize a variety of maps.

## Providing Additional Resources to Teachers

Budget cuts have plagued school districts across the country over the past 10 years and have had a devastating impact on curriculum. As a result, parents need to stay closely involved with their local school budget and monitor any imminent or long-term detrimental changes. If you notice something that needs to be addressed, get involved.

- **Funding additional teaching resources.** Parents can work through the appropriate PTOs or PTAs to provide additional resources to school libraries and teachers, including maps, globes, books, DVDs, puzzles, games, music, "discovery bags," and other teaching aids.

- **Stepping in to fill a need.** Parents may have an ability in a certain language, a global background, or a special skill that can be shared with classrooms. Talk with teachers about ways to incorporate this into existing classes or programs. If a subject is cut, consider stepping in to help teach it on a volunteer basis.

- **Recommending continuing education training.** For teachers who haven't had any formal training in global education, parents can recommend appropriate continuing education courses to school administrators. These can be funded either by the school or the PTO/PTA.

- **Writing grants.** Parents can take the lead in identifying and writing a grant application for additional funding for global education programs.

- **Creating an International Night.** Another effective way for parents to get involved is by putting on or sponsoring an International Night or Week as this can play an important role in helping children appreciate diversity and become globally aware. For maximum effectiveness, it's important to have a diverse cross-section of parents work to create an event that accurately reflects the school's population.

- **Funding international exchanges.** There are many teacher exchange programs available (see a detailed list below) and some require additional funding. Nominating teachers and raising funds are ways parents can help.

- **Hosting international teachers.** Inviting teachers from outside the United States to spend time in our schools is an excellent way for students to get firsthand experience with another culture. Parents can help by being supportive and offering to host a teacher while he or she is in the community.

- **Volunteer to serve on school curriculum committees.** Parent advisory groups are often formed to provide input into curriculum content. Your voice can be heard if you are a member of these committees.

- **Speak up.** Let your school principal, board members, and superintendent know that you support global education and offer suggestions to globalize the learning opportunities in your school.

- **Get local civic clubs involved.** Both Rotary International and Civitan International have programs and sponsorships that support local schools, programs which may be able to fund teachers to participate in international study programs.

*The United States is more global than we think or recognize in our daily lives. People are connecting internationally for professional and personal reasons in thousands of communities across the United States, but it's not often happening in an organized fashion. School administrators, teachers, and parents can try to tap these individual resources and harness the collective, global power of the community for the benefit of our students.*

                                                            survey respondent

*Our school had its social studies teacher cut for budget reasons, and the kids weren't getting any geography. So I stepped in and taught an elective class for fifth to seventh graders on geography on a volunteer basis. It's been so popular that it's been over-subscribed now for years, and now that my son is aging out of the school, we're discussing whether or not there's funding to pay me part-time to keep it going.*

                                                            survey respondent

The point to remember here is that communication and collaboration can go a long way in satisfying mutually beneficial objectives in global education.

## Incorporating Cultural Exchange into Core Curricula

Virtual international exchange programs with sister schools in another country help children develop direct communication with kids their own age living under significantly different circumstances. Studies have shown such exchanges not only facilitate cross-cultural competence and a sense of global community, but also enhance critical thinking, problem solving, communication, collaboration, creativity, and innovation. In addition, the students tend to be more engaged and interested after having learned new perspectives from their virtual exchange program peers, and they demonstrate increased levels of comprehension, retention, and confidence.[3] Teachers see such exchanges not only as an exciting way to impart geography, history, language, and science, but also as a vehicle to forge connections that push children beyond cultural stereotypes. Students have the opportunity to "travel" to another country without leaving their own school.

The number of networks and organizations dedicated to connecting students and teachers around the world is growing. Although each organization does it a little differently, they all create an educational and cultural exchange that enriches the lives of the students, teachers, and administrators. The organizations listed below each offer an opportunity to learn through global connections:

- **ePals** is one of the most widely known online learning exchange networks with classrooms in 200 countries and territories. The organization provides project-based collaboration on a variety of topics from natural disasters to holidays and festivals. Students, teachers, and families can all sign up to be part of this international learning network.

- **Environment Online (ENO)** is a global virtual school and network for sustainable development that is based in Finland. Environmental themes are studied throughout the school year and issue-based campaigns are scheduled simultaneously around the world. More than 10,000 schools from 150 countries have taken part since 2000.

- **Global Nomads Group** was created in 1998 to deliver interactive educational programs for students about global issues. The organization delivers four different types of video conferences in which students learn about and discuss subjects with their peers from around the world on a variety of international issues. GNG also connects schools and provides lesson plans, as well as teacher training for its interactive programs and projects.

- **Global School Net** was established in 1984 to enhance education through global collaboration. It offers a variety of project-based resources and activities that bring the world together. The organization engages teachers and students in meaningful e-learning projects that develop science, math, literacy, and communication skills. Competitive scholarship contests are offered on a global basis.

- **iEARN** is an organization based in Spain that works in more than 140 countries, in 30 languages, and with 50,000 educators and two million youth. It's a project-based site that encourages teachers and students to facilitate or take part in international collaborations. It also offers in-person and online professional development courses for teachers and administrators on how to integrate global collaboration projects into the curriculum.

- **Model United Nations (MUN)** is an academic simulation of the United Nations for secondary school students. It offers exploration of pressing world issues through interactive simulations and curricular materials while preparing and promoting active global citizenship. The organization provides detailed guidelines on how to participate in existing MUN programs, as well as how to start a MUN Club or plan a MUN Conference.

- **Project Explorer** was founded in 2003 to bring the world into the classroom via free multimedia content and lesson plans that improve students' global awareness and cross cultural understanding. Designed for families and classrooms, ProjectExplorer.org provides students with access to people and places they may never knew existed in an effort to foster global understanding.

- **Schools Online** is an education network for teachers and students dedicated to using technology for cultural exchanges. The organization has created more than 130 Internet Learning Centers (ILCs) worldwide, each of which offers students and teachers the chance to participate in global service learning projects focused on technological advancement and education. It also offers in-person exchange programs that give participants an opportunity to see the effects of their collaboration firsthand.

- **Sister Cities International (SCI)** helps schools create a Sister School relationship that connects youth from different parts of the world through collaborative projects between classrooms, schools, or after-school programs. Students gain international awareness by learning from their international peers and view the world from a new perspective. Project-based learning encourages teamwork, teaches project management, and promotes cognitive development and active student participation. Students learn how to plan, conduct, and complete a project—all while creating bonds that surpass boundaries with their Sister School peers. SCI provides material to help a school get started.

- **Students of the World**, which originated in France, is a networking site that connects pen pals as well as classrooms. Teachers complete an online registration listing details of their classrooms to then be matched with a classroom similar in age and make-up in another part of the world. The goal is to help children discover new cultures, exchange ideas, and improve knowledge of places outside the students' home country. Designed primarily to connect people and classrooms, the site has inspired more than 200 million visitors, one million pen pals, and 12,000 blogs since its founding in 1995.

- **World Wise Schools** is a Peace Corps Program that, since its inception in 1989, has matched more than 3 million U.S. students with Peace Corps volunteers abroad. The program's main goal is to infuse global issues and 21st-century skills into the classroom. It also provides many online resources for implementing a global curriculum and encourages cultural exchanges which benefit students, teachers, and Peace Corps volunteers alike.

## Encouraging More Exchange Programs

Exchange programs provide students and teachers with an opportunity to both live and study in another country. But it's not just the travelers who benefit—so, too, do the schools they visit. Exchange students and teachers usually live with a host family or in a designated place such as a hostel or an apartment. Costs for the program vary according to country and institution, with participants being able to fund their participation via scholarships, loans, or their families. Parents can support the addition of international exchanges by offering to host a student or teacher and helping with fundraising. They can also advocate for more such programs at the national level since international exchange programs are affected by foreign affairs policies and thus require broad public and congressional support. For more on this topic, see the section on advocacy below.

One group that advocates for the general health and welfare of international exchange programs is the Alliance for International Educational and Cultural Exchange, an association of 80 nongovernmental, international educational and cultural exchange organizations here in the United States which serves as their collective public policy voice. The Alliance's mission is to formulate and promote public policies that support the growth and well-being of international exchange links between the people of the United States and other nations. Its guiding principles are:

- The experience and relationships gained through international exchange are essential to furthering global peace, freedom, mutual understanding, international cooperation, economic prosperity, and the growth of human knowledge.

- International exchanges enhance the effectiveness of the United States in dealing with other nations by building the global competencies of U.S. citizens and other skills increasingly important in the world of the 21st century.

- Participating in an international exchange program contributes fundamentally to a person's intellectual development.

- The conduct of the international exchange program must embody the highest standards of quality, integrity, and professionalism, and must offer the fullest possible equality of opportunity.

- The international exchange community in the United States has a responsibility to advocate public policies needed to sustain and strengthen international linkages with other countries through educational and cultural exchanges.

For more information on the Alliance, as well as to learn how to support and advocate for more exchange programs, visit their website.

## Supporting Teachers in their Quest for International Professional Development

As noted in Chapters 6 and 7, one of the best ways to broaden your child's global awareness is for him or her to spend time abroad. Another is to be taught by teachers who have done it, and there are a wide range of summer programs to which educators can apply, some of whose costs are automatically covered. For the others, PTOs/PTAs may be able to raise the necessary money, either on a case-by-case or ongoing basis.

*It is important to provide opportunities for teachers to gain international experience and expertise which they can impart to their students. Whether analyzing historic works of art or telling a riveting account of an ancient civilization, teachers are the ultimate conduits to help students expand their world view and cultural literacy. Teachers with a global perspective will help foster increased cultural understanding and support more young people around the world to think, act, and live as global citizens.*

**Dr. Allan E. Goodman,** leader in international education, former dean and professor, and father

Founded in 1919, The Institute of International Education (IIE) is the oldest and most experienced private, nonprofit U.S. educational exchange organization. It is also the undisputed leader in developing and administering international professional development programs for educators, with some 29,000 educators annually participating in some of the world's largest and most prestigious programs. Governments, foundations, corporations, research centers, universities, bi-national and international agencies, and NGOs all serve as sponsors. IIE administers the following programs for U.S. educators:

- **The Fulbright Classroom Teacher Exchange Program** is sponsored by the State Department's Bureau of Educational and Cultural Affairs (ECA) and offers educators the opportunity to exchange teaching positions with a counterpart from another country for either a semester or an academic year. By living and working abroad, Fulbright Teachers improve their understanding and appreciation of another culture and education system. With this enhanced awareness, participants expand the global perspectives of students and colleagues in their home and host communities and have a positive impact on the quality of classroom instruction. The program is open to teachers from the Czech Republic, France, Hungary, India, Mexico, the United Kingdom, and the United States. Applications are accepted in October for the following school year.

- **The Distinguished Fulbright Awards in Teaching Program** recognizes and encourages excellence in teaching in the United States and abroad. U.S. and international teachers receive grants to study at a university, observe classes, and complete a project pertaining to their field of educational inquiry during their time abroad. The program, which is sponsored by the ECA, is open to teachers from the United States and other selected countries.

- **The Fulbright English Teaching Assistantship (ETA) Program** is also sponsored by the ECA. Fulbright ETA participants spend an academic year at one or more host institutions where they serve as language learning assistants to English teachers. They help strengthen English language education there while providing firsthand cultural knowledge of the United States. In addition to their classroom responsibilities, Fulbright ETAs may also give presentations on topics related to the United States such as culture, society, and history, lead programs in language labs, conduct English conversation clubs, tutor, participate in sports, language, and drama clubs, and volunteer at local organizations, such as hospitals. Additionally, Fulbright ETAs act as resource people both at the host institutions and in communities.

- **The Japan–U.S. Teacher Exchange Program for Education for Sustainable Development (ESD)**, operated by Fulbright Japan, is an exchange between Japanese and U.S. teachers aimed at enhancing ESD-related curricula in both countries. Teachers from Japan visit the United States in the spring while those from the United States travel to Japan in early summer. At the end of the program, all of the teachers participate in a joint conference. The program raises awareness of ESD-oriented school programs, deepens the sense of global interconnectedness between teachers in Japan and the United States, and advances collaboration in the four vital areas of ESD focus: food and sustainable nutrition, environment, energy and resources, and international understanding and cooperation.

- **The Toyota International Teacher Program** is sponsored by Toyota Motor Sales, U.S.A., Inc., and offers two-week, fully funded study tours for U.S. secondary school teachers in Costa Rica and the Galapagos Islands. Through exposure to model conservation initiatives, lectures and discussions, and hands-on activities, the program advances environmental stewardship and global connectedness in U.S. schools and communities.

Non-IIE administered programs for teachers include:

- **The College Board Chinese Guest Teacher Program** is designed to help U.S. schools develop Chinese language and culture study programs and to promote cross-cultural exchange between the United States and China. Made possible through a collaboration between the College Board and Hanban/Confucius Institute Headquarters (Hanban), the program serves hundreds of K–12 schools in districts nationwide and reaches tens of thousands of U.S. students each year.

- **The Teachers for Global Classrooms Program (TGC)** provides a professional development opportunity for middle and high school teachers from the United States to participate in a program aimed at globalizing teaching and learning in their classrooms. TGC is a program of the ECA and administered by IREX, an international nonprofit organization providing thought leadership and innovative programs to promote positive lasting change globally.

Programs specifically for language teachers include:

- **The Cultural Service of the French Embassy** offers 10-day teacher training sessions at a center specializing in French foreign language instruction. These scholarships are intended for French teachers at elementary or secondary schools or in immersion programs who wish to improve their knowledge of the French language and culture, and to develop new teaching skills and methods for French instruction. The French government covers the costs of the training and the round-trip ticket from Paris to Provence (international flights must be covered by the participant), and a stipend to cover part of room and board costs. The French Consulate in Boston regularly organizes free teacher training workshops for French middle and high school teachers as well as university professors in New England.

- **The Goethe-Institut** is the Federal Republic of Germany's cultural institution operating worldwide to promote the study of the German language abroad and encourage international cultural exchange. The Institut offers online educational training for German language teachers in 80 countries around the world, including Germany.

- **The Hanban Chinese Teacher Training Program** is designed to provide trainees/teachers with systematic, professional knowledge in Chinese language teaching methods and Chinese culture promotion techniques based upon the established teaching practices of their home country. Applicants cannot be native Chinese speakers or citizens of China. The program is administered by the Ministry of China Education and Office of Chinese Language Council International (Hanban).

- **The Instituto Cervantes** was founded in 1991 by the Spanish government to teach and promote the language and culture of Spain as well as the co-official languages of Spain and Spanish-speaking countries. The Instituto Cervantes offers a comprehensive teacher training program designed to cater to the needs of teachers of Spanish as a second/foreign language in different stages of their careers.

- **The Japan Foundation (JF)** offers a variety of training and fellowships to promote the teaching of Japanese based upon its Japanese-Language Course program. As of 2012, approximately 10,000 people are studying

Japanese through the JF language course in 26 countries. The Foundation also responds to overseas demands for Japanese-language education by dispatching specialists to overseas Japanese educational organizations and training Japanese language teachers at its two Japanese Language Institute centers, one in Urawa and the other in Kansai. Japanese Studies Fellowships are awarded annually for the purpose of promoting Japanese studies overseas; the program provides support to pre-eminent foreign scholars in Japanese studies to give them an opportunity to conduct research in Japan.

In addition, many of the programs recommended for teens in Chapter 7 invite teachers to participate as chaperones, instructors, and guides.

## Parents and Teachers Working Together for Language Learning

While global education can be infused throughout the curriculum through a variety of strategies and tactics, language learning is different. It is a core subject and, as such, needs to be integrated into the overall curriculum in a systematic way in order for our children to achieve proficiency by the time they graduate. We can't begin programs just to cut them and then start anew with whatever language or teaching method is currently "hot." We can't require only 2 years of mandatory language for high school students and then expect them to be able to master the language in college. And we can't choose who gets language instruction and who doesn't: According to a study by the bipartisan not-for-profit Council on Economic Development (CED), foreign language instruction is offered in only one-quarter of urban public schools, compared with about two-thirds of suburban ones. We need to follow a logical process of incorporating language learning for every student just as we do in math and science by establishing a solid foundation in elementary school that is then built upon throughout secondary school and then college.

To make matters worse, governments at all levels in the United States are investing less per capita today in foreign language education than they were 40 years ago. We're going backwards at a time that we ought to be moving steadily forward. We can't prepare our students for a global world without giving them foreign language instruction. Making foreign languages available to all K–12 students in the United States is certainly a worthy long-term objective. But we must be realistic; our school systems cannot be changed overnight. For starters, we just don't have the teaching resources available to do that. Many experts agree that it will take a full generation to completely infuse our national curricula with the combination of foreign language learning and intercultural learning necessary to prepare all students. But we must begin somewhere.

Some parents already have by successfully lobbying for stronger foreign language programs in the public school districts in which they live. Never underestimate the power of a few dedicated parents and teachers to change the availability of foreign languages in our schools—or to effect any desired change in schools. The following is a list of proven steps to take; your local school district's foreign language policy will determine your ultimate objective.

- **Find out the facts.** Ascertain your school or district's current policy and history with foreign language curriculum, including sources of funding. Most of this can be found on the school/district website, but asking fellow parents may shed some light as well. Supplement these facts by:

  - Attending local town hall meetings, especially those concerning board of education and budget issues. In the tight budgets of today, many language programs are being cut because administrators or politicians consider them "extra" or "nice to have," thinking only in the short term.
  - Get to know your superintendent, principal, and/or foreign language director/coordinator (if one exists).
  - Get involved with your school's PTO/PTA, Parent Team, School Planning and Management Team, or other controlling organizational body.
  - Find out which civic organizations, service organizations, senior citizens groups, and other community groups might be interested in supporting language learning.

- **Support your local foreign language program.** If your school district has a program, do everything you can to support it. Treat your child's language lessons as being as important as math, science, and history; it's a core subject after all! Don't take the program for granted:

  - Let your board of education, superintendent, and/or principal know, in writing, that you support the program and appreciate the school's dedication to language learning.
  - Get to know your children's language teachers and thank them for teaching such a worthwhile subject.
  - Encourage other parents to speak up and show their support as well.
  - Take advantage of any and all language learning tools, summer camps, or after-school programs to show support.

- Use local media to showcase media-worthy language learning projects so as to spread the word locally.

- **Add or expand a foreign language program.** If you don't have a foreign language program at all or you'd like to have the current offerings start earlier, meet more frequently, or include additional languages, use traditional advocacy techniques to accomplish your objectives (go to ACTFL's website for detailed information).

  - Begin by reading up on successful programs to get a sense of what makes these programs work. For two such examples, read about the Glastonbury (CT) Public School Language Program in Chapter 4 and the Fairfax County (VA) story at the end of this chapter.
  - Survey parents on levels of interest in learning foreign languages, and which languages are of greatest interest.
  - Consider surveying local employers, especially large companies, on which languages are of greatest interest, and what support they might offer to local schools supporting those language offerings.
  - Call or write your governor and state legislators; your city, county or town legislators, and/or your mayor; and your superintendent and principal. Be specific about your request and your rationale and use data or statistics to back up your argument.
  - Collect signatures of support from other parents and local businesses and include these signatures with your advocacy letters, as well as when approaching the media.
  - Use print and broadcast media to spotlight the issue and generate broad public support via opinion editorials, letters to the editor, and calls to radio talk shows.
  - Evaluate realistically how much money can be raised within the school, in the community, and through outside philanthropic and/or corporate grants, and set your objectives accordingly. Will it be enough for a pilot program? A summer course? A half-time teacher? A full-time teacher?
  - Review what government funding might be available to support teaching the desired program in your school or district or encouraging students to pursue their language skills in high school and into college. Some targeted federal funding sources include:
    - » STARTALK grants for pilot summer programs,
    - » National Security Language Initiative for Youth (NSLI-Y) grants for high school students,

» International and Foreign Language Education (IFLE) grants for college students,

» The Language Flagship for college students,

» David L. Boren Scholarships for undergraduates and fellowships for graduate students, and

» Project Go.

- Track down a school parent or community volunteer with grant-writing experience and access to donor and philanthropic databases, and begin researching grants that might be available to schools in your area for the language learning courses you desire. Sometimes language-specific placements can be made through not-for-profits involved with language and cultural exchange in the country the target language comes from. Other times foundations or corporations will sponsor programs that benefit children in a particular area, or of a particular socioeconomic background. Leave no stone unturned! You never know what grants are out there just waiting to be tapped until you start looking.

- Consider meeting with members of local immigrant and refugee communities, foreign students, and others in your community fluent in the target language to see whether or not they might be available on a volunteer or semi-volunteer basis for pilot enrichment programs during the school day or after school. In many areas, both district rules on teacher certification and union rules on minimum required compensation and benefits can be altered or waived for volunteers or for those working less than 20 hours.

*In the 1990s, there was funding at the state level in Iowa to start FLES (foreign language in elementary schools) programs. When the funding went away, almost all of the programs were cut. Within the last few years, however, the number of programs is once again increasing. Parents are behind the push to start the programs this time in Iowa. They see that their children will not be prepared to compete if they do not begin learning languages early. They also understand the positive effects of learning a second language.*

**Tammy Dann,** teacher and mother

There is no doubt that local efforts are the ones most likely to have the biggest direct impact on your children. But to strengthen these efforts—and possibly to make the cause you're fighting for easier—consider sharing your advocacy efforts with others through ACTFL. If the voices of hundreds of thousands of parents who believe in the benefits of foreign language learning as a core subject to be taught to all American students are combined, we stand a better chance of being heard and thus making a lasting difference not only for our own children, but all American children. Advocacy comes in all shapes and sizes, and although we mentioned some of these initiatives before, they're worth repeating again:

- Vote in any and all elections—not just local ones, but state and national level ones as well. Who gets elected and what policies they enact affects our lives today and tomorrow. By voting, we send a message to all those on the ballot, whether they win or lose, about whether their views are supported or not. But whoever wins has the power to make an impact on our lives.

- Start a petition or letter-writing campaign to local, state, and federal legislators advocating for continuing, enhancing and/or incorporating second language programs as a means to keep our children globally competitive.

- Use media to raise awareness of the need for language learning. Opinion editorials and letters to the editor are great ways to get a message across. But so, too, are social media channels like YouTube, Facebook, and Twitter. Whether it's a personal story or photo, or you're posting good news of others, be sure to share it as far and wide as possible.

- Stay informed by following experts, leaders, and not-for-profit organizations on blogs, Twitter, and Facebook.

- Seek broader, nationwide access for foreign languages via joint advocacy with groups such as:
  - American Council on the Teaching of Foreign Languages (ACTFL),
  - Joint National Committee for Languages-National Council for Languages and International Studies (JNCL-NCLIS),
  - National Network for Early Language Learners (NNELL),
  - Institute for International Education (IIE),
  - Asia Society,
  - World Affairs Council (WAC),
  - IREX, and
  - Global Teacher Education (GTE).

We hope that your eyes have been opened to the undeniable benefits and practical necessity of raising global children in today's increasingly global world marketplace. Unfortunately, most Americans still don't think global exposure serves much purpose. They don't see that developing a collective global mind-set in our children is critical to both their individual child's—and ultimately the nation's—long-term success. Perhaps, in fact, you didn't believe it yourself for quite some time. If so, then you know that getting others to believe in the im-portance of global awareness is not easy.

But it is still something that we must work on since each "true believer" can be a force for convincing others within his or her own immediate sphere of influence. We ask, therefore, that you commit to helping others understand and appreciate the value of instilling a global mindset in their children by learning another language, paying attention to global news, and encouraging them to start traveling, both domestically and internationally. If you have some, share your own stories of cross-cultural competency and success with them. If we don't each do what we can now to bring about the necessary change, first in attitude, then in practical policies, we will all be the losers for it later. But no one will suffer more than our children. The battle is tough, and we will need a groundswell of support from small towns to big cities if we are to effect national and lasting change in our quest to raise global children.

## Real Stories from Real People

### Sandy Knox, *mother and parent advocate*

I am a stay-at-home mother of two sons in Fairfax County, (Northern) Virginia. In 2007, when my youngest son was in kindergarten, I learned at a PTA meeting that our elementary school was one of 16 elementary schools in the county being considered for the next round of installments of a new foreign language program called FLES (Foreign Language in the Elementary Schools). The pro-gram provided two 30-minute sessions twice a week, in which core curriculum subject matter would be reinforced using only the target language unique to each school (Spanish, French, Chinese, Japanese, Italian, or German). I also learned that community interest in the program would be one of the selection criteria and that the Fairfax County Public Schools (FCPS) system would be facing a budget crisis in the coming years, the result of which was that they might have to cut back on implementing FLES in new schools.

Up until this point, my parental volunteering had been limited to going into my son's classrooms to help the teachers with copying, reading and playing learn-ing games, and chaperoning field trips. But I agreed to look into what parents at his school would need to do in order to increase our chances of being selected for the next round of FLES implementation.

I started with our local school board representative and learned everything I could about the school and the county budget process. In order to motivate other parents, I also did a lot of research about early language learning so that I could explain why we should fight for our children to have this opportunity, one that would truly increase their chances of actually mastering a second language.

I encouraged other parents to speak at public budget hearings and to write letters to the school board. As the process unfolded, funding for the upcoming school year was first cut from 16 new school implementations to eight. It was then eliminated entirely. But we didn't give up. In the end, our school was chosen to be one of only four schools in which the FLES program would be implemented. I have no doubt that my leadership enabled the students at our school to have the opportunity to benefit from this wonderful program.

Because of all the time I had invested in bringing FLES to our school and the ongoing debate by some in the larger community as to whether elementary language instruction is a "luxury" that should be cut during tough budget times, I felt compelled to stay informed in the following budget years. As it turned out, there were no additional FLES implementations, but many parents became complacent and assumed that if they already had the program in their school, it was "safe" from being cut.

But in the fall of 2009, FCPS proposed cutting not only all 32 existing FLES programs, but also the lottery-based partial-immersion programs at 12 other schools that had been around for 20 years. Because it was a new program and had not yet proven itself, there was a very good chance that FLES would indeed be cut completely. I had worked so hard, but I knew that I could not be the sole motivator to save the programs at all 44 schools.

I sprang into action by contacting PTAs at all the schools with language programs. I found another parent, Tina Meek, whose daughters were in a Japanese immersion program and we went full force planning our advocacy campaign. We had about 30 attendees at our first meeting, and decided to call ourselves Fairfax FLAGS (Foreign Language Advocacy for Grade Schools). We tapped into the talents of others in our group and found someone to set up a website, a contact database, and a graphic designer to design a logo.

Tina and I were a great team and our skill sets complemented each other nicely. I had several years' experience closely following the budget and public hearing processes and learning the political side, especially working with the school board and building up contacts. I am also a former project manager and that helped with organization efforts. Tina had a marketing, writing, and public relations background. We always had a PowerPoint presentation and posted information on our website and Facebook pages, which I think made us look more professional.

In grass-roots advocacy, time is of the essence. Our Fairfax FLAGS group began organizing in late October 2009, and we soon had over 3,000 signatures on a petition. Most importantly, we were able to contact them via our email database. This was critical in requesting action on the part of our supporters. We created magnets with our Fairfax FLAGS logo with the slogan "The World is Not Monolingual," and our supporters drove all over the county advocating for our language programs. We also had Fairfax FLAGS liaisons at most of the elementary schools with language programs to help motivate parents there to take action, and we had monthly meetings that quickly grew to have over 100 people in attendance.

The defining moment of our campaign was when we coordinated over 100 people to provide testimony in support of early language learning at the January 2010 budget public hearings. The speakers included students from different programs learning different languages, parents, and other community members who spoke about the benefits of language learning, including the cognitive, academic, and cultural benefits as well as enhanced career options in the government and military. We made sure that the messages covered different angles so that we provided a host of strong arguments, but that our testimony did not become repetitive. We encouraged personal stories and emphasized that our elementary language programs were important to maintaining Fairfax County's reputation as a world-class school system.

The School Board listened to our community and reinstated funding for both elementary language programs. But there was even more work to do as we had to continue to rally our group to advocate to the Commonwealth of Virginia and the Fairfax County Board of Supervisors to fund and maintain our schools' high academic standards in other programs as well, including music and full-day kindergarten. Leading this advocacy effort was more than a full-time job, but it paid off—not only did we save our programs that year, but FCPS started slowly expanding them to additional schools.

Personally, I feel very good about my work as an advocate. My life has changed a lot since getting involved in this effort. In the beginning, I just thought it would be cool for my child to learn a second language. Now I believe that knowing a second language is truly a necessity for our kids if they are going to be able to compete in the global economy, whether they are college bound or not, whether they work in the international marketplace or in a service industry.

Grass-roots advocacy can work! There has to be one really passionate person to take charge, but it can't be a one-person effort. You have to network and find other interested parents who are willing to help. You have to be willing to work hard, be persistent, and "bug" those people who say they believe in something to take action and not accept "I'm busy" as an excuse. So don't be afraid to step outside of your comfort zone and get involved in something that you don't know much about but believe is important for your children. I believe it is important for my kids to be global citizens, and I will continue to do whatever I can to provide them with opportunities to experience other cultures and learn at least one other language.

### Claire González, *teacher educator, former teacher, and mother*

While growing up, I spent a fair amount of time traveling, hosting exchange students, and being around people from everywhere. I saw it as normal! Now, I realize how lucky I was to have these experiences, and how the transformative power of language has shaped me in my personal and professional life.

In college, my majors were French and Spanish. At age 21, I began a 16-year career teaching Spanish and French, which spanned all Grades K–12. This time was incredibly rewarding and I would not have traded it for anything. I eventually married someone who had immigrated from Mexico, and we settled in the United States, raising two bicultural children.

In 2009, I began an amazing adventure working at the Center for Latin American Studies (CLAS) at Vanderbilt University, a Title VI National Resource Center on Latin America. As Assistant Director for Outreach, one of my main roles is organizing teacher workshops and institutes on the topic of Latin America, bringing experts from inside and out of the university to K–12 teachers to both improve their own knowledge of the area and facilitate their implementing this knowledge into their classes through curriculum development. CLAS offers book clubs, film institutes, and has organized trips to Latin America to build curriculum.

Recently, we partnered with Tulane University's Stone Center for Latin American Studies to found an institute at the University of Georgia entitled "Exploring Brazil: A Window in the Language and Culture of a Country on the Rise." Teachers received instruction in Portuguese, explored Brazilian literature, watched Brazilian films, and toured a Latin American ethno-botanical garden on the campus of UG-Athens.

Our center co-coordinates a Children's and Young Adult Book Award called the Americas Award, presented each year at the Library of Congress. The rationale of the award, which is sponsored by the Consortium of Latin American Studies Programs, is to encourage and commend authors, illustrators, and publishers who produce quality children's and young adult books that productively portray Latin America, the Caribbean, or Latinos in the United States, and to provide teachers with recommendations for using them in their classrooms.

The most rewarding part of my job is working with teachers—all kinds of teachers. I am constantly amazed and inspired by what they are able to accomplish with their students; opening up the world to them by teaching about it. Often, they work with only limited support and resources, but are still able to offer some of the world to their students. Our country needs them—and they need each other—more than anyone realizes. In a time when there is a great need for understanding to replace fear of other cultures, teachers are huge, and often underappreciated, agents of change. I hope that through the support and resources our center offers them, we are also able to make a difference.

### Dr. Randa J. Duvick, *professor*

In June of 2012, I participated in an International Faculty Development Seminar organized by CIEE in Senegal. During the trip I met a high-school English teacher from the village of Popenguine, Mr. Amadou Sall, and proposed that we set up a correspondence exchange between my students of French and his students of English. Mr. Sall suggested that we set up a Skype exchange, and I readily agreed.

I incorporated the project into a unit in my third-semester French class at Valparaiso University. In this unit we focused on Senegal, using some of the materials that I had gathered during my short trip. Mr. Sall had two classes participating in the Skype project, one with students in their second year of high school, and one with students in their final year.

There were some scheduling challenges caused by the differences between the academic calendars of Senegal and the United States, but we managed to set up two 40-minute sessions during which our students spoke to each other via Skype.

To prepare our students beforehand, Mr. Sall and I both had our students write short paragraphs describing themselves (my students wrote in French and his in English). He and I e-mailed these paragraphs to each other, and we distributed them to our students. These paragraphs gave a fascinating look into similarities and differences between the lives of our students. My students also read a number of short texts in French that acquainted them with Senegalese history and society. We also brainstormed topics for questions that we wanted to ask during the Skype session.

During the two sessions, the students took turns asking and answering the prepared questions. Despite a small problem with sound quality, the two groups were able to hear each other. But it was the visual aspect that was so compelling for my students. We were able to see Mr. Sall and his students live in their uniforms in their classroom, and to see them interact with each other and with us—with very much the same kinds of reactions that we had: a little self-conscious, working hard to understand the foreign language, giggling a bit at times. It was both very memorable and rewarding for all involved, so much so that Mr. Sall and I plan to repeat the project again this fall because it's not difficult and doesn't cost much. All we needed was a computer hooked in with Skype, while Mr. Sall used a laptop computer equipped with a camera and access to the Internet.

Since the Skype sessions were part of an entire unit focused on Senegal, my students came away with a better understanding of Senegal's history and contemporary culture. But just the e-mail exchange of paragraphs followed by the Skype session proved of immense value. Any exchange like this can help students understand that the people about whom they are learning are real individuals, with voices and personalities, likes and dislikes. And while the worlds from which the two groups of students come are very different, I think that both groups came away from the experience realizing just how similar they are as human beings. Students can also make discoveries about their communication skills in the second language—"They really did understand me when I spoke French!" This is real communication, a time when all that practice in the classroom bears fruit.

## Rita A. Oleksak, *public school administrator, teacher, and mother*

As educators, parents, and lifelong learners, it is our responsibility—better yet—our duty, to prepare our children to become competent, successful citizens, capable of maneuvering the intricacies of living in a globally connected world. Children today need to be equipped with a rigorous set of 21st-century skills as well as curricular content knowledge in order to interact and participate productively in our ever-changing global society. It is our role as parents and educators to guide, prepare, and educate today's youth with the skills necessary for a successful life. Innovation, collaboration, and creativity are infused into the mainstream of education since our future and the well-being of our world is counting on tomorrow's leaders to problem-solve and co-exist in harmony with others who share the same concerns, but may be thousands of miles away.

Foreign language education and the development of intercultural competence are integral components in raising global children. Learning a foreign language opens doors to communication as well as creates a thirst for what lies across the many bodies of water that surround us, all while developing an appreciation of another culture and people. My own firsthand experience as director of foreign languages in the Glastonbury (CT) public school system has shown that students become more empathetic as they expand their knowledge of another language and culture. They are also building the foundation of an understanding of how to live and work together for the betterment of our world.

I am fortunate to lead an articulated, sequential Grades 1–12 foreign language program with a 50+ year history. Foreign Language in the Elementary Schools (FLES) begins with Spanish in first grade as students learn how to function in another language and develop an understanding and appreciation of another culture while learning to negotiate meaning through the different modes of communication (interpersonal, interpretive and presentational). At the same time, they develop reading, writing, listening, and speaking skills in a culturally appropriate context.

We're fortunate to have a very strong program in Glastonbury. But like so many other districts around the state and country, we too have faced budget cuts in recent years. But thanks to strong community support and ongoing program advocacy, we have prevailed. I am always keenly aware of the importance of connecting to the other core subject areas which has helped to reinforce cross curricular connections in language learning. Administrators, parents, teachers, and our local Board of Education see the value of language learning and its lifelong impact. Implementing international language exchanges with six different schools in other countries has enhanced language by extending a cultural component into our local community.

As program director, I also believe that it is important to advocate not only locally but nationally in support of K–16 language learning. I meet regularly with other district supervisors in Connecticut and annually through our national association. I also meet annually with senators and members of congress to ask for more funding in support of languages. As president of the American Council on the Teaching of Foreign Languages (ACTFL) in 2007, I testified on Capitol Hill asking for greater support for foreign language learning.

Perhaps even more important in today's ever-changing global society is intercultural competence. According to the definition developed by the participants in the Intercultural Competence Course in Glastonbury in 2013: *Intercultural competence is not about knowing another culture, but rather recognizing cultural nuances and being able to adapt/understand without judgment. It is understanding that culture is a very complex and changing concept and you cannot look at it just from the surface. It is not about answers, but rather the questions that are generated by curiosity and observation.* In our foreign language classes in Glastonbury, we have worked to promote the development of intercultural competence in our students as they learn the perspectives, practices, and products of the culture of their language of study. Students graduate high school with a heightened awareness and empathy towards other people along with the ability to interact, appreciate, and communicate with people from different backgrounds in their native language.

Technologies are changing at a rapid-fire pace, and we can only guess what will be the norm in as little as 5 years. What will not change, however, is the importance of each of us—administrators, teachers, and parents—doing our individual parts to ensure that every student receives an education that includes language learning and intercultural competence in order to prepare them to be productive global citizens.

# AFTERWORD

# Toward a New Global Order

Instilling a global mindset in the youth of today is now as critical to the long-term economic success of the United States as it has been for years to many smaller and less inherently self-sustainable nations—ones who realized long ago that they could not go it alone. Part of that sea change is no doubt the result of geometric progressions in technology, which, by and large, have obviated the checkpoints and border crossings of even the late 20th century. This is not to say that the sovereignty of individual nations is no longer important. But increasingly, the ability of individuals and nations to interact effectively and expeditiously with those beyond their own borders makes the difference between individual success and failure, and national prosperity and poverty. Technology also enables people from widely disparate parts of the world to work together to resolve issues that concern all humanity, such as eradicating diseases, conserving natural resources, and reducing poverty and illiteracy.

Inevitably, the process of raising global children has to begin at home. But it must also be reinforced and expanded upon at school. In both situations, the most effective way to build a global mindset is not in short, separate installments—as you might with math or manners—but rather by infusing it into everything we teach our children, overtly or tacitly. The more global their overall perspective becomes, the better their long-term opportunities. And isn't doing what's best for our children in the long term what parenting is all about?

## Stacie's Story

I've often tried to pinpoint when in my life I made the global turn. In retrospect, I think that my global awareness began when I was 8 or 9 years old and first saw the Taj Mahal on the cover of *National Geographic* in my parent's family room and started turning page after page, enthralled by the splendor of India's physical and cultural riches. I came to realize that the big world out there was very different from my sheltered suburban life in Florida and that I was inherently curious. As you have no doubt realized after reading the many and varied stories in this book, there is no one specific path that leads a child to global awareness, but there are many pathways that can help.

Take for instance one of my favorite family stories, and one that inspired me from a young age: that of my maternal grandmother. At the age of 18, she left her home in southern Poland with the intention of visiting her aunt who had immigrated to the United States and was living in Montana. But she never made it, opting instead to head to northeast Pennsylvania after hearing about opportunities in the coal mining industry from another relative living there. Speaking very little English, she made her way from Ellis Island to Hazleton, eventually met my grandfather, and never saw her mother again as they both recognized that this new life, difficult as it was, was still much better for her than what she faced back in rural Poland in the 1910s and '20s.

Both my parents were first-generation Polish Americans, and on both sides of their respective families. Like most children of immigrants, they were raised bilingual, with Polish traditions being a major part of their everyday life. In turn, they passed these customs on to me and my seven siblings (I was number 6), infusing Polish foods, customs, and traditions into our otherwise typical American family life. Unfortunately, they didn't teach us the Polish language, something they both later regretted.

But they did get out of Hazleton and the coal industry, which had fallen on tough times after the war. My father used the GI Bill to go to college and flight school to become a commercial pilot for Delta Airlines, which had him move in his early career from New York to Houston to Miami and then to Coral Springs, just outside of Fort Lauderdale. My mother, a trained biologist who had worked on various vaccine formulas at Lederle Lab, left her career to follow my father and became a stay-at-home mother.

One of the great benefits of having an airline pilot for a father was the number of vacations we were able to take to various destinations, both domestic and international. These adventures allowed us to enjoy people, places, and things outside our comfort zone yet within the safety of a loving family. Our many adventures included walking along the streets of San Francisco, exploring the palaces of Portugal, enjoying high tea in London, and swimming in the warm waters off many Caribbean islands. Growing up and traveling as a large family was a wonderful experience and, although we competed for attention, we were also encouraged to be independent self-starters. My father loved to play games with us that involved the capitals of states and countries, and geographical coordinates. We were all taught to read at a young age and encouraged to become avid readers in order to explore our own interests. Our individuality was celebrated, and we were brought up to be self-confident, free thinkers.

Recently, I chatted with my mother (my father passed away in 1995) about my childhood and how I came to be as internationally oriented as I did. She was adamant about two things. First, she said that I was a voracious reader from a very young age, and that she believes reading opens up many worlds to young people. Second, she told me that I asked questions constantly. My mom said that she and my dad sometimes felt exasperated by my constant barrage of questions, but never wanted to stymie my curiosity. So sometimes they fobbed me off on older siblings, or on neighbors, teachers, friends, or books. But they always encouraged curiosity, open-mindedness, and awareness of the world.

I would build on this global curiosity in college, where the friends I became closest to all turned out to be international students, three of whom (one French, one Italian, and one Moroccan) remain among my closest friends today. After graduation, I moved to Washington, D.C., to look for a job. I chose to interview only at large international public relations agencies because I wanted an international career. Having left my comfort zone to seek opportunity, I was lucky enough to land a great job with Burson-Marsteller, where I worked for 12 years. For as long as I can remember, I have wanted to explore. International cultures have always seemed exciting rather than scary to me. That curiosity and excitement evolved over time, allowing me to work successfully all around the world. I came to realize that my success on global accounts depended on intercultural skills, which included my ability to work with diplomats in Pakistan, business leaders in Hong Kong, and colleagues in Paris.

It was at Burson-Marsteller that I met my future husband, Mike, who shared my love of international adventure, and we began to travel together; our first big trip was three weeks in Nepal. The day after our wedding, Mike and I moved to Hong Kong (en route, we stopped to see the Taj Mahal, thus fulfilling a lifetime goal), where I had been transferred from the D.C. office for three years. I almost went to Buenos Aires, but I didn't have the Spanish language skills that Burson leadership thought I needed to succeed. So I went to Hong Kong instead, even though I did not speak any Chinese. But in 1996, I really didn't need to: Hong Kong was still a British colony, poised to pass over to Chinese rule. I studied Mandarin twice a week in the evening when I was there, and although it was difficult, I managed to learn key phrases in Mandarin, as well as the Cantonese dialect spoken in Hong Kong. Because I worked across East and Southeast Asia, I had to learn about multiple cultures and practice key phrases in many languages, and I tried my best in Japanese, Korean, Malay, and Hindi. I don't have a knack for languages like some people, but I always got high marks for trying. What I found I did have was an ability to work across cultures, and I counseled clients and managed teams from Korea to Australia. I also watched how fast China and India were growing and knew that my Asian experience would come in handy later on. We moved back to Washington, D.C., and my career took off as I moved quickly up the ranks despite taking time off to give birth to our twin daughters, Connie and Betty. My initial love of travel and adventure had turned into a global career.

Six years later, and now living in Connecticut, I left the corporate world to co-author a book on international careers. Since then I have written three additional books, developed a national reputation as an expert on international careers, and launched my own business, consulting, writing, and speaking about the global workplace. Although remaining in the corporate world full-time would have allowed me to relocate abroad again and take our daughters, Mike and I decided against it. We weighed the pros and cons and believed it would be more beneficial to us as a family to ground our children in a stable upbringing here in the United States while exploring the world together through travel, language, food, and friendships with people from many lands.

## Mike's Story

Although blessed with the ability to do so, travel was something that my family just didn't do often. This came from reluctance on my father's part. He had spent the better part of his own coming-of-age years, 19–22, traveling (particularly flying) all around the country for, as he called it, "his Uncle Sam" before eventually ending up in the cockpit of a B-29, based on the Pacific island of Guam. At the conclusion of the war, all he wanted to do was return home to Ohio, marry his sweetheart, and get on with his interrupted life, which first took the form of a job as a traveling petrochemical salesman based initially in Tulsa, Oklahoma, and then in Houston, Texas. By the time I showed up, he was all traveled out, and vacations for us were return visits to established family destinations in northern Michigan and the Adirondack mountains in upstate New York. The one exception was a vacation in spring 1966 when he actually suggested that we go to Jamaica, where he had trained for several months in the winter of 1945. He felt that he had not seen the real Jamaica then, and wanted to have that experience.

Fortunately for me, there was my mother's youngest brother, Mike. Uncle Mike had taken a job with the World Bank in Washington, D.C., and not only loved to travel himself, but got to do so—and do so extensively—as part of his work. Moreover, the places he generally went—Ethiopia, Afghanistan, India, Pakistan, and Nepal—seemed quintessentially exotic, at least to me, a stay-at-home-in-Ohio youth. One summer he took his whole family—including my four cousins—to Jordan, and I was green with envy. A couple of summers later, when I was 14, he got a similar opportunity in Morocco, and asked my mother and me to join them. We did, and that summer was my introduction to the world outside the United States. It began with 10 days in Portugal and southern Spain, where we traveled from city to city as quintessential American tourists.

In Morocco, however, we had a rented house outside of the capital of Rabat, where we settled in for about eight weeks, interspersed with occasional three- or four-night excursions. In retrospect, it was that homestay experience that I believe was most responsible for the global citizen that I eventually became. As an introduction to foreign cultures, Morocco was just about perfect. Everything about it seemed exotic: the land itself, the people and the way they dressed, the religion (and especially the five times daily call to prayers), the food, and the music. Then there was the Arabic language, whose sounds were unrecognizable and whose script was undecipherable.

Had they only spoken Arabic there, I might have been completely intimidated. But as a former French colony, they also spoke the language that I had been learning for the past five years in school. That allowed me to read signs, make myself understood, and understand enough of what they were saying in response that I was never completely lost or confused. Considering that we were allowed out and about in our little residential neighborhood, this made all the difference in the world. My cousins and I wandered the streets almost at will, ran errands for our parents, and stopped in any store that interested us. I wouldn't call us downright intrepid, but neither were we nonplussed in the least, not then or when we would visit large and what could well have been overwhelming cities such as Tangiers, Fez, and Marrakesh with their mysterious *casbahs* and vast covered *souks*. Moreover, Morocco was just plain fascinating—everything the Moroccans did they did differently than we did it back in the States, but it all worked (even the obligatory bargaining) and made perfect sense. I was inspired to learn more, see more, and especially continue with my French, which had proven to be so useful.

Five years later, I had the opportunity to study abroad in college and I took it—living and studying in the Loire Valley of France, feeling now quite competent in my French. Every other long weekend saw groups of us "part-time" students heading to the local train station for Eurail excursions to Belgium, the Netherlands, Germany, Switzerland, or Italy, where we took in the museums, palaces, and historical sites of Western Europe—the very places that we had all read about in high school and were now learning about in college. Of course, it wasn't all just "Western Civ in real time." There was also a fair amount of pleasure involved as well, mostly in the form of experiencing other cultures firsthand and accumulating the kind of collective knowledge of the world and its multitudinous ways that only travel can bring.

This was followed up by a summer studying Spanish in Salamanca, and a year working as a business journalist in Sweden, where I was in charge of a Swedish multinational's internal magazine which had to be in proper English (not "Swinglish") since they had operations in 23 countries worldwide. When I returned to the States, I was a committed internationalist and I sought a job in the U.S. Foreign Service. I passed the written exam and moved to cosmopolitan Washington, D.C., in anticipation of soon beginning my training. But I ended up flunking the orals and eventually found a job writing and editing natural resource management reports on sub-Saharan Africa and Asia for a subcontractor for USAID for 5 years. Two years later, when Stacie and I moved to Hong Kong, I was able to re-indulge my love of off-the-beaten path travel, this time as a travel writer for a Hong Kong company that published the in-flight magazines for several Asian carriers.

When we returned to the United States in 1999, I stayed with the career of travel writer, though my subjects, of necessity, became much less exotic. But a writer's life has many rewards, one of which is flexibility. When our daughters arrived in the winter of 2000, I had primary responsibility for them (albeit with daily professional help) as Stacie continued to work full-time. Whenever she could, she would join us on our forays in and about Washington, D.C., which is a great place to introduce children to the world. Not only are there so many things there to captivate and entertain formative young minds (museums, galleries, historic sites, etc.), but most of them are absolutely free, courtesy of your federal tax dollars. Nor was there any shortage of international or multicultural experiences for them to have, whether in ethnic neighborhoods or events, or just through the obvious diversity of Washingtonians going about their daily business. By being "different" ourselves—I was often the only father at the playground or museums—the girls learned to appreciate that different is OK at a very early age.

As the girls have grown and been more able to travel with me, my writing has come to focus more on family travel, primarily domestic, but with an international trip thrown in as often as feasible, both time-wise and financially. I have never lost my love of foreign lands, my fascination with the infinite variety of social and cultural practices, and my appreciation that we are all human beings and that we are all in this together. Hopefully, I've been able to impart a little of that to them.

## Our Global Family

For both of us growing up and coming of age in the 1970s and '80s, acquiring a global mindset was very much a fortuitous bonus—something we probably didn't really need to have, but that was a definite asset, both personally and in terms of the additional doors it opened up career-wise. Thirty-plus years on, we no longer believe that raising global children is an option. Since our daughters were born, we have been committed to opening the world to them, both by sharing our own knowledge of the world and by instilling in them a desire to proactively learn and explore it for themselves. We believe instilling global awareness in children is a crucial element of a well-rounded education and intellect, one that is just as important as excellent nutrition and physical fitness, spiritual fulfillment, and emotional strength and stability.

We took our daughters on their first international trip to the Dominican Republic when they were seven months old and now, at the age of 13, they have explored significant portions of the United States, Eastern Canada, Western Europe, Central America and parts of South America and East Asia. They have swum with whale sharks in the Philippines, savored crêpes in Paris, learned to surf in Nicaragua, and climbed Mayan temples at sunrise in Guatemala. They are learning how to travel—with backpacks, travel guides, maps, and a lot of patience—and so far, they seem to really enjoy it and remain open to all kinds of cross-cultural experiences. We are also encouraging them to take full advantage of the Spanish language courses offered beginning in first grade in our local public school system, to which they have added Mandarin Chinese in seventh grade and possibly a third language in ninth. Our daughters have participated in the summer STARTALK Chinese language camps, and we are planning to spend parts of the next few summers in intensive Spanish-language programs or traveling in Spanish-speaking countries. We write op-eds, call members of Congress, and attend local Board of Education meetings to show support for language learning, and we encourage other parents to do the same.

But it's not only about travel and languages. We all enjoy foods from other cultures, and we make at least three meals a week involving international elements. We listen to a variety of music, watch travel and cultural documentaries, and talk about politics, economics, religion, and world events at the dinner table every night. Eating together as a family is one of the most important things we do for it allows us to ask and answer questions of each other. We have taught them to respect and appreciate others' opinions. Overall, though, the most important life lessons they are learning are to be open-minded and empathetic, appreciate diversity, and respect difference.

As it already has done for our two daughters, exposing children to a wide variety of cultural experiences will help them become more aware of the world beyond our borders, minimize the fear of the unknown, and encourage them to think critically about global issues. In addition to just making them better and wiser people, such awareness should eventually also help them find jobs and better serve our nation—as well as the world—in the near future. After all, globalization is here to stay and preparing our children for the world they will soon enter as adults is the very least that we believe we should do for them. If you, the reader, have made it this far, you must feel the same.

# Acknowledgments

This book is written for parents and their children, and teachers and their students from all walks of life. As such, we would like to first thank the parents who are already doing their best at home to raise global children and advocating for better global education in our schools, and the teachers and administrators from preschool through graduate school who are working to bring the wider world into the classroom. Our children's future depends on you.

This book could not have been written without the assistance of many people, and we would like to thank all of them. At the top of the list, however, has to be Rebecca Weiner, dear friend and fellow author, who spent untold hours researching, drafting, and editing the text, and countless others debating and encouraging us. We simply couldn't have done it without her.

Thanks also go to our many global friends who contributed their experiences and ideas about raising global children with us in hundreds of discussions over the past few years. Several of these individuals also agreed to read drafts of the manuscript and offered sound advice as to how to make it better; their constructive criticism, personal and professional experiences, and overall belief in the importance of the subject have collectively made the book much stronger. In appreciation, we would like to acknowledge our indebtedness to them specifically: Morgan Abate, Curtis S. Chin, William B. Johnston, Jeanette Miranda, Steve Miranda, Rita Oleksak, Indira Pulliadath, Scott D. Seligman, and Becky Todd York.

We are also grateful to the dozens of people who participated in lengthy indepth interviews, during which they told us their personal stories, provided successful strategies and tips, and contributed the quotes and anecdotes that help bring the text alive, thus greatly enriching the reader's experience. Their stories not only added the human touch necessary to create a more enlightening and interesting text, but encouraged us to continue believing in the power of our central idea. A complete listing of all quoted contributors can be found on the following pages. We are also grateful to the more than 1,000 people who took our online surveys, and who, by the strength of their numbers, thus enabled us to cross-check our research with a fresh set of empirical data.

In addition, we would like to thank our publisher, the American Council on the Teaching of Foreign Languages (ACTFL), and its staff who helped make this book a reality. Marty Abbott, Howie Berman, and Chelsea Bowes provided insightful comments to the drafts and clear guidance throughout the process, while Sandy Cutshall did a thoroughly professional job of copy editing and proofreading. We are also grateful to Katie Kotchman, agent extraordinaire, for her unwavering faith in this project, and HDN Studio, Inc., for their creative and effective jacket design and layout.

Last but not least, we are grateful to our daughters, Connie and Betty, who each contributed ideas, advice, and personal stories as requested, but inspiration without even knowing it.

# Contributors

**Mackenzie Abate** is an undergraduate nursing student at Temple University who plans to study abroad and travel to as many places as possible; in her free time, she enjoys photography and being with friends and family.

**Morgan Abate** is an undergraduate student at Elon University pursuing international studies and communications with a minor in Spanish who plans to study abroad in Latin America; she wants to pursue a career that allows her to travel, work, and live abroad.

**Martha G. Abbott,** Executive Director of the American Council on the Teaching of Foreign Languages, has served as a language teacher and public school administrator and has been involved in standards and assessment development; she enjoys working on language advocacy issues and traveling internationally.

**Liz Allred** serves as the Program Director for Global Enrichment in the Huntsman School of Business at Utah State University.

**Amanda** attends high school in Europe and enjoys spending her free time with her family and dog.

**Betty Berdan** is an eighth-grade student who enjoys playing soccer and basketball, horseback riding, and learning foreign languages; she looks forward to a lifetime of traveling.

**Connie Berdan** is an eighth-grade student who lives in New England and likes to ride horses in the summer and ski in the winter.

**Anna C. Catalano** is a board director with an international business background, speaker, and mother, who is interested in people and companies that are making a difference in the world.

**Curtis S. Chin,** an international business executive and former U.S. ambassador, has enjoyed a career living and working in Bangkok, Beijing, Hong Kong, Tokyo, Manila, and across the United States and Switzerland so far, and remains a globetrotting, third culture kid and child at heart.

**Don V. Cogman** is a communications, public affairs, and advertising executive who formerly lived and worked in New York and Washington, D.C., where he had global responsibilities.

**Beth Cubanski** is a senior at American University studying medicine and Spanish; she hopes to combine the two for a career with Doctors Without Borders.

**Laura Cubanski** has been an at-home mother (baker, medic, chauffeur), a lawyer, an author, and a tutor, but traveling with her family is her greatest joy.

**Tammy Dann** teaches Spanish at the elementary-school level and, as such, spends so much time speaking Spanish to her students at school and her daughter at home that she sometimes forgets English.

**Dr. Randa J. Duvick** is a Professor of French at Valparaiso University in Valparaiso, Indiana, where she also teaches Francophone cultures and literatures.

**Steve Finikiotis** is Principal at Osprey LLC, where he leads a team of specialists that helps companies access international markets, especially high-growth ones.

**Claire González** is Assistant Director for Outreach at the Center for Latin American Studies at Vanderbilt University, where she has the pleasure of working with teachers and the community to promote education about Latin America.

**José D. González** is an instructor of management and entrepreneurship at the College of Business Administration at Belmont University, a father of two, and a study abroad enthusiast who has led students to seven different countries.

**Dr. Allan E. Goodman** is the President and CEO of the Institute of International Education (IIE), the leading not-for-profit organization in the field of international educational exchange and development training.

**Diane Gulyas** is the President of DuPont Performance Polymers; she has lived and worked in Switzerland and Belgium and has traveled to 48 U.S. states and 45 countries, but there are still many places left that she wants to explore.

**Patricia Guy** has lived in Verona, Italy, for more than 20 years where she writes about wine, food, culture, and Sherlock Holmes.

**Julian Ha** is a native New Yorker who has lived and worked in Hong Kong, London, and Singapore and who is now a Washington, D.C.-based executive recruiter.

**Alex Hager** is a high school junior who is an avid sports fan and world traveler; he is interested in international cultures at home and abroad.

**Roya Hakakian** is an award-winning poet and journalist whose byline regularly appears in the *New York Times, Newsweek, Wall Street Journal* and elsewhere, and who has also developed programming for CBS's *60 Minutes*; a noted human rights advocate, Roya is also co-founder of the Iran Human Rights Documentation Center and serves on the board of Refugees International.

**Clancey Houston** is a mom, writer, and senior executive who counsels global teams on market entry and expansion strategies in the Asia/Pacific and Africa regions, with a focus on access, education, and engagement in the health care sector.

**Angela Jackson** is a global education leader working to expand educational opportunities for disadvantaged students.

**Hope Johnson** is currently a Fulbright English Teaching Assistant in Russia who loves creative writing, playing basketball, and spending time with her family in Maine.

**Michelle Morgan Knott** lives in the Washington, D.C., area and enjoys home-schooling her three kids while trying to keep her sanity and sense of humor.

**Sandy Knox** is an involved parent advocate and adventurous stay-at-home mom who values education (inside and outside of the classroom), loves to travel and see new places, and never stops planning for the next fun family vacation or local "field trip."

**Bernie Lee** is a stay-at-home father of two teenagers, a part-time high school tutor, and an ardent supporter of Arsenal Football Club.

**Jennifer Maniscalco** is a Senior Marketing Manager for Stericycle, Inc., and as a xenophile has a passion for making the world a better place for all children because they are the caretakers of the future.

**Brenna McStravick** is an adventuresome high school student who loves traveling the world, listening to music, and meeting new friends.

**Dr. Salvatore Menzo** is Superintendent of the Wallingford Public School District in Connecticut.

**Adam L. Michaels** is the father of two sons and the head of North American integrated business planning at Mondelez International.

**Abraham Minto** has lived in New York, London, China, Panama, Cyprus, and Colombia, and currently resides in Miami, Florida.

**Jeanette Miranda** enjoys dividing her time between Brown University's race car building team and adventures around China by plane, train, and minibus.

**Steve Miranda** is Managing Director at the Cornell Center for Advanced HR Studies, and a globe-trotting nomad.

**Therese Miranda-Blackney** is pursuing an MBA and a Master's Degree in Sustainable Systems at the University of Michigan in hopes of finding ways to get more energy-efficient products into the hands of consumers.

**Rita A. Oleksak** is the Director of Foreign Languages/ELL in Glastonbury, Connecticut, who loves traveling, spending time by the shore, and watching her sons play golf.

**Jennifer M. Olshan** first found a photograph of the Cotswolds' Arlington Row in middle school and vowed to see it in person; her passion for overseas travel has taken her and her family to remarkable destinations—ones that always leave her yearning for her next great trip.

**Dr. Jeffrey W. Overby** is Director of the Center for International Business and the Edward C. and Helen J. Kennedy Chair of Excellence at Belmont University, and part of a family of avid world travelers and international foodies.

**Chris Page** likes to travel the world with his children and wife; he lives in Napa, California, makes wine, and spends more time than is normal talking to complete strangers in Trader Joe's.

**Paige** lives in Connecticut with her parents, brother, and cat and enjoys playing soccer and practicing the piano.

**Ben Pauker** is a senior at The George Washington University concentrating in finance and marketing; he hopes to continue his language learning throughout his professional career.

**Laura Perry** is a registered nurse who spent eight years in the U.S. Air Force, much of it overseas; now grounded, she is the mother of two teenage daughters and enjoys the opportunity to help them see the world and master Spanish, which she never could.

**Mike Perry** began his career as a Navy flier and participated in the first Gulf War before turning his talents to chemical engineering for United Technologies where, with more than 50 unique patents, he leads research initiatives on advanced clean-energy technology.

**Mitchell Polman** works on public diplomacy programs, on international elections monitoring missions, and with foreign journalists.

**Indira Pulliadath** is married with two kids and works as a research scientist in the health care industry; in her spare time, she loves to cook and enjoy diverse cuisines with her family and friends.

**Brent Riddle** is a devoted husband and father, an aspiring BBQ pitmaster, and a Taekwondo blue belt who revels in international travel and Texas Longhorn Football.

**Dr. Liesl Riddle** fell in love with and married a world traveler, Brent Riddle, became an Associate Professor of International Business at The George Washington University, and now looks forward to exploring the world with her sons who teach her something new every day.

**Dr. Frank D. Sanchez** is deeply committed to assisting underserved student populations and is invested in both access and success for future generations of college students.

**Scott D. Seligman** is a writer, historian, genealogist, retired corporate executive, and career "China hand."

**Elizabeth Shutt** is a high school student and lover of animals—friends call her "the dog whisperer"—and she loves traveling, shopping, and sports.

**Jacqueline Stack** is a lifelong learner who also happens to be a social science teacher.

**Jennifer Stassen** enjoys the challenge of tutoring students from Grade 1 through college while taking care of her three children and two dysfunctional dogs.

**Sharon Elliott Sullivan** is an international educator, living at her sixth post, who believes in global education, teaching tolerance, and conflict resolution.

**Kristi Vitelli** is a lifetime learner who enjoys gardening, cooking, reading, and exploring the world through travel.

**Sara Vitelli** is a high school student who loves acting, singing, lacrosse, rowing crew, horseback riding, and traveling the world.

**Rebecca Weiner** is co-founder and co-director of Strebesana Resources, a consulting firm that supports the U.S.–China medical optics trade; she is also a mom, foster mom, community volunteer, real estate investor, and dedicated urban chicken farmer.

# About the Publisher

**The American Council on the Teaching of Foreign Languages (ACTFL)** is the national association for language education professionals from all levels of instruction and representing all languages. With more than 12,000 active members, ACTFL provides innovative professional development opportunities, acclaimed training and certification programs, and widely cited books, publications, scholarly journals, research studies, and language education resources, including *Foreign Language Annals* and *The Language Educator* magazine.

As part of its mission and vision, the organization provides guidance to the profession and to the general public regarding issues, policies, and best practices related to the teaching and learning of languages and cultures. ACTFL is a leading national voice among language educators and administrators and is guided by a responsibility to set standards and expectations that will result in high-quality language programs.

Learn more at **www.actfl.org**.

# Notes

## Chapter 1

1 http://www.dni.gov/index.php/about/organization/national-intelligence-council-global-trends.

2 http://www.pwc.com/en_GX/gx/world-2050/assets/pwc-world-in-2050-report-january-2013.pdf.

3 http://www.randstad.com/press-room/news/randstad-news/global-employment-trends-in-clients.

4 Ibid.

5 Munro, John, "Learning Internationally in a Future Context," from Hayden, Mary, Jack Levy and Jeff Thompson, Eds., *The SAGE Handbook of Research in International Education*, (London: SAGE Publications, 2007), p. 118.

## Chapter 2

1 http://www.ncssfl.org/papers/BenefitsSecondLanguageStudyNEA.pdf.

2 Schliecher, K., Ed. *Nationalism in Education*, (New York: Peter Lang, 2003).

3 Kirkwood-Tucker, Toni, *Visions in Global Education* (New York: Peter Lang, 2009), pp.3–24.

4 Cunningham, Gregg L., *Blowing the Whistle on Global Education* (Denver: Regional Office, United States Department of Education, 1986); cited in Gaudelli, pp. 15–16.

5 http://www.whitehouse.gov/the-press-office/2011/03/28/remarks-president-univision-town-hall.

6 https://www.stanford.edu/dept/lc/language/about/conferencepapers/panettapaper.pdf.

7 http://www.americanprogress.org/wp-content/uploads/2012/08/USChinaIndiaEduCompetitiveness.pdf.

8 http://www.thelanguageflagship.org/images/documents/what_business_wants_report_final_7_09.pdf.

9 Heater, D.B., *Peace Through Education* (London: Falmer Press, 1984); cited in Gaudelli, p. 8.

10 Nussbaum, Martha C., *For Love of Country?* (Boston: Beacon, 2002), p. 6; cited in Parker, Walter C. "International Education: What's in a Name?" *Phi Delta Kappan*, Vol. 90, No. 03, November 2008, pp. 196–202.

11 http://globalmindset.thunderbird.edu/sites/default/files/gmi-tech-report_0.pdf.

12 Yeatman, C. Perry and Stacie Nevadomski Berdan, *Get Ahead By Going Abroad: A Woman's Guide to Fast-track Career Success* (New York: HarperCollins, 2007), pp. 13–17.

13 http://www.leeds.ac.uk/educol/documents/00003495.htm.

14 Swiniarski, Louise A, Mary-Lou Breitborde and Jo-Anne Murphy, *Educating the Global Village: Including the Young Child in the World*, (Columbus, OH: Merrill/Prentice Hall, 1999), p. 6.

## Chapter 3

1   Ibid, p. 130.

2   Pollock, David and Van Reken, R.E., *The Third Culture Kid Experience: Growing Up Between Worlds* (Yarmouth, ME: Intercultural Press, 1999), cited in Hayden, Mary, Jack Levy and Jeff Thompson, Eds., *The SAGE Handbook of Research in International Education*, ("SAGE Handbook": London: SAGE Publications, 2007), p. 103.

3   Gunesch, Konrad, "International Education's Internationalism: Inspiration from Cosmopolitans," in ibid, p. 93.

4   Mischel, Walter; Ebbe B. Ebbesen, Antonette Raskoff Zeiss (1972). "Cognitive and Attentional Mechanisms in Delay of Gratification." *Journal of Personality and Social Psychology* 21 (2): 204–218.

5   In the UK: http://www.dailymail.co.uk/news/article-480895/Over-protective-parents-robbing-children-childhood-experts-warn.html, and in Australia: http://www.news.com.au/national/childrens-play-equipment-too-safe-for-their-own-good-expert-warns/story-e6frfkvr-1226065260649.

## Chapter 4

1   England's new foreign language requirements: http://www.guardian.co.uk/education/2012/jun/10/foreign-languages-compulsory-aged-7, and Scotland's: http://www.telegraph.co.uk/news/politics/9273117/Four-year-olds-to-start-learning-two-foreign-languages.html.

2   http://www.thelanguageflagship.org/images/documents/what_business_wants_report_final_7_09.pdf.

3   http://blog.nafsa.org/2012/02/15/we-have-a-listening-problem-if-we-arent-learning-foreign-languages/.

4   http://www.sde.ct.gov/sde/lib/sde/PDF/Curriculum/Curriculum_Root_Web_Folder/BenefitsofSecondLanguage.pdf.

5   Ibid.

6   http://www.sciencedaily.com/releases/2011/08/110829070559.htm.

7   http://www.earlychildhoodnews.com/earlychildhood/article_view.aspx?ArticleID=38.

## Chapter 7

1   http://worldsavvy.org/.

2   Berdan, Stacie Nevadomski, Allan Goodman and Cyril Taylor, *A Student Guide to Study Abroad* (New York: Institute of International Education and AIFS Foundation, 2013).

## Chapter 8

1   http://www.worldaffairschallenge.org/wp-content/uploads/2012/01/Global-Issues-in-the-Elementary-Classroom.pdf.

2   http://www.longviewfdn.org/122/teacher-preparation-for-the-global-age.html.

3   http://www.athgo.org/about_us/news/athgo_10_april_22.html.